DESTINED TO RULE THE SCHOOLS

SUNY Series, Educational Leadership

Daniel L. Duke, Editor

Destined to Rule the Schools

Women and the Superintendency, 1873–1995

Jackie M. Blount

State University of New York Press

Chapter 4 is a revised version of Jackie M. Blount, "Manly Men and Womanly Women: Deviance, Gender Role Polarization, and the Shift in Women's School Employment, 1900–1976," *Harvard Educational Review*, 66:2 (Summer 1996), pp. 318–338. Copyright © 1996 by the President and Fellows of Harvard College. All rights reserved.

Cover photograph: Ella Flagg Young; ICHi–26962; (n.p.); (n.d.); Creator—Louise Betts (American). Reprinted with permission from the Chicago Historical Society.

Cover design: Adrienne Klein

Published by
State University of New York Press, Albany

© 1998 State University of New York

For information, address the State University of New York Press, 90 State Street, Suite 700, Albany, NY 12207

Production by M. R. Mulholland
Marketing by Anne M. Valentine

Library of Congress Cataloging-in-Publication Data

Blount, Jackie M., 1959–
    Destined to rule the schools : women and the superintendency.
1873–1995 / Jackie M. Blount.
        p.   cm. — (SUNY series, educational leadership)
    Includes bibliographical references (p.) and index.
    ISBN 0–7914–3729–9 (hc : alk. paper). — ISBN 0–7914–3730–2 (pb : alk. paper)
    1. Women school superintendents—United States—History.
2. School management and organization—United States—History.
I. Title.   II. Series: SUNY series in educational leadership.
LB2831.72.B53   1998
371.2'001—dc21   97–25555
                                                                CIP

10 9 8 7 6 5 4 3 2 1

To Ann Highsmith Fleming, Kellie McGarrh,
and Ella Flagg Young

CONTENTS

FIGURES

TABLES

ACKNOWLEDGMENTS

This project could not have been undertaken without significant assistance from a number of persons and organizations. First, I extend my thanks to the Spencer Foundation for funding my dissertation research. Since then, Iowa State University has supported my efforts and graciously allocated resources to help me complete this project. I am particularly grateful to the kind staff at Parks Library for helping me track down documents from around the country.

I could not have begun this work had Richard Phillips not recognized my passion for research and invited me into the Social Foundations of Education doctoral program at the University of North Carolina. As counselor, guide, and friend, he maintained faith in my work even when I did not. I also thank George Noblit for constantly knocking me out of easy, unquestioned patterns of thinking. His generous insights throughout my graduate studies greatly inspired me.

I owe a tremendous debt of appreciation to John D'Emilio both for his personal help as well as for the impressive examples of his scholarship and political work. His books have deeply influenced my thinking about gender, sexuality, and history. To Catherine Marshall I extend my gratitude for introducing me to a wide range of issues associated with women in school administration. Her careful mentoring of my early scholarship has significantly shaped my research focus and affected my willingness to ask difficult, often painful questions about the meaning of gender in school administration. Jim Garrison I thank for challenging me with an endless series of questions and for his kind assistance with projects. I also credit him with first alerting me to the scarcity of women superintendents.

Shawnel Seifried, a talented undergraduate research assistant, practically lived in the library for months to help me with all sorts of mundane research tasks. Her help and unending enthusiasm have made this project much more manageable. Siné Anahita, Kayt Sunwood, Carolyn Blount, and BeJae Fleming graciously read drafts of this work and made thoughtful, critically important suggestions along the way. Through the years a number of other persons have stimulated my thinking and provided me with wonderful resources, ideas, contacts, and models of outstanding leadership: Amy Bailey, Camilla Benbow,

Jill Blackmore, Edward Bostley, Geraldine Buford, Joan Burstyn, Sara Campbell, Nancy Clifton, Joe Daniels, Nancy Dillingham, Linda Eisenmann, Gladys Graves, Sandra Gupton, Karen Harbeck, Alice Henderson, Ashley Hinson, Polly Welts Kaufman, Barbara Licklider, Brian Matney, Mike Price, Penny Richards, Dan Robinson, Kate Rousmaniere, Charol Shakeshaft, Ann Thompson, Lucy Townsend, Wayne Urban, Kathleen Weiler, John Wilson, and Dick Zbaracki. Though I have not met them, I am grateful to David Tyack and Elisabeth Hansot, whose scholarship has inspired me and provided important motivation for this project. Several graduate students with whom I have worked closely over the past few years have richly stimulated my thinking and made my work far more enjoyable: T. J. Larson, Pat Leigh, Lowell Monke, Kelli Jo Kerry Moran, and Chris Ohana.

A woman who particularly influenced my thinking this last year was Kellie McGarrh, whom I met at an academic conference. Kellie and I had been working on similar, though separate projects; but when we discovered each other's research interests, bystanders could not pull us apart as we skipped sessions, compared notes, and frantically discussed our work for hours at a stretch. We exchanged dissertations after the conference and committed to working together on historical projects about women school leaders. Her untimely death a few weeks later has made me redouble my efforts to share some of her work and ideas.

I appreciate Priscilla Ross, my editor at the State University of New York Press, for her confidence in this project and her limitless help. Megeen Mulholland skillfully shepherded this volume through the publication process, Anne Valentine coordinated its marketing, and David Hopkins completed the copyediting.

My mother I thank for her unending faith in me. She always wanted to write a book—so I hope this volume will encourage her in that direction. I in turn have faith in her. I also thank my father who smiled when I built radios and otherwise turned out to be a science nerd. When I told him I was writing my first book, he suggested I attempt a best-selling pulp novel. This book may not be what he had in mind. I simply could not have completed the superintendent database without the help of my "other mother," Ann Highsmith Fleming. Ann sacrificed several months of time to assist me with the mammoth task of entering data into the superintendent database. She was undaunted by the thousands of names that stretched between Alabama and Wyoming, and she entered them with flawless care. Although she did not see the completion of this volume, her memory has richly motivated it onward.

Finally, BeJae Fleming has offered me help beyond description. She has encouraged, challenged, comforted, and assisted me all the way through this project. Also, her original acoustic music has provided the inspiring backdrop for my daily writing routine, which otherwise would have been embarrassingly mundane. To her I extend my love as well as my deepest thanks. Now it is my turn to help while she works in the studio.

INTRODUCTION

Ella Flagg Young savored the magnitude of her accomplishment. In 1909 when she became the first woman superintendent of the Chicago schools, she declared:

> Women are destined to rule the schools of every city. I look for a large majority of the big cities to follow the lead of Chicago in choosing a woman for superintendent. In the near future we will have more women than men in executive charge of the vast educational system. It is woman's natural field, and she is no longer satisfied to do the greatest part of the work and yet be denied leadership. As the first woman to be placed in control of the schools of a big city, it will be my aim to prove that no mistake has been made and to show cities and friends alike that a woman is better qualified for this work than a man.[1]

Young's enthusiasm for women's school leadership reflected the palpable momentum among women's activists of the time. After all, in a mere fifty years women had progressed from having few means of employment outside the home to dominating their new profession of teaching, accounting for around 70 percent of all teachers by 1900.[2] Women's ascendance into formal school leadership positions could not be far behind, especially as steady suffrage victories had cleared the way for women to wage and win campaigns for elected superintendencies west of the Mississippi River.

In the early decades of the twentieth century, thousands of women succeeded in attaining school leadership positions during what Elisabeth Hansot and David Tyack have called a "golden age" for women school administrators.[3] During this time school districts added formal bureaucratic structures and administrative layers, a trend that resulted in a proliferation of administrative positions. Women moved into these positions, becoming lead teachers, teaching principals, supervisors, mid-level administrators, and sometimes ultimately superintendents. Feminists considered attainment of the superintendency as a particularly important goal for women because it was a position from which they could wield considerable educational influence. It also symbolized women's increasing social, political, and economic power. When Young took the reigns of the Chicago schools, women held around 9 percent of all superintendencies and their numbers appeared to be heading higher (see figure I.1 and the appendix). Even though many of these women superintendents served in small or rural county school systems typically deemed undesirable by men, nonetheless women ambitious for educational leadership were urged to go west to seek these opportunities.[4]

The golden age for women school leaders continued until after World War II in spite of economic depression and a backlash movement against women's social and political advances. Then from the end of the war to 1970, women's representation in most school administrative positions declined quietly, yet rapidly. The percentage of women superintendents, for example, plummeted from 9 to 3 percent during these decades and has risen only slightly since. Ironically, in spite of Ella Flagg Young's optimism and even though numerically women have dominated teaching throughout this century, proportionately fewer women lead school systems today than did in her day, leaving unfulfilled her vision of women "in executive charge of the vast educational system."

This volume, then, tells the story of women and school leadership in America from the common school era to the present. In a broad sense, it is an historical account of how teaching became women's work and school administration men's; it also explores how this gendered division of roles and power in education has been maintained in spite of ever-shifting tensions and contests between organized gendered constituencies. It describes how school administrative positions were created, analyzes the meanings individual women and men have attached to attaining them, and explores the complex social interplay among those who have sought to shape and control the superintendency. It is written from a feminist perspective in that it particularly seeks to understand how power in school employment has been structured unequally by gender. And finally, it focuses on the superintendency because an important component of the effort to establish control of schools has occurred in contesting the definition of this position.

This book is unique in that it seeks to integrate historical scholarship describing school administration with that concerning teaching. Histories of school administration, with the notable exception of works by David Tyack and Elisabeth Hansot, have tended to detail the development of school administration as though only administrative men and a small circle of their powerful allies organized and controlled the profession—both the administrative profession and the larger profession of educators. Typically these narrow accounts have minimized the expansive presence of teachers and women in education. Such approaches have ignored the ways in which some male administrators have defined themselves in relation, or sometimes in reaction, to the larger "feminized" profession. In this volume I argue in part that the superintendency was a creation of some men who wanted to establish a safe, acceptably masculine place for themselves in a profession increasingly identified with women. Educational administration scholarship that ignores teachers and women, then, is incomplete because it misses an important structuring force in the creation of this traditionally male-identified educational domain.

Historical projects concerning the lives and experiences of teachers must, in reciprocal fashion, devote attention to the matter of school administrators. Historical accounts that segregate teachers from administrators risk perpetuating gender polarization in educational employment because important defining interactions between teachers and administrators may be obscured. Segregation hides the embattled territory between men and women where socially constructed gender roles are created and reified. It also renders women school leaders invisible because their experiences lie outside the central focus of either discourse. To understand clearly the mechanism of gender-role polarization in educational employment, it is important to look closely at the cases of persons who have crossed socially defined gender lines, in this case women who have challenged the bounds of a traditionally male domain. This volume attempts to integrate and synthesize histories of school administrators and teachers while maintaining an emphasis on women superintendents.

This project would have proved exceedingly difficult twenty years ago because the most abundantly available historical resources typically minimized the voices of women educators. These sources, which include professional journals, newspapers, magazines, official printed histories of professional education organizations, biographies of prominent educational leaders, and other printed documents, traditionally have been written by men for audiences consisting primarily of men. More recently, however, feminist scholars such as Kathryn Kish Sklar, Polly Welts Kaufman, Kate Rousmaniere, Kathleen Weiler, Geraldine Clifford, Lucy Townsend, Joan Burstyn, Linda Perkins, Linda Eisenmann, Kellie McGarrh, Maxine Schwartz Seller, and many others have endeavored to recover lost female voices by piecing together historical accounts of women's experiences in teaching. The painstaking collection and interpretation of scattered personal documents have yielded fresh insights into the complexities of women's roles in educational employment. This volume owes a great debt to such scholarship. In addition to these works, this analysis also draws from traditional printed

primary source materials and secondary accounts, including dissertations and research monographs. Overall, it offers a synthesis of these
varied sources.

My interest in this research began during my doctoral studies
when a friend mentioned that of all the superintendents who served in
1990, only 3 percent were women. I quickly attempted to verify this sta-
tistic, but found that nearly all of the studies describing the number of
women superintendents were based on limited surveys rather than
comprehensive tallies. These studies offered widely divergent results
and sampling techniques as well. Historical reports suffered from the
same shortcomings. For months, however, I continued the search, hoping to find some obscure, yet illuminating body of research describing
women's representation in the superintendency during the twentieth
century. This search eventually proved both frustrating and unproduc-
tive. When discussing statistical reportage from earlier in the century,
Tyack and Hansot capture the perplexity of the situation when they conclude that "amid proliferation of other kinds of statistical reporting in
an age enamored of numbers . . . data by sex became strangely inacces-
sible. A conspiracy of silence could hardly have been unintentional."[5]

If it were possible that this information had been squelched inten-
tionally, then I felt irresistibly compelled to understand why as well as
to produce and reveal it. I subsequently launched into the laborious task
of compiling the data myself by constructing a superintendent database
from a comprehensive listing of all school administrators who have
served during this century. The 50,000+ record database that emerged
contains detailed data about every chief school officer serving in the
years 1910, 1930, 1950, 1970, and 1990. With this database I have produced and analyzed historical patterns of women's representation in
the superintendency. (See the appendix for detailed information about
the statistical study of school superintendents.)

Several patterns are evident in this data. First, women attained
numerically and proportionately more intermediate (county) superintendencies than either state or local positions. Hundreds, perhaps even
thousands of women served as county school superintendents during
this century. Persons holding these positions typically enjoyed less prestige, lower salaries, and less control of building-level school affairs than
their peers in local systems. Also, intermediate superintendents frequently were chosen by election, while local and state superintendents
usually were appointed by school boards or other officials. Second, the
decades from the middle of the century to the present witnessed significant school-district reorganization. The number of intermediate districts plummeted from 3,095 in 1950 to one-fifth that number by 1990.

FIGURE I.1

Women Superintendents of All District Types Combined, 1910–1990

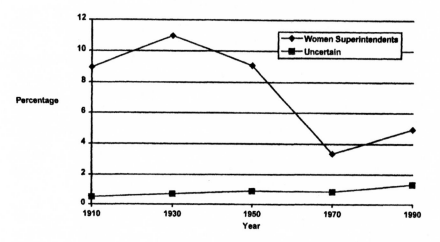

At the same time, the number of local districts with superintendents doubled. Because women have held far more intermediate superintendencies than any other kind, their employment has been affected disproportionately by the demise of the intermediate unit. Third, the total percentage of women superintendents remained fairly stable for the first half of the century before dropping after World War II, recovering only slightly since.

These results cast doubt on commonly held views about the history of women superintendents. The first view maintains that while women have never held many school leadership positions, currently they are making rapid progress after the social changes produced by the modern women's movement. This is an ahistorical assumption, however, because this data demonstrates that recent participation rates of women in the superintendency pale in comparison with those from before World War II. The second view speculates that the decline of women school administrators has occurred gradually throughout this century. My analysis clearly shows that the decline happened both abruptly and relatively recently. A final view contends that women have never held many superintendencies, so their current low numbers are not surprising. While women have never held a majority of school leadership positions, they used to preside over proportionately twice as many school systems as at present.

Even though the numerical data disputes these traditionally held notions, it also raises more questions than it answers. For example, who were these women who became superintendents earlier in the century? What caused the leveling and eventual decline of women's rate of attaining school superintendencies in spite of Ella Flagg Young's belief that increases would continue until women "ruled the schools of every city"? How have women attained superintendencies? Who has supported them? Why? Have there been differences in the ways men and women have constructed their work in this position? What contributed to the steep decline in the number of women school leaders in the 1950s and 1960s? Of immediate concern, why do women seldom hold controlling influence over what was once considered "women's true profession"? And most importantly, what does this persistent gendered division of power reveal about the messages perpetuated by schools, institutions charged with helping to socialize our nation's children?

This book explores these questions. Briefly, the first two chapters survey the creation of sex-segregated employment in nineteenth-century schooling. The first chapter traces the story of how teaching in this country first came to be identified with women, and the second chapter examines how a few men established and assumed school administrative positions. Chapters 3 through 6 elaborate the complex interactions of various gendered constituencies in the campaigns to control the distribution of power in public education. Finally, the appendix elaborates the details of the superintendent database study, including methods, data, and analysis.

The nineteenth century witnessed a dramatic shift in the teaching force. At the beginning only men taught, but by the end women held over two-thirds of all teaching positions. Chapter 1 details how teaching became "feminized" after long having been a profession for men. It explores how women first argued for their right to be educated in formal institutions such as academies, and then how they leveraged that right into an opportunity for their employment outside the home as teachers. The confluence of women's twin desires for education and employment fit well with the ideologies and organizational needs of common school reformers like Horace Mann, who enthusiastically promoted the notion of women teachers. Schools needed women teachers, he argued, because they provided a cheap and readily available source of labor for the burgeoning common school enterprise. There were other benefits as well. Women would welcome the opportunity for independence; they would undertake teacher preparation in earnest; and once hired, they could easily be controlled, especially young, single women. Advocates such as Catharine Beecher persuaded remaining critics that women teachers would be well prepared to assume their rightful duties as wives and mothers; therefore they would not jeopardize their traditional roles for this new venture into the world of salaried employment. As women trickled and then flooded into classrooms in every state and territory, men found diminishing rewards in teaching. With women garnering wages one-half to one-third of men's, school districts found little incentive for raising men's salaries. The increasing presence of school administrators made the work of teaching less independent, more regimented, and more tightly controlled than it had been previously, a shift that male teachers generally despised because it stripped them of authority and therefore part of their masculine prerogative. Some men simply disliked being part of a woman's profession. Men generally took at least one of four courses of action: they deserted teaching; they continued teaching in spite of public doubts about their virility; they created male teacher associations that sought to upgrade their status in the profession and affirm their masculinity; or they moved into administration, the newly created, male-appropriate niche in school employment.

Men who became school administrators modeled their work closely on such hierarchical social institutions as the military and industry where roles, status, power, and authority were defined with position. They customarily refused positions that made them subservient to women, whom they regarded as lower in status. School boards eager to preserve any male presence in schools responded by offering men teaching positions with the promise of rapid administrative advancement. Men effectively rose to the top layers while women remained at the bottom of this new hierarchy.

The administrators holding these desirable higher positions grew increasingly isolated from other school employees, not only in terms of rank, but also because of the physical separation between their new, centrally located offices and the schools they governed. Male administrators had created an inherently isolated new profession. To remedy this sense of detachment, they reached out across districts to connect with each other through professional associations. Groups such as the Department of Superintendence of the National Educational Association tended to promote camaraderie, defend schools and administrators against critics, lobby for greater public recognition of schooling, and help members advance to better positions. Chapter 2 explores the gendered contexts in which school administration developed. It describes the mechanisms by which administrators created associations to systematize and legitimize their work. It also discusses the manner in which administrative associations sought to create an exclusive profession that promoted the interests of members while effectively keeping others out, particularly women, who had begun to encroach on this male sanctuary by the turn of the twentieth century.

Chapter 3 discusses how the turn-of-the-century women's movement pushed women into school leadership positions in spite of, or perhaps because of informally enforced gender barriers. This movement embodied women's larger desires for education, connection with one another, and action for the social good. In the early decades of this century, millions of women participated in a range of social and political organizations that actively campaigned for woman's suffrage, such as the General Federation of Women's Clubs and the National Woman Suffrage Association. Women gained political power as each state granted them the right to vote. Eager to exercise their democratic rights, women not only voted, but they also frequently worked for the election of promising female political candidates. Local women's groups and teachers' organizations vigorously campaigned for the election of women to school superintendencies, positions that symbolized their growing social, political, and economic clout. As a result of these campaigns, thousands of women became local, intermediate, and even state school superintendents, especially in midwestern and western states where women had won suffrage early and superintendencies tended to be elected positions. As the number of women superintendents increased, however, the predominantly male Department of Superintendence lobbied diligently to eliminate the elected superintendency, opting instead for the appointment of "professionals" trained in men's postsecondary institutions. Chapter 3 details the rise of women superintendents during these years and describes the bases of support these leaders found. The chapter also examines how superintendents' organizations simultaneously lobbied for structural changes that would effectively reduce the number of women in their ranks and elevate the social stature of school administration.

In the midst of the golden age of women superintendents, another important, yet little-documented obstacle emerged to erode women's momentum: the practice of stigmatizing and suppressing women who crossed traditional gender-role boundaries. With the social, economic, and political successes of the women's movement, some men perceived that they were losing their traditional places of power in an increasingly gender-stratified society. Those who felt threatened trained their sights on women who defied traditional gender roles, including unmarried women educators. In 1900, well over 90 percent of all female teachers were single or widowed, and many women superintendents were single as well. In a backlash movement, critics portrayed single women teachers as threats to the masculinity of male educators and students. They accused spinster teachers of contributing to the demise of the (White) race. Finally, they used the works of turn-of-the-century sexologists to link spinsterhood with lesbianism, thus creating a climate where single women teachers seemed socially dangerous. This change in ethos regarding single women educators eventually affected policy and hiring practices in the 1940s and 1950s. As a result, the proportion of unmarried women educators decreased rapidly, especially after World War II. In this context, women school administrators faced a particularly difficult dilemma. On one hand, if they performed their supervisory and leadership roles well, they were perceived as masculine because men traditionally controlled social structures and issued orders in this gender-stratified employment scheme. Supposedly masculine women were considered abnormal and undesirable for working with children. On the other hand, if women administrators performed their leadership roles with a feminine demeanor, they were regarded as weak and ineffectual. Chapter 4 documents this postsuffrage backlash movement and the resulting gender-role polarization. It explores how a higher proportion of married women became school administrators and how at the same time women administrators generally struggled to project feminine exteriors while performing work increasingly configured as masculine, a feat so difficult that it contributed to the end of the golden age.

World War II produced major changes in the landscape of public schooling and its leadership. First, millions of veterans returned from service seeking civilian employment. Patriotic school districts anxiously recruited, hired, and promoted them in an effort to increase the number of men in schools. Second, organizational and psychological theories developed by the military later permeated educational-administration training programs and eventually the structure of school systems. Third, credentials obtained in institutions of higher education soon replaced "rising through the ranks" as the predominant means of advancement in school administration. Male veterans with G.I. Bill benefits pushed large numbers of women out of their college and university enrollment slots to obtain these credentials, a gender shift further exacerbated by the fact that many credentialing programs imposed low quotas on the number of women who could be admitted. Finally, immense social pressures forced women who had worked outside the home during the war to return to the home, give their jobs to veterans, marry, and bear children. As a result of these and other changes, women's representation in the superintendency declined to the lowest point of the century in the postwar decades. Few educators discussed this enormous shift in the gender composition of school administration, though. When the topic was raised, women were blamed for their lack of credentials and career commitment. Chapter 5 elaborates this story of how women administrators had, as one article described the postwar trend, "gone the way of the buffalo."

The modern women's movement inspired discussion about women's economic, political, and social opportunities. In education circles, a spate of reports, journal articles, books, conferences, and other public forums devoted attention to the debate over women's roles in the education profession. Women's activists, inspired by the judicial successes of the NAACP and frustrated by women's continued lack of power in educational decision-making, pursued legal remedies and pushed for legislation to eliminate sexual inequities in schooling. Eventually after much wrangling, federal legislation such as Title IX (1972) was passed. Agencies charged with monitoring compliance with this legislation, though, performed anemically at best as strong lobbies quietly pushed for shelving any federal effort to document women's success in attaining school leadership positions. Also, enforcement of many provisions of sex equity legislation was nonexistent. Chapter 6 documents the ways that women's advocates in education attempted to work through the legal and judicial systems to eliminate persistent sexual inequities in schooling and educational employment. It also explores the multiple forms of overt and subtle resistance that greeted and eventually eroded most of these efforts even as journals published reports about women's progress in attaining school leadership positions.

1

THEIR FIRST GREAT PUBLIC PROFESSION

"Everywhere they were demonstrating their capacity as teachers; and, in some places they were becoming superintendents and principals of schools. Because of their prominence in this, their first great public profession, it came to be generally recognized that they should have a voice in the control of school affairs." So wrote Thomas Woody in his 1929 classic work, *A History of Women's Education in the United States*, as he explained how women's participation in school work had moved them closer to full suffrage.[1] Woody's observation would have seemed absurd a century earlier because men, not women, taught children and tutored aspiring young scholars. By the time he penned these words, however, teaching had witnessed a dramatic transformation in which women not only had filled the ranks of teachers and gained "a voice in the control of school affairs," but some hoped that through leadership of their new profession women would demonstrate to the world the public service of which they were capable.

The emergence of women teachers in the 1800s is remarkable considering long-standing Western traditions prohibiting women from this work. In one of the first recorded instances of formal teaching, ancient Sumerian priests passed the lucrative craft of accounting on only to their sons. Through the millennia various religions have disallowed the education of females, and they have certainly prohibited the engagement of women as instructors, tutors, guides, or religious leaders. Christian biblical dictates proscribing women from teaching influenced the early New England Puritan settlers who forced Anne Hutchinson to cease her popular public scriptural lessons.[2] Tradition demanded that men provide the religious wisdom to their communities, not women. Within the home, literate males led their families in scripture readings and taught children to read well enough to participate. Women were to respect and rely on men's authority; thus they were thought to have little need of education, much less were they to provide it.

Eventually as the lives of European settlers grew more complex, socially interconnected, and economically differentiated, tutors and schoolmasters offered their services to families who could afford them. Some of these early colonial instructors were indentured servants working off their transcontinental travel expenses. A few had studied for a time in European colleges and universities. Such men tutored boys in the community to make extra money in addition to other employment. Occasionally schoolmasters established schools and academies and otherwise undertook full-time teaching duties. Only relatively well-to-do colonial families could afford tuition to these institutions.

As colonial populations grew, the demand for schooling increased. In the mid-seventeenth century, Massachusetts passed laws requiring parents to ensure that their children received an education. After the colonies declared independence, Massachusetts and Connecticut enacted legislation requiring local school tax collection to provide education for children whose families could not otherwise afford tuition to private institutions.

This expansion of schooling obviously required the services of an enlarged pool of qualified schoolmasters; however, such teachers were not abundantly available. A few of the men tapped for teaching duties had attended college and hoped to undertake promising careers in the ministry, law, medicine, business, or politics. These men usually did not envision school teaching as their final profession. Instead, they undertook the work as a means of establishing themselves in their communities while providing a socially valuable, yet relatively inexpensive service.

Typically, however, communities struggled to find educated and capable men willing to serve as schoolmasters. Ambitious men frequently pursued lucrative opportunities in other endeavors, and few communities taxed themselves sufficiently to support a well-recommended schoolmaster. As a result, men desperate enough to accept the meager wages and difficult working conditions of the classroom acquired the reputation as ne'er-do-wells who could succeed at little else. This reputation was further sullied by the popular perception that schoolmasters were inclined toward harsh disciplinary methods.[3] Walt Whitman evoked the pedagogue archetype when he wrote that "the word schoolteacher is identified with a dozen unpleasant and ridiculous associations—a sour face, a whip, hard knuckles snapped on tender heads, no gentle, fatherly kindness, no inciting of young ambition in its noble phrases, none of the beautifiers of authority, but all that is small, ludicrous, and in after life productive of indignation."[4]

In spite of the paucity of well-educated and respected schoolmasters, communities initially refrained from hiring women for school teaching duties. First, women were considered less intelligent than men and therefore an education would be wasted on them. Second, because women generally received little, if any academic preparation themselves, they had little to offer others. Besides, young working-class and poor White women commonly worked long hours as domestic servants in middle-class homes; therefore they hardly enjoyed the opportunity to attend school, much less teach. And in the plantation economy of the South, Black women who labored in enslavement faced severe punishment, sometimes death, if they sought or obtained any measure of formal education, on which appointment to teaching positions was contingent. Middle-class White women who might have had the time and resources to pursue education sufficient for teaching responsibilities would have lost status by venturing into the realm of paid labor. Any work outside the home would have conflicted with the traditional expectation that they manage their own households, thus pleasing their husbands and ultimately submitting to male authority.[5]

A few notable persons disagreed with the worthiness of providing formal education for women, however. In the year of American independence, Abigail Adams contended that the young democracy, grounded in Enlightenment faith in reason and respect for humanity, should offer educational opportunities to women as well as men. Adams implored her husband, John, that "if we mean to have Heroes, Statesmen and Philosophers, we should have learned women."[6] While Adams's plea was ignored, Benjamin Rush, a physician and another proponent of women's education, offered a different argument. He asserted that women could serve the country best by providing some modest instruction to their own children, especially their sons; therefore women should receive sufficient education to enhance their motherly duties. He explained: "The equal share that every citizen has in the liberty and the possible share he may have in the government of our country make it necessary that our ladies should be qualified to a certain degree by a peculiar and suitable education, to concur in instructing their sons in the principles of liberty and government."[7] Thus Rush provided generally accepted rhetoric justifying education for females: women should receive education for the benefit of their sons, and by extension, the republic. Consequently, Rush's ideology of republican motherhood failed to challenge existing gender roles and relations deeply, perhaps a requirement for its acceptance at the time.

In spite of its flaws, the ideology of republican motherhood justified a surge in women's opportunities for formal education from 1790 to 1850. During these years a variety of educational institutions at all levels emerged to serve the growing needs of women eager to avail themselves of this new privilege. Seminaries, academies, and colleges opened their doors to female applicants. Some schools admitted females and males on an equal basis, while others were established only for single-sex education. Though curricula varied by institution, female academies in particular offered young middle-class women rigorous liberal studies that in some cases rivaled the quality of elite male academies.[8]

Women who pursued formal studies later usually taught their own children rudimentary academic skills. Some women took in neighboring children and offered them instruction as well. These "dame schools," as they were called, prepared children for eventual enrollment in schools or academies. Although dame schools are generally recounted in contemporary histories of education as an interesting, though hardly critical development in the rise of American schooling, Sally Schwager argues that dame schools represent a high point of women's authority in education because women set the schools up in their own homes, designed their curricula, prepared materials, admitted students, and in every respect controlled the conditions of schooling without oversight by supervisors or other governmental agencies.[9] They exercised their enlarged duties for republican motherhood in a spirit of independence unmatched by other endeavors available to them at the time. They saw as their mission the inculcation in youth of civic virtues as well as reading, writing, and other skills necessary for civic participation. Through teaching they believed they were performing a patriotic duty by contributing to the vitality of the young democracy, which consequently justified their larger role in community work.

Eventually women's opportunities for teaching broadened beyond dame schools. Some communities experimented with hiring women to teach in local schools when men were unavailable or otherwise needed assistance. And because the number of marriageable males in some East Coast communities declined as young men pushed westward to seek their fortune, parents quickly recognized the value of preparing their unmarried daughters for possible school-teaching responsibilities. These "surplus women," as they were called, could support themselves through teaching, however modestly, and ease the economic burden on their families.[10]

By the early nineteenth century, both single and married women had begun to distinguish themselves in the work of schooling. For middle-class women, the stigma of working outside the home had begun to vanish as school teaching became a respectable occupation. At last some working-class and poor women also enjoyed access to the formal education and preparation necessary for teaching; they typically supported themselves through teaching even as they pursued their own studies.

A few enjoyed exemplary careers, such as the handful of New England women who worked their way through district schools and academies and eventually established prominent women's educational institutions. Sarah Pierce started her academy in Litchfield, Connecticut, in 1791. The academy quickly grew as enrollments increased and as she garnered financial support from the community.[11] Catharine Beecher taught at Pierce's academy before establishing her own seminary. In 1823, Beecher rented a modest room for her classes in the center of Hartford. From these humble beginnings, she created the Hartford Female Seminary complete with a large building, a full faculty, and an eminent board of trustees. Kathryn Kish Sklar notes that the Hartford Female Seminary was widely recognized as "one of the most significant advances made in early nineteenth-century education for women."[12]

Emma Willard founded the Troy Female Seminary in 1821, an institution designed primarily to offer women academic preparation as intellectually rigorous as that offered in elite men's colleges. So determined was Willard to see Troy realize this goal that she appealed to the governor of New York for funding by arguing that only educated mothers could foster the kind of individual character that would create prosperity; and because it was the government's duty to provide for national prosperity, the government should fund women's education.[13] Even though the governor did not allocate funds for Troy, the seminary eventually became an important center of women's intellectual, political, social, and economic growth. Finally, beyond Pierce, Beecher, and Willard, Mary Lyon established yet another school for women. After having worked with Zilpah Grant at the Ipswich Seminary, Lyon launched Mt. Holyoke in 1837, the first fully endowed women's institution.[14]

Like other women's institutions of the time, these seminaries prepared women for future careers as teachers. Pierce, Willard, Beecher, Lyon, Grant, and other leading educators of women advocated the notion that females were intellectually capable and that they should be trained specifically for a profession. Since teaching had become acceptable employment for White women across economic strata, the preparation for such work offered added reason for women to seek formal education. When women graduated, teaching opportunities awaited them. There was a catch, though. Most of these early jobs existed outside the Northeast and in remote regions of the continent. Many of them required young women to face physical danger in transit, difficult working conditions, and meager wages when communities had bothered to collect school taxes at all. Occasionally a woman arrived in her designated new community only to discover that no schoolhouse

existed. In spite of such daunting challenges, these women demonstrated their independence, resourcefulness, and intellectual capabilities. They impressed their communities, who in turn accorded them a
large measure of respect.

While some extraordinary women graduates of seminaries and
academies proved their mettle through teaching in far-flung locations,
not everyone greeted educated women with open arms. When a Kentucky college for women opened in 1835, a writer for the local paper
complained that the degrees awarded by the institution such as M.P.L.,
or Mistress of Polite Literature, took women outside their acceptable
places in polite society. If the institution were to continue, he argued in
the satirical piece, the degrees should be replaced by the "M.P.M. (Mistress of Pudding Making), M.D.N. (Mistress of Darning Needle)." "Well
qualified Professors," he continued, could be found "from among the
farmers' wives, and especially from some of the best regulated kitchens,
to teach the young ladies the useful art of house-wifery." In the end, if
graduates succeeded in "making their husband's fireside comfortable,"
then they could happily anticipate receiving the high degrees of "R.W.
(the Respectable Wife), H.H. (Of a Happy Husband); and M.W.R.F.
(Mother of a Well Regulated Family)."[15]

In spite of such resistance to women's formal education and to
their expanded roles outside the home and in school teaching, women
continued to pursue educational opportunities with a thirst and drive
characteristic of persons long deprived. Perhaps American women possessed unique character qualities of independence and awareness that
were forged in revolutionary times and further shaped by the rough
wilderness and uncharted opportunities of a developing nation. Alexis
de Tocqueville certainly thought so. In his landmark 1835 study, *Democracy in America*, the visiting Frenchman observed that "nowhere
are young women surrendered so early or so completely to their own
guidance."[16]

Yet even though single American women may have enjoyed an
independence far greater than their European counterparts, de Tocqueville paradoxically noted that "the independence of woman is irrecov-
erably lost in the bonds of matrimony. If an unmarried woman is less
constrained there than elsewhere, a wife is subjected to stricter obligations . . . [living] in the home of her husband as if it were a cloister."[17]
While young single women might perhaps leverage the right to formal
education and work outside the home into an independence somewhat
unavailable to European women at the time, these rights met their strict
limits in the institution of marriage. Thus women might enjoy radically

new opportunities at one stage of their lives while being expected to return to conservative, traditional limits at another.

Sally Schwager describes women's educational opportunities during this time as configured to satisfy both sides of the paradox simultaneously: "that education for women served the conservative function of preserving dominant cultural values of domesticity and subservience, while at the same time it provided women with the skills, the insights, and the desire to advance nontraditional values and, in some cases, even radical change."[18] Such a system ultimately set limits on the extent to which women might resist their traditional roles, even though it also allowed them to leverage such roles into expanded opportunities. Perhaps nowhere was this as true as in the formal creation of teaching as "women's true profession."

In the first half of the nineteenth century, hundreds of ambitious women taught in schoolhouses scattered through remote regions of the country. In spite of women's increasing presence in teaching, men still presided over most classrooms, especially in urban areas. The rapid spread of common schooling throughout the states and territories, however, created such an intense need for new teachers that local school officials struggled to find people qualified to fill available positions. Traditional factions preferred males, but they found it impractical to locate men willing to work for relatively low wages. Some communities dared to hire women, especially after hearing success stories about the capable women teachers educated and inspired by the likes of Emma Willard and Catharine Beecher. However, for large numbers of communities to hire women rather than men, voting, taxpaying citizens needed justification for the practice, justification powerful enough to compel the reversal of thousands of years of tradition.

Catharine Beecher was more than prepared to address this matter. She had long maintained that women made natural teachers. For one thing, she argued they were better suited to working with children than men. More importantly, though, Beecher believed that women should have dominion over the domestic sphere, and by extension, any work associated with the home. Because children were considered part of the domestic sphere, Beecher contended that it should be women's duty to care for them and teach them. She held that teaching "is woman's natural profession. . . . It is ordained by infinite wisdom, that, as in the family, so in the social state, the interest of young children and of women are one and the same."[19]

Horace Mann, the first state secretary of education in Massachusetts and a childhood friend of Beecher's, faced the immense problem
of identifying a capable and readily available source of teachers. When
Mann assumed the position of secretary in 1837, he confronted the challenge of transforming the state's poorly funded and ragged collection of
district schools into well-funded models of excellence and consistency.
Although Mann's position initially carried very little power, he maxi-
mized his influence by studying the schools of the state thoroughly and
compiling a series of twelve widely distributed annual reports that he
hoped would embarrass apathetic communities into upgrading and improving their schools.

Mann devoted an entire report to addressing the impending shortage of qualified and trained teachers. He concluded that the practice of
hiring women teachers would offer the most viable solution to the
teacher shortage. He agreed with Beecher's contention that women
made natural teachers because they inherently possessed several
unique qualities. For example, he lauded women's natural maternal
qualities. He held that the "greater intensity of the parental instinct in
the female sex, their natural love for the society of children, and the superior gentleness and forbearance of their dispositions . . . lead them to
mildness rather than severity, to the use of hope rather than of fear as a
motive of action, and to the various arts of encouragement rather than
to annoyances and compulsion in their management of the young."[20]

Another supposedly natural quality possessed by women teachers was their womanly affection. Mann held that women's affectional
qualities outstripped their intellectual abilities, which made them quite
suitable as teachers of the young. Moreover, he regarded the tender nurturance of the emotional needs of children as women's distinct calling:
"If the intellect of woman, like that of man, has the sharpness and the
penetrancy of iron and of steel, it must also be as cold and as hard. No!
but to breathe pure and exalted sentiments into young and tender
hearts . . . this is her high and holy mission."[21]

Some advocates of women teachers went beyond merely arguing
that women made natural teachers to contending that they were clearly
superior to men. The New York Committee on Hiring Women Teachers
concluded that "while man's nature is rough, stern, impatient, ambitious, hers is gentle, tender, enduring, unaspiring. One always wins; the
other sometimes repels; the one is loved; the other sometimes feared."
Beecher elaborated further: "That young women are the best teachers
has been proved and acknowledged by those men who have made trial
of the gentle sex in schools of the most difficult description, because of
the superior tact and moral power natural to the female character."

Catharine's sister, Harriett Beecher Stowe, agreed. She contended that "if men have more knowledge they have less talent at communicating it, nor have they the patience, the long-suffering, and gentleness necessary to superintend the formation of character."[22]

Women, it was argued, would also bring a host of other advantages to the classroom if the public would only hire them. To begin with, Beecher explained that women tended to put their work first because of their self-denying nature. A second argument she forwarded played insidiously on Protestant fears of Catholic domination in the states. Since Catholics in recent centuries had begun to support the education of women and their employment as teachers, Protestants would have to consider doing so as well, she argued.[23]

Perhaps the most compelling argument for the hiring of women teachers concerned cost. Because women had few other job opportunities available outside the home, and many women eagerly anticipated the chance for economic independence, education, and public service, large numbers of women enthusiastically pursued teaching. Consequently, they could be hired for relatively little money, certainly much less than that demanded by men. Male teachers customarily would not work for the wages offered by some districts. Beecher maintained that women needed lower salaries because they "can afford to teach for one-half, or even less, the salary which men would ask, because the female teacher has only herself; she does not look forward to the duty of supporting a family, should she marry; nor has she the ambition to amass a fortune."[24] In school districts where barely enough money could be raised to build a schoolhouse, much less to sustain an educational program, the prospect of hiring inexpensive labor proved irresistibly enticing.

Not everyone shared the enthusiasm for women teachers professed by Beecher and Mann, however. One of the greatest problems voiced by critics concerned women's ability, or perhaps inability to control their students, especially older males. Women were thought to be delicate and unable to discipline disruptive students properly. Certainly discipline concerned many communities because students were known to beat or even throw unpopular male teachers from the schoolhouse occasionally. One superintendent wrote in 1865 that "it must be acknowledged that in a few cases the 'big boys' are a little unruly."[25] Another simply indicated that a woman teacher should not be hired "for the same reason that she cannot so well manage a vicious horse or other animal, as a man may do."[26]

In spite of complaints about women's purported inability to control students, school districts around the country cautiously hired women teachers, largely because in the final analysis the choice seemed expedient. Within a few years, however, school districts not only hired women, but actively sought them out. Horace Mann summarized: "Six or eight years ago when the employment of female teachers was recommended to school committees, not a little was said against the adoption of the suggestion. But one committee after another was induced to try the experiment and the success has been so great that the voice of opposition is now silenced."[27]

As teaching opportunities opened to them, hundreds of thousands of women prepared themselves for their new careers. In spite of the difficult working conditions and low wages, women found that school teaching offered them advantages previously unimaginable. First, women who intended to teach were justified in seeking their own education. When asked why they wanted to attend institutions of higher education, they could assure skeptical friends and family members that they needed education for their career plans. Some from humble homes might be able to study only at a district school before being summoned into local service. Others could seek higher education at a variety of institutions such as normal schools, academies, seminaries, and colleges. Higher education was no longer viewed only as ornamental or unnecessary for these women.

A second advantage offered by teaching was that because of the wages paid, large numbers of middle-class women were able to live independently of their families for the first time. Previously, daughters were expected to perform domestic duties within their family's home until they married and undertook these same duties for their husbands. Women customarily did not pursue paid labor because it demanded that their allegiance be split between work and their husbands or fathers. Teaching offered women a chance to pursue work that did not conflict with their expected social roles, yet still allowed them a measure of economic independence. Working-class and poor women whose economic needs outweighed their concern for social propriety could earn wages in the teaching profession, which had the added benefit of conferring middle-class status.[28]

With economic independence came a third benefit of teaching: social independence. Fewer women felt compelled to marry. Women had previously faced the choice of marrying men—even ones they despised—depending on their families, or living in poverty with no one to support them. Some women who married favorably found that the institution of marriage robbed them of their independence and self-reliance. A few chose to teach rather than marry. Others taught until a suitable marriage offer presented itself. Clearly teaching offered women new options.

A fourth advantage of teaching was that women could control a physical space of their own: the schoolhouse. There were not many such female-controlled areas, especially public places. Arguably, married women governed the functions within their homes; however, their husbands still exercised ultimate authority there. Even though schoolteachers were supervised periodically by district administrators who rode from schoolhouse to schoolhouse, the women who taught in schoolhouses largely determined when the school day would begin and end, who could enter and leave, the arrangements within the building, and other conditions. In some cases the schoolhouse even provided women teachers with a place to live. The privacy afforded them granted a measure of freedom from the watchful eyes of community members, privacy they could not have enjoyed while boarding in the homes of community families or local boarding houses.[29]

A fifth important advantage women found in teaching was that it made them feel they were contributing to the public good. Said one teacher, "No profession affords greater opportunities for doing good than that of teaching; and we consider this as being the highest inducement to influence a person to engage in it."[30] Such idealism extended into several different social arenas. First, Beecher advocated the notion that women's work in teaching would aid in national unification. It was women's patriotic duty to teach and further the cause of nationalism.[31] Other women who felt socially empowered through teaching went on to become temperance workers, abolitionists, and suffragists.[32] If women had been confined to the home previously, teaching allowed them to expand their reach to the public sphere, where they might address larger social problems.

Women's willingness to take on the work of school teaching solved a thorny employment problem that otherwise would have stunted the common school movement and the promise of basic education for American children. However, not only did these ambitious women fulfill a social need, but they also reaped several significant benefits in return. Through their increased economic, political, social, and intellectual standing, they continued pushing the limits of women's traditional roles. In some ways, teaching allowed women to attain privileges previously available only to men.

As women filled classrooms around the country in the mid-nineteenth century, male teachers found themselves part of an increasingly "feminized" profession, feminized in that women constituted a growing proportion of the teaching ranks, but also feminized in the sense that the work had changed to fit traditional notions of women's work. Some men departed the schoolhouse in disgust or in search of better wages. A few wondered what it meant that women held the same jobs previously reserved for learned men. Feeling socially isolated among ever-larger numbers of women, schoolmasters developed several strategies for preserving or enhancing their identities as teachers. One strategy involved establishing associations of schoolmasters where men in "women's true profession" could meet each other socially and discuss educational issues among those whom they regarded as their intellectual and social peers.

Associations and fraternal organizations were not uncommon in America during that time. Such groups proliferated in the middle decades of the nineteenth century, facilitated by at least two key technological developments. The penny press, which had made its way to America around 1830, offered an inexpensive means for organizations to publish newsletters and journals by which members could communicate from a distance.[33] Also, improved transportation through better roads, steamboats, and regional train systems allowed widely scattered members to gather from time to time. Teacher associations formed and dedicated themselves to sharing professional knowledge as well as to socializing. In describing the 1886 establishment of the Michigan Schoolmasters' Club, Leslie Butler explains:

> What was the driving force that caused the pioneer educators to assemble despite extremely difficult travel, considerable discomfort, and expense involving a depletion of their meager resources? Some of the answers were that teachers— 1) Are more than ordinarily gregarious. 2) Desire to obtain solutions to problems common to all. 3) Are interested in new methods and techniques of teaching. 4) Anticipate profit and pleasure from exchange of experiences. 5) Desire to hear addresses by noted authorities from foreign countries and other states on new subjects and educational projects appearing on the educational horizon. 6) Desire to continue friendly and stimulating relationships.[34]

Male teachers found that the opportunity to socialize with each other held great appeal. Often schoolmasters felt limited in their social outlets because teachers generally were expected to live proper, upstanding lives relatively free of the vices such as drinking or slovenliness that had often tarnished the reputations of early schoolmasters. However, as Willard Waller explained, men who did not "smoke, drink, swear, or tell risqué stories" would tend to be excluded from "the confraternity of men in general, from all barber shop, pool room, and men's club fellowship."[35] Thus if schoolmasters adhered to unwritten professional standards of behavior, they effectively were barred from socializing with other local men where such behaviors were customary and perhaps a demonstration of proper masculinity. Male teachers found a solution to this difficult dilemma by gathering in exclusively male teacher organizations. They did not have to chomp cigars or swill liquor to be accepted, yet they could still socialize with other men. Perhaps even better for them in the long run, these organizations eventually endeavored to improve the status and conditions of schoolmasters. The men in these groups eventually mastered civic affairs and became skilled political strategists at the local, state, and federal levels.

One of the earliest and most influential of these organizations was the American Institute of Instruction, organized in Boston in 1830. Membership in the institute was generally limited to elite educators and scholars of the time, mainly from New England. Most founding members taught in academies and the majority were college graduates. All members were men. Among other accomplishments, the institute was instrumental in lobbying for the creation of the office of the State Superintendent of Schools in Massachusetts, the position first held by Horace Mann. The group also successfully campaigned for higher teacher salaries. The institute provided members with a chance to talk, debate, and then to put their ideas into action utilizing political mechanisms.[36]

Even though women increasingly filled teaching positions through the middle of the 1800s, the American Institute of Instruction did not allow them to join until 1867. Women then quickly pushed the membership of the institute steeply upward. However, as women's numbers in the previously all-male organization increased, many male members, especially the older, better-educated, and more highly placed members, decided to leave. Some even left school teaching altogether to become professors or business executives. Essentially, as women moved into the organization, men chose to leave and were not replaced. This trend paralleled that of the larger teaching profession. Historian Paul Mattingly sadly recounts how this "incursion of females" signaled the end of the highly influential organization.[37]

Another such organization, the National Teachers Association, which was established in 1857 and later merged with two other groups to become the National Education Association (NEA), initially allowed women to join as honorary members, but only with the approval of the board of directors. Once approved, they could attend meetings, though they were not allowed to speak publicly at such gatherings. If women wished to address their colleagues, they could only discuss topics assigned to them and even then they needed to prepare speeches to be read by male officers of the association. Generally, even though women constituted a significant proportion of teachers by this time, they were not well represented in the proceedings of teacher associations, nor were they allowed any meaningful leadership roles.[38]

Occasionally there were showdowns over women's circumscribed roles in teacher associations. At a gathering of New York teachers in 1853, Susan B. Anthony wished to join a discussion about why teachers were not as well respected as lawyers, ministers, or doctors. At first the chair denied her the floor because the association's rules prohibited women from speaking at such meetings. Anthony, however, caught many off-guard when she challenged the rule and requested permission to speak. A long, contentious debate ensued over whether she should be granted a special dispensation. Finally, when permitted to speak, she said:

> It seems to me, gentlemen, that none of you quite comprehend the cause of the disrespect of which you complain. Do you not see that so long as society says a woman is incompetent to be a lawyer, minister, or doctor, but has ample ability to be a teacher, that every man of you who chooses that profession tacitly acknowledges that he has no more brains than a woman? And this, too, is the reason that teaching is a less lucrative profession, as here men must compete with the cheap labor of woman. Would you exalt your profession, exalt those who labor with you. Would you make it more lucrative, increase the salaries of the women engaged in the noble work of educating our future Presidents, Senators, and Congressmen.[39]

Later, a man in attendance told her: "As much as I am compelled to admire your rhetoric and logic, the matter and manner of your address and its delivery, I would rather follow a daughter of mine to her grave, than to have her deliver such an address before such an assembly."[40] Essentially, the fact that she had spoken publicly with force and intelligence had disturbed this man even more than her provocative message, which challenged the gender stratification of power and status sought by schoolmasters.

Even three decades later when women clearly dominated the teaching profession numerically, women were only grudgingly allowed the floor during association meetings. At the 1884 annual meeting of the NEA, May Wright Sewall had been invited to address the assembly in a panel discussion devoted to the topic of women in education. No pushover, she began by describing the rather unconscious manner by which males in the association seemed to speak only among themselves even with large numbers of women in attendance:

Notwithstanding the fluttering of fans and the fluttering of ribbons, and the gay waving of plumes, and the glancing smiles, and the eloquent blushes from the audience, speakers have persisted in addressing their audiences as "gentlemen." Doubtless a preconceived supposition of who would be here has been more to them than the testimony of their eyes, and notwithstanding the major part of their audiences, save the audience of superintendents convened this afternoon, notwithstanding the major part of every audience has been constituted of women, gentlemen have absolutely been enabled to see them, and have persistently addressed the remarks, which women were assiduously endeavoring to hear and profit by, to men.[41]

A second way that male teachers bolstered their status was to promote the skills and qualities that only they supposedly could bring to the classroom. Schoolmasters argued that men were instrumental in shaping the character of children in ways that women could not duplicate.[42] Without men's help and guidance, children would grow into socially incomplete persons. More generally, male educators contended that their mere presence was needed in schools to lend a masculine tone to an otherwise female-dominated institution. Leonard Ayres in 1911 listed the specific masculine qualities he thought only men brought to their work:

Positive influences distinctly masculine in character. Masculinity. Man's viewpoint of life. Power. Elements of strength, of deliberative judgment, of logical power, of executive force. Positive convictions, practical sense, breadth of vision and sound judgment. Manly influence. Man's point of view on questions of civics, ethics and conduct. Vigorous, aggressive and ambitious attitude toward life. Man's interest in mechanical contrivances, helping to develop the practical inventive faculty in boys. Man's interests in and understanding of the fundamental principles of government and man's duties as a citizen.[43]

Perhaps one of the most important arguments articulated on the need for male teachers, though, was that men alone enforced proper discipline. A group of male teachers contended that to produce properly masculine men, "a boy needs forceful, manly control. He should learn the grip and control of a man. If he is to become a manly man, he should hardly be deprived of the daily contact of a virile man. He also needs the strength of a man to control and direct his strong, boyish proclivities."[44] Conversely, to keep boys from becoming feminine, Henry Armstrong wrote in 1903 that to "develop a virile man," there should be more male teachers in schools. Otherwise, "the boy in America is not being brought up to punch another boy's head or to stand having his own punched in a healthy and proper manner . . . There is a strange and indefinable feminine air coming over the men; a tendency towards a . . . sexless tone of thought."[45] However, just as those who initially had resisted employing women teachers in the first place had maintained that women could hardly manage rowdy older boys, the new advocates of male teachers employed essentially the same argument, but this time to bolster men's value in a predominantly female profession.

In the mid-1800s, an interesting trend in educational employment developed in parallel with the emergence of women teachers. Local and state officials created the domain of school administration, a realm reserved from the beginning for men. Just as communities eventually had welcomed women into schoolhouses to perform duties derived from the notion of republican motherhood, so too did school districts hire men to assume new authority positions configured suspiciously like institutionalized, idealized versions of the family man, husband, and father. Though there was no flurry of editorials debating the merits of employing men in roles reminiscent of traditional male heads of household, a few school districts adopted the practice at first, and then as though finding a resonance in the collective psyches of local school officials, the practice proliferated with breathtaking speed. After all, when women had ventured into the classroom, they not only had broadened their acceptable sphere of work, but they also had stepped dangerously close to setting an unsettling new precedent for autonomy and independence from men's controlling influence. The danger was quickly circumvented, however, when male administrators appeared and exercised a measure of authority. School officials lauded the notion of paid male school administrators who could monitor female teachers and keep them from getting out of line.

The school supervisor was one of the first such administrative positions established, with supervisory duties varying by school type and perceived community needs. In urban schools, supervisors controlled instruction by administering promotional exams to students and by evaluating teachers' mastery of approved pedagogical techniques. They also assisted with disciplinary matters, but the ultimate disciplinary authority resided in the male superintendent.[46] Supervisors of rural schools performed slightly different duties. They certified teachers and supervised teacher preparation programs. They also periodically made the rounds of country schools to observe teachers at work and to assess the quality of student recitations.

In urban school districts, the schoolmaster/principal teacher preceded the appearance of the supervisor. Boston schools, for example, employed schoolmasters in the early 1800s to head the instructional work performed in large, two-room schoolhouses. In these schools, schoolmasters typically taught older students in the second-floor room, while women assistants instructed younger children downstairs. Women assistants generally received little training for their work.[47] They also were expected to refer difficult disciplinary matters to the schoolmaster upstairs.

Eventually urban schools built multiclassroom, graded schools. From the beginning of these new institutions, school boards employed women to teach in individual classrooms and a male principal teacher or full-time principal to oversee the functioning of an entire school. With such a configuration, the charge that women were poor disciplinarians could be countered with the explanation that male principals in each building could handle any disciplinary problems that women might face.[48]

Women who taught in these schools, while perhaps not as physically daunting as some of their male colleagues, nonetheless found their own unique ways to manage their classes. Many of them reportedly prevented disruptions from older male students far more effectively than did their male colleagues.[49] May Sewall in 1884 described what she regarded as one of the finest contributions women had made to teaching:

> The first visible effect of women's entrance upon the profession of teachers was the amelioration of discipline in the school-room. . . . [This] was the direct result of [their] inferior physical strength . . . which compelled women to substitute for the physical agencies that had before been used, spiritual ones. . . . It is true indeed that softer discipline, that moral suasion, that spiritual force, were resented by the big boys. He demanded the birch and the rawhide and ferule upon his teacher's desk as external symbols of the superior animal force by which alone he wished to be bound. Notwithstanding the big boy's resentment, which for a time worked out its purpose, and confined women teachers in the country to district schools in the summer, when the big boy could

not be there, notwithstanding that, the spiritual agencies substituted by women were necessarily soon adopted by men, and the growth of the moral powers, which had, perhaps by accident, or, at least unconsciously, been discovered by women, was thenceforth conscientiously and studiously developed.[50]

Regardless of their actual success in managing their students, the popular contention that women needed men's help with disciplinary matters persisted. In describing the tenacity of this view, David Tyack concludes that, "the presumed superiority of men as executives and disciplinarians seems to rest more on male vanity than on evidence."[51] The rationale that men were needed for disciplinary control was employed to justify hiring male administrators in multiclassroom schools in spite of contradictory information. Strober and Tyack observe that "from the beginning, sex segregation was part of the design of the urban graded school."[52]

Rural school districts also added supervisors, or superintendents as they sometimes were called, but ostensibly for somewhat different reasons. Elected school officials generally thought that teachers needed significant guidance, particularly as women moved into the work. School committees, while willing to offer advice, did not necessarily know how to teach well themselves because teaching experience was not a prerequisite for committee service. Rural school districts solved this perceived problem by hiring supervisors who then rode the district circuit of one-room schoolhouses to oversee teachers' work. Though many of these early supervisors had little or no instructional experience from which they might offer teachers assistance, what they reliably brought to their work was the fact that they were men.

One reason proffered by school committees on the need for supervisors' guiding presence was that women as a group tended to move in and out of teaching quickly. Some taught only briefly before leaving for marriage. Others departed because of difficult working conditions or to care for family members needing their daughters' assistance. Such transience was deemed unprofessional.[53] However, men moved in and out of teaching, too; but they typically left for better pay, improved working conditions, or greater authority and prestige. Their transience was not criticized as it was for women. Instead men were thought justified in seeking better opportunities. Clearly in most school districts, though, teachers of either sex hardly were paid sufficiently or treated well enough to remain firmly committed to the work for extended periods, leading historian Thomas Morain to conclude that teaching was not women's work, but rather it was youths' work.[54] As long as

women teachers were perceived as transient, though, school committees easily could justify hiring supervisors.

By some accounts, early rural school supervisors did little to improve teachers' work. To begin with, school committees assigned supervisors the herculean task of visiting numerous schoolhouses spread
over great distances. For instance, a study of rural Pennsylvania teachers revealed that supervisors visited their classes only fifteen minutes to
eight hours in a year.[55] Once supervisors made it to the classroom, they
could offer little guidance in structuring the educational program because they generally lacked curricular training. This state of affairs led
Willard Ellsbree to conclude that "infrequent visits of the superintendents, coupled with the absence of any well-defined program of studies, could not conceivably result in any appreciable improvement in
teaching."[56]

If rural supervisors generally were unable to effect significant im-
provements in the quality of work done by district teachers, one won-
ders why they were hired at all. After all, they commanded higher
salaries than teachers, and their employment reduced the pool of
money otherwise available for teacher salaries. They were not hired to
any appreciable degree when teaching was performed primarily by
men. That men were systematically granted authority over women
whose positions became ever more subordinate is a fact that cannot be
dismissed as irrelevant. Even as women escaped the immediate control
of husbands and fathers by becoming teachers, male supervisors may
have been viewed as surrogate family males who made certain that
women stayed within their culturally defined gender-role boundaries.[57]
Language used to describe the relationships between female teachers
and male supervisors frequently evoked male-centered family relationships. For example, Aaron Gove, superintendent of Denver schools, explained that any advice teachers might have for their superiors "is to be
given as the good daughter talks with the father."[58] Women generally
had little choice in accepting this new layer of control, leading Strober
and Tyack to conclude that "difference of gender provided an important
form of social control."[59]

Not surprisingly, teachers did not always welcome the addition of
supervisory personnel in their work. However, superintendents
charged with the task of compiling local annual school reports generally did not see fit to include teachers' opinions on this matter. Neither
did reports that included the statements of school committee members.
In spite of the omission of their voices in official reports, teachers found
ways of expressing their dismay with the controlling element added to
the profession. A Rochester teacher complained that the supervisory

system "needs not much trial to secure its abandonment at once," and further that the $1,000 annual superintendent salary could well be cut and used for the tuition fund.[60] Rural teachers had little supervision and preferred it that way. A survey of Nebraska teachers suggested that even with sporadic and marginally helpful visits by supervisors, only 4 percent believed that better supervision was necessary.

When Vermont schools moved from one-room schoolhouses to multiclassroom buildings with building supervisors or principals, the women teachers believed they had lost much of their independence, pride, and sense of purpose. One teacher explained: "For so many years I had been the one who settled everything. . . . That was one of the hardest things for teachers who had always been in a country school to come into a graded school—because you had to follow rules and regulations." Another explained that in one-room schoolhouses "you were on your own. You didn't have to answer to anyone." One teacher summarized: "I was the boss—that's why I liked it better, I suppose."[61]

As school districts hired administrators, the structure and practice of school teaching changed. Teaching was reconfigured in incremental steps to align ever more closely with the traditionally acceptable duties, roles, and constraints of women. It became "feminized" in a functional sense. Even before individual teachers faced their first classes, these transformations had already affected the means by which they received training and superintendents selected them. Institutions that prepared teachers shifted the focus away from subject matter such as mathematics, science, and literature, and toward pedagogical methods. Horace Mann initially had recommended this curricular change for normal schools, which a variety of teacher preparation programs later adopted. Some argued that requiring teachers to learn advanced academic concepts wasted everyone's time because teachers only needed to know what they would use in the classroom. As a result, normal schools and teacher training institutes increasingly required teachers to study how they would convey their lessons more than they considered the content itself. Teacher certification exams changed accordingly. This curricular shift arguably repelled some men who might otherwise have been interested in teaching.[62] It also reduced the possibility that intellectually talented women could engage fully with challenging subject content as their male peers could in other programs or institutions of higher education. By so restricting the content of teacher preparation programs, college-educated administrators could, through their supposedly greater intellectual authority, exercise increased control over teachers.

A second important shift occurred in the amount of preparation prospective teachers needed for certification. School administrators set progressively stiffer certification requirements. This in turn meant that teaching candidates needed to attend special summer programs or enroll in lengthy teacher preparation institutes. These changes effectively discouraged potential male teachers for several reasons. Because men tended to supplement their regular teaching salaries by holding agriculture-related summer jobs, they would have had to sacrifice some of their traditional wage-earning activity to attend summer school. Besides, teachers were expected to attend these programs at their own expense.[63] Generally, men calculated that the additional training required for their certification was hardly worth the low wages they would earn as teachers. Women, however, had few other alternatives; thus they were more willing to bear the greater load and expense. This situation led Edward Thorndike to conclude in 1912 that "there is evidence that raising the requirements quickly increases the percentage of women among those securing [teaching] positions in elementary or secondary schools."[64]

Teachers also lost autonomy, status, and authority to the same degree that administrators simultaneously gained in these three areas. Essentially, power in educational employment shifted upward as administrative strata emerged. Administrators expected greater deference from teachers. While teachers had not previously enjoyed much job security, administrators increasingly certified, examined, and otherwise set requirements for teacher employment. These broadened powers essentially gave administrators more control over teachers and their tenure. Teachers knew not to cause trouble or their certification might not be renewed. Superintendents who hired teachers preferred women because they were less likely to question administrative authority and policies than men.[65] Likewise, administrators favored single, rather than married women because the latter had husbands who occasionally complained about district practices. In time, administrators imposed progressively greater restrictions on teachers' employment and practices, thereby tipping the power balance further toward themselves.

These three changes and others arguably constituted the construction of teaching as women's work. Men were less inclined to study pedagogy than subject content. They were not as likely to increase their level of preparation for teaching without commensurate monetary, status, or power rewards. And they undoubtedly were discouraged by the increased subservience demanded of teachers especially because submission was deemed a desirable quality for women at the time, but anathema to a properly masculine demeanor.

The gradual construction of teaching as women's work intensified what was already a strong trend in hiring women teachers. In the mid-1800s, women constituted a significant and growing segment of the teaching force. After the Civil War, however, they accounted for the majority of all teachers and their numbers continued to increase well into the twentieth century. Men, on the other hand, left teaching in droves. From 1899 to 1906 alone, the number of male teachers in the United States dropped by 24 percent.[66] This happened even as the overall number of teachers continued to increase. Apparently this did not occur because women crowded men out of teaching positions, but rather because men decided to leave.[67] Thomas Morain, in his study of nineteenth-century male teachers in Iowa, suggests that "departure, not displacement seems to have been the pattern."[68]

Not all men chose to leave, however. The men who remained struggled to redefine themselves in a profession not only increasingly made up of women, but also restructured around women's traditionally defined gender roles. School boards and superintendents charged with hiring teachers usually sought male candidates, but they tended to avoid hiring the men who applied because such men often did not fit traditional standards of masculinity.[69] Supposedly masculine men would not have been attracted to the positions as they were increasingly configured. Sociologist Willard Waller cruelly concluded that teaching had therefore become "the refuge of unsaleable men and unmarriageable women."[70]

By the turn of the twentieth century, women accounted for over 70 percent of all teachers.[71] At that point, the shift in the makeup of the teaching force had become inescapably clear and it stimulated a flurry of public discussion. Suddenly, school men, journalists, academics, school officials, and a variety of other concerned citizens expressed outrage over the phenomenon.

One reason widely advanced for men's exodus from teaching concerned the low salaries that many regarded as unattractive to capable men. To produce salaries likely to entice men back into teaching, though, taxpayers would have faced increased school taxes, a change likely to ignite protest. Not everyone agreed, however. In his 1908 article, "Why Teaching Repels Men," C. W. Bardeen explained that "it is not a matter of wages. Professionally fitted men teachers get a higher average salary than the average incomes of lawyers, physicians, clergymen, and business men in their communities." Rather, other factors were more important, he argued. Bardeen did admit that men were deterred from teaching younger children because of the low salaries, though.[72]

A more important reason for the decline of male teachers, according to Bardeen, concerned the fact that men regarded teaching as poor work. He explained that "teaching usually belittles a man. . . . His daily dealing is with petty things, of interest only to his children and a few women assistants, and under regulations laid down by outside authority, so that large questions seldom come to him for consideration." He continued:

> It is a hireling occupation. . . . The ordinary man teacher is entirely at their [school trustees'] mercy. The law makes them the authority as to course of study, regulations, selection of teachers, equipment, and supplies. . . . They are in a state of dependency upon trustees elected to office without special knowledge of the needs of the schools or the relative qualifications of teachers. . . . It is otherwise with the lawyer, the physician, the business man. Provided they earn enough to keep out of debt they are their own masters. They can come when they like, go when they like, do what they like.[73]

Ella Flagg Young concurred with Bardeen's assessment. She explained in her 1900 doctoral dissertation that perhaps the most potent influences keeping men from teaching were "the mechanism, drudgery, and loss of individuality which the method of organization and administration has tended to make characteristic of the graded school."[74]

Essentially, as teaching had been constructed as women's work, it had become far less desirable for men. A group of male teachers explained, "the profession has become so feminized that men have felt a loss of social standing while engaged as teachers."[75] One writer distilled the situation: "The business of school teaching is coming to be considered a woman's business, and therefore, offers less attraction to young men than formerly."[76]

Men disliked being associated with women's work and they also frequently complained about working with women. One New Jersey superintendent said:

> Of my own knowledge many young men have been driven from school because of their intense dislike to being (using their own words) "bossed by women." . . . Those men, many of them, were forced out of school because of their intense individualism, because they were strong, because they had reached an age where it was imperative that they be instructed, directed, controlled by one of their own sex, and by a man larger and broader, both physically and mentally, than each youth felt himself to be.[77]

A final reason commonly offered for why men left the classroom concerned the Civil War. Thousands of men left teaching to fight in the war and women typically replaced them. When the war ended, though, men did not return to teaching in significant numbers, partly because some had died or suffered wounds in battle, and partly because the postwar salaries available were insufficient to attract them when greater opportunities existed elsewhere.[78]

The men who continued to teach needed to find ways to preserve their sense of masculinity among their female colleagues. One way for them to do this was to aspire toward becoming educational heroes or martyrs. Within schoolmasters' clubs and associations, the great educators in American history were hailed as models of the profession. Icons of educational leadership and innovation, and the lone champions of scholarship amid armies of apparent mediocrity were visions that inspired male teachers everywhere to distinguish themselves in this otherwise degraded work.[79]

A second means of bolstering men's flagging masculinity involved recruiting more of them into teaching to form something of a critical mass of males. Male educators usually led these efforts. The Male Teachers' Association of New York City, for example, published a pamphlet in 1904 describing why they believed more men were urgently needed in schools:

> At the present time over ninety percent of all the boys in the United States leave school without ever coming in contact with a single male teacher. . . . The elementary schools of the great cities of our country are almost entirely under the control of women teachers. The few men that are in the elementary schools are largely in administrative work. . . . Formerly women were employed as teachers because such a practice was deemed expedient. Men were then considered the ideal teachers. While this ideal has largely passed away among administrative agents, and the tendency is rapidly gaining ground to place all the agencies of education in woman's hands as her particular function, yet we have found, as teachers, that parents decidedly prefer men teachers. The increase in the number of women in the schools has been a most rapid change, and unprecedented in the educational history of the world. It has had as yet scarcely the sanction of a generation.[80]

In 1911, Leonard Ayres circulated a survey to leading male educators in New York City requesting their opinions on the need for hiring men. One survey question concerning whether schools needed men was answered in the affirmative by a resounding 98 percent of the respondents.[81] He then presented the results of this survey to the city commission on teachers' salaries hoping that a large-scale recruiting effort might result. Other groups similarly sought to increase men's presence in schools. Districts throughout Oklahoma actively sought and hired male teachers even though a number were unqualified. Some received rapid promotions to superintendencies to help preserve male leadership.[82] In 1938, Phi Delta Kappa, an entirely male organization of educators, published a widely circulated pamphlet designed to encourage promising young male students to become teachers.[83]

A final important means of making teaching more appealing to men involved the creation of male-identified niches such as coaching, vocational education, other manual trades, and certain high school subjects such as science and mathematics. Administrative positions held particular appeal because supervisory work had been structured from the start to suit masculine-appropriate gender definitions. Bardeen idealized the position of the superintendency because "the kinds of men chosen for these places are those who are least subject to . . . defects. . . . But the rank and file of men teachers are still seriously deficient."[84]

FIGURE 1.1

Percentages of Male and Female Teachers, 1870–1950*

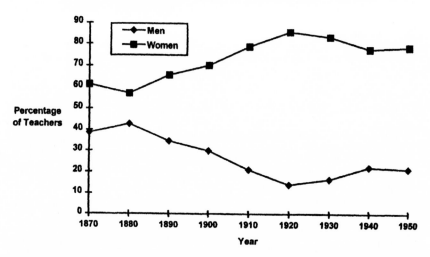

*For a detailed breakdown of the data charted in this figure, see *The Statistical History of the United States from Colonial Times to the Present* (Stamford, CT: Fairfield Publishers, 1965), 208.

In spite of these efforts to end the shortage of male teachers and recruit men into the profession, the overall percentage of male educators continued to decline until well into the twentieth century. In 1870 women held 60 percent of all teaching positions compared with 40 percent for men. Three decades later in 1900, women held 70 percent and men 30 percent. By 1920, the overall percentage of women educators peaked at 86 percent, while men held only 14 percent of all school positions, *including* supervisory and administrative jobs.[85]

Hidden within these larger statistics on the percentages of female and male teachers are subtle geographical, economic, and cultural variations. Katz and Ellsbree have maintained that urban schools were feminized before rural ones. While there is evidence to suggest that this was the case for some areas, it did not occur consistently. For instance, rural areas of Canada that either were poor or had lumber jobs for men were feminized before government-funded schools in urban areas. Also, Quebec saw faster feminization because the region had a long-standing cultural tradition of Catholic nuns who served as teachers.[86]

Strober and Tyack have speculated that the feminization of teaching correlates with the formalization of schooling, where formalization is defined as a measure of the length of the school term and the number of teachers per school.[87] Formalization entails longer school years, state standards for funding, "more 'professional' and intrusive" supervision, a decrease in the female/male salary ratio, uniform curriculum and certification regulations. They explain, "we suspect that it was not only economic factors but also this increasingly administrative direction [toward control] that made rural school teaching less attractive to men."[88] John Rury has argued, however, that feminization may not have been tied so closely with formalization as much as with high levels of school participation. Additionally, percentages of male teachers varied by geographic regions according to the degree to which men also could work in the learned professions. In such areas, the proportion of men teachers was the highest.[89]

The nineteenth century witnessed a remarkable transformation in the demographic characteristics of teachers. While at the start of the century, men accounted for virtually all of the teachers in the country, one hundred years later women held the majority of teaching positions. The number of teachers increased dramatically, too, as education progressed from a privilege reserved for the social and economic elite to a benefit, if not a right, of all American children. Women helped alleviate the chronic shortage of qualified teachers resulting from the popular common school movement. While early teachers, male or female, were people whose families could afford to educate them—which necessarily meant that they had some degree of privilege—by the turn of the twentieth century, persons of virtually every social and economic class could aspire to teaching. Finally, while most teachers were White, after the Civil War, Black men and women rapidly entered teaching, especially in schools built for Black children throughout the South. By 1900, as many as 20 percent of women teachers in the South were Black.[90]

During the nineteenth century the structure of teaching also changed. While in 1800 male teachers generally worked by themselves in schoolhouses with little, if any supervision, by 1900 teachers increasingly found their curricula structured, their work monitored by an expanding system of administrative supervisors, their certification requirements regulated, their salaries centrally fixed, their work days and years extended, and their loads increased. The independence and curricular freedoms that teachers had enjoyed previously were minimized as administrators, mostly male, took on the work of making decisions for them.

I argue that it was not coincidental that teachers' independence and decision-making powers were stripped away just as women dominated the profession numerically. The male educators who remained had to assert their masculine qualities somehow, thus many became administrators to control the labors of women just as fathers and husbands long had done in the home. Administrators did not appear in significant numbers until women began filling teaching positions. As administrators assumed more control, male teachers felt less comfortable remaining in the classroom. They either left teaching or found other ways to pursue masculine-appropriate work within the profession. Teaching had become a woman's profession—controlled by men.

2

A DISTINCTLY HIGHER WALK

Charles Francis Adams Jr. stood to address his attentive audience at the 1880 meeting of the National Education Association. The direct descendent of presidents John Adams and John Quincy Adams, this Harvard-educated railroad executive had been invited by the association to offer a lay perspective on the superintendency.[1] In a prepared speech that undoubtedly offended some in the assembly, he described three evolutionary stages of the superintendency, or what he labeled the material, the pseudo-intellectual, and the scientific phases. The earliest superintendents, he explained, faced immediate logistical challenges in building and equipping schools with "the school-house, the out-house, the desk, the map, the slate, and the text-book. The low, dark, ill-ventilated, dirty room, with its long rows of benches and continuous desks, hacked and disfigured by the jack-knives of successive generations, had slowly to give place to something better . . . and this was the first work of the superintendency." He argued that those who filled the positions were not particularly well trained for their work that mainly consisted of managing repairs.[2]

Adams contended that by the 1840s and 1850s, the work of these early superintendents had given way to the pseudo-intellectual phase where superintendents structured schools into "huge, mechanical, educational machines, or mills" that resembled the "cotton-mill and the railroad" and "the state's prison." In such schools "the organization is perfect. The machine works almost with the precision of clock-work" and further, classes as a whole moved "with military precision to a given destination at a specified date." [3]

Finally, however, Adams contended that the superintendency was moving into a third, mature phase where scientific inquiry could be applied to education, schooling, and the processes by which children learn. "The superintendent of the future is thus a Baconian in his philosophy," he explained, a scholar who uses the scientific method to improve schooling. Graduates of normal schools would be inadequate for such a challenge because normal schools "educate teachers . . . but the work in hand is something more than direct teaching;—it is the philosophy of teaching. It is a distinctly-higher walk of the profession. It accordingly implies . . . a preceding groundwork of general education not required in the pupils of our Normal Schools. It is in fact a legitimate portion of University training, which always supposes the groundwork of an undergraduate course." [4]

Indeed, Adams hoped that superintendents might create for themselves a true profession grounded in a scientific, disciplined inquiry into the process of learning. He challenged colleges and universities to treat the superintendency with the seriousness of the medical, legal, and religious professions and therefore to establish programs to prepare superintendents for their "distinctly-higher walk." Even as thousands of women poured into normal schools, seminaries, teachers institutes, and other preparation programs, Adams urged his male audience of superintendents to take their guidance from universities, nearly all of which excluded or severely limited women's enrollment at the time. By so preparing themselves, superintendents as a class finally might deserve the mantle of "school executive," standing elbow-to-elbow with the captains of industry and other civic leaders. Through creating and studying the philosophy rather than the practice of teaching, superintendents might distance themselves from the continued encroachment of women into all levels of school work.

Those in attendance listened to Adams's words carefully. Within two decades, several universities responded to his challenge by establishing programs of study for administrative candidates. Increasing numbers of superintendents enrolled in such programs, forged connections with their professors, and otherwise strengthened their ties to a growing national network of power brokers in school administration. As school administrators organized and consolidated their power, teachers simultaneously lost autonomy and authority in the schools. And as the percentage of women teachers increased, administrators sought ever more vigorously to distinguish themselves in stature from teachers, even as they purported to represent and control the entire education profession.

In the first half of the 1800s, the American educational landscape included a broad range of institutions such as church schools, small district and township schools, dame schools, academies, seminaries, colleges, schools associated with philanthropic societies, loose affiliations of students with private tutors, and other configurations. Among publicly supported schools, the principle of local control assured that school districts functioned in ways appropriate for each unique municipality. The motley character of education gave way to greater uniformity, though, as state-regulated public schools became the predominant educational institution for American youth by the end of the century.

Early-nineteenth-century schools depended on the kindness of benefactors, the willingness of families to pay tuition, or the public will to assess and collect taxes for local school support. When townships opted to tax themselves for schools, local citizens demanded that governance of school affairs reside with the taxpayers, leading one British observer to note that "local self-government is the mainspring of the American school system."[5] Citizens elected school commissioners or board members who assumed responsibility for monitoring the school budget, recruiting and employing teachers, and otherwise overseeing school business.[6] Communities essentially charged these elected board members with safeguarding the public's investment in education. As the responsibilities of school boards grew, some hired superintendents or supervisors to carry out much of the administrative work.

Some communities, however, refused to levy taxes on themselves to support schools. Because of this, common school advocates despaired over denying children who lived in unsupportive communities the opportunity to attend school. Advocates maintained that statewide governmental agencies should provide the overarching authority to intervene in educationally resistant areas. To them, a measure of state-level school control would increase the fairness of educational opportunities.

State Superintendents

Advocates of state control in school matters justified their position with a provision of the Land Ordinance of 1785 requiring states to reserve "the lot No. 16, of every township, for the maintenance of public schools." The governance of these lands necessitated the oversight of state officials.[7] In 1812 New York became the first state to assign a school superintendent specifically to direct the use of school land, and other states eventually followed suit.[8] Iowa's first state superintendent, for example, declared in 1848 that he had selected 500,000 acres of land to be used or sold for school purposes.[9] State superintendents distributed the proceeds from these land sales to local schools through intermediate governmental officials.

As local school communities accepted state funding, they also relinquished some of their tight local school control. Schools that accepted state funds needed to abide by state school laws and as such, state superintendents then assumed the additional duty of assuring that schools complied. To do this, state education officers documented and published detailed annual reports describing the conditions of common schools, much as Horace Mann had in Massachusetts. Describing these reports, one scholar noted in 1875 that "every detail of organisation is subjected to a microscopic examination, and every rotten place is discovered and exposed."[10] State superintendents also traveled to communities throughout their states to explain school laws and urge compliance. As their duties expanded, state superintendents added personnel to their offices, creating an administrative machinery that increasingly controlled and connected the state's disparate school districts.[11] Essentially, the provision of centralized funding had promoted the establishment of a new state governmental agency, and it also reconfigured the power structure of local schooling.

In time, state superintendents' work grew even more complex. The job increasingly demanded persuasive public speakers who could travel the state convincing reluctant taxpayers about the benefits of supporting schools. State legislatures also pressed superintendents into service by consulting with them in drafting education-related bills. Generally, the job required visionary leadership and expert knowledge about the conditions of the state's schools.[12]

County Superintendents

The county school superintendency evolved not from a grassroots school organization, but rather was created to assist state superintendents in overseeing distribution of state funds and in assuring local school compliance with state laws.[13] Most states and territories established county school systems with superintendencies in the mid to late 1800s. County superintendents performed several key functions with some state-by-state variation. First, they channeled state funds to local schools. Second, county superintendents became indispensable partners in compiling school statistics because they could more easily visit isolated schoolhouses to verify information than could state officials. They counted students, reported conditions of outhouses, and described the usability of wood stoves. As populations shifted and land use changed, county superintendents also assumed the heinous task of adjusting school district lines, a matter that frequently triggered bitter feuds among communities. County superintendents needed tact and diplomacy to handle these and other disputes that inevitably surfaced as schools grew, changed, and adapted to local and state requirements.

A particularly important component of county superintendents' work involved examining and training teachers. Superintendents set requirements for teacher licensure. They also organized county institutes where teachers learned about new curricular content, innovative teaching techniques, and the heavily debated educational issues of the time. Some superintendents hired inspirational speakers to ignite the energies of local teachers. In 1872 one state superintendent enthusiastically asserted: "No other agency has done more to strengthen and vitalize our system of public education than these meetings of teachers, school officers, and friends of common schools, known as Teachers' Institutes."[14] Beyond these duties, county superintendents visited every school in their counties to observe teachers, listen to student recitations, and otherwise ascertain that teachers conducted classes in compliance with all requirements.[15]

From its creation in the mid-1800s through the first quarter of the 1900s, the county superintendency expanded to encompass greater responsibilities and power. These increases occurred even as local district superintendents sometimes saw their roles diminish. Part of the growing responsibility experienced by county superintendents came from above as state education agencies granted them increased authority. Some of the expansion, however, also came from below as county superintendents absorbed greater portions of the work previously performed by local supervisors or superintendents. The overall growth of the county superintendency led Ellwood Cubberley in 1916 to explain that "the office of the county superintendent of schools has to-day, in many of our American States, evolved into an office of large potential importance."[16]

As intermediate officials, county superintendents served the interests of their local communities as well as those of the state. To establish local accountability, eligible voters in the community usually elected county superintendents. Superintendents in turn worked to assure that decisions about funding, school locations, district boundaries, and personnel matters did not alienate key constituencies.

Although the work was fraught with political dangers, initially there was a sense that most any competent citizen could fulfill the requirements of the position. Early county superintendents therefore needed no special training. Men from a range of backgrounds undertook the work, many having no experience with schools whatsoever.[17] In some cases the men who ran for the position did so only for the meager salary rather than for any deep-rooted concern for educational improvement. One state official complained:

> The wide-spread and painful incompetency in this branch of the school work, is due to the fact that the office, being awarded politically and very poorly paid, is sought for by those who design

making it simply collateral and subsidiary to something else. The lawyer seeks it, that he may use the per diem of an occasional jaunt through the county, in enlarging the field of his practice, and filling up the deficit of a livelihood his slender fees will not supply. The Minister finds, in this way, a convenient method of supplementing the very meager salary his Sabbath services will command.[18]

School systems frequently employed county superintendents on a part-time basis, which divided the incumbents' attention. Aggravating these problems were elected terms as short as one year, which caused a great deal of instability in the position. Though colonial schoolmasters a century earlier had tutored students in addition to their other employment, or in preparation for assuming legal or clerical careers, county superintendents in the mid-1800s were criticized for their dual allegiances, and for failing to discharge their public duties adequately, especially as the county superintendency grew into a full-time position. Finally, a number of these early superintendents reportedly were simply derelict in their duties.[19] Clarence Aurner explained that Iowa legislators even attempted unsuccessfully to abolish the county superintendency in 1872 because of "assertions that the office was doing no good; that it cost more than it was worth; that the persons selected for the office were of no benefit to the schools; and that the office was too often filled by 'politicians and incompetents.'"[20]

In spite of these early shortcomings, some county superintendents invested themselves fully in their work and in their mission to upgrade and maintain the quality of schools in their districts. Said one Kansas county superintendent in 1872: "I honestly cannot conceive of a position more . . . difficult to fill . . . than that of a county superintendent. . . . His duties and responsibilities are . . . simply enormous."[21]

District Superintendents

At first, districts, townships, parishes, and other small local communities administered their school affairs through school boards. These boards eventually hired superintendents to assume administrative duties as the work grew beyond what unpaid, elected board members were willing to shoulder. Some superintendents had served as teachers before becoming administrators, but often local men without teaching experience were hired simply to establish some oversight of the teachers' work. Most local superintendents worked in exceedingly small communities that could not afford to pay them high salaries; therefore reputedly more capable men aspired to positions in counties or urban systems with higher tax bases. The lack of prestige associated with district or township superintendencies compelled the argument that small village school districts should be collapsed into the more natural county unit, which indeed happened eventually in many cases.[22]

City Superintendents

City school districts, like small rural ones, originally were administered by unpaid volunteer school boards. Then, as in the case of small districts, board members' duties quickly outstripped what they could contribute as otherwise fully employed citizens. Frequent turnover resulted. Eventually, school boards hired superintendents to manage school business. Although city board members were usually chosen from the business community because of their supposedly greater organizational and fiscal expertise, they quickly fell into the role of directing work done by superintendents rather than doing it themselves. In 1837, Buffalo and Louisville appointed school superintendents. Other cities rapidly followed suit.[23]

City superintendents, however, also experienced quite different circumstances from either county or small district superintendents. In the second half of the 1800s and well into the 1900s, cities witnessed phenomenal growth fueled by rapid industrialization, immigration, and a nationwide population shift away from rural agricultural areas. The numbers of school-age youths exploded during this time. To accommodate these changes, cities quickly constructed large, multiclassroom school buildings; purchased quantities of textbooks and other classroom materials; hired legions of teachers, usually women, and mostly for low wages; and offered salaries sufficient to attract men into the rapidly expanding school administrative class. Further adding to the enticement of urban administration was the innovative reputation city school systems enjoyed. City superintendents tended to experiment with school configurations and programs in a manner somewhat unconstrained by tradition, often to deal with the enormous social and economic flux of the time. For these reasons male educators regarded city districts as the most exciting and prestigious places to work.[24]

City superintendents performed some of the same duties as their rural counterparts. They typically visited schools to observe teachers. Some cities required these visitations, and state education reports frequently included the tallies of such visits. However, unlike isolated one- or two-room rural schoolhouses, cities increasingly constructed multiclassroom structures supervised by lead teachers or principals appointed by the superintendent. In one school visit, a superintendent could observe the work of several or perhaps many teachers.

In addition to dropping in on classes, city superintendents also conducted ongoing instructional meetings for teachers. While county superintendents organized summer teacher institutes, city superintendents instead required teachers to attend administrative and instructional meetings, usually on Saturdays. City superintendents also faced a broad array of other administrative tasks, including examining students and assigning them to grades, keeping track of attendance records and enrollments, choosing texts for classroom adoption, and hiring school personnel such as custodians, teachers, clerical staff, and principals.[25]

Gradually city superintendents assumed greater shares of school administrative duties. To accommodate this expansion, they increased the personnel in their central offices and also appointed principals to govern the schools directly. Their central office personnel handled much of the system's clerical work, but in addition, superintendents also hired supervisors and assistants who each assumed particular portions of the superintendent's supervisory work and thus constituted a new administrative layer.[26] These new administrators, usually men, received salaries considerably above those paid to teachers. Meanwhile, since city teaching largely had become women's work and also since women teachers usually earned one-third to one-half of what men received, the practice of hiring women teachers made the creation of these new administrative positions financially feasible. In response to the charge that women educators were systematically paid less than men, one superintendent simply explained: "The apparent discrimination against women in the average salaries paid, is accounted for chiefly by the fact that a large proportion of men occupy the positions which command the higher salaries."[27] And, in fact, as well-paid administrative positions emerged, men aggressively sought them, usually to the exclusion of women.

The creation of the various kinds of superintendencies addressed several education-related concerns of the nineteenth century. First, the existence of county superintendencies allowed state governments to extend their controlling reach to local schools. Second, district and city superintendents eased the workloads of school boards, who had increasingly taken on routine administrative and clerical work. Third, male educators appreciated the existence of the superintendency to the extent that it offered them a new route for promotion within a profession that otherwise held diminished appeal. Superintendents received substantially higher salaries than teachers; they assumed more masculine-identified supervisory duties; they maintained their offices in central locations near local male power structures; and the title offered incumbents some stature in their communities. Administrative work offered a gender-appropriate way for men to stay in education.[28] Fourth, for communities concerned about employing young, single women, the oversight provided by male superintendents offered some reassurance that women teachers would not overstep their traditional gender boundaries. Males would be present to define and enforce those bounds, much as husbands and fathers did in the home.

The model of the superintendency, as it was constructed in the second half of the nineteenth century, was borrowed from other institutions of the time. David Tyack and Elisabeth Hansot suggest that the remarkable success of the American Sunday School Union (ASSU) early in the nineteenth century may have inspired common schools to adopt some of its structural practices. By 1828, the ASSU enrolled and taught around one-seventh of all American school-age children. This enviable reach was achieved through careful marketing, organizing, and supervision performed by superintendents. Comparing superintendents of the ASSU with those of public schools, Tyack and Hansot observe that "long before public-school systems acquired their superintendents, the Sunday School superintendent was a familiar male authority figure organizing the work of his unpaid, mostly female teachers."[29]

Horace Mann, in his 1843 Massachusetts common school report, described a configuration of power he found worthy of broad emulation. He had visited Prussia and admired the strong centralized model of authority that characterized their schools and contributed to an efficient, smoothly functioning system.[30] Mann advocated adopting Prussian organizational structures. Not everyone agreed with Mann's assessment, however, as critics such as Orestes Brownson argued that widespread adoption of such centralized authority in schooling would contribute to increased authoritarianism in society as a whole and was therefore not worth the short-term benefit.[31]

Industry provided a third model for the superintendency. In the nineteenth century, industrialism swept through many parts of the country and fueled rapid economic growth, produced some astoundingly wealthy men, and figured heavily in American metaphorical thought. Not surprisingly, educators spoke of schools in industrial terms; politicians and experts sought to build schools on industrial models; and personnel structures in schools eventually resembled those in manufacturing sites. Ellwood Cubberley reflected on the connection between schooling and industrialism when he explained that, "our schools are, in a sense, factories in which the raw materials (children) are to be shaped and fashioned into products to meet the various demands of life."[32] Factories not only shaped raw materials, but a supervisory class of men ran them. This administrative feature seemed desirable to some community leaders, usually businessmen, and provided a ready model for those seeking to build schools. Josiah L. Pickard, superintendent of Chicago schools from 1864 to 1877, described the need for a school superintendent whose functions and roles resembled those of the industrial supervisor:

> In every branch of human labor the importance of supervision has grown with the specialization of labor. The more minute the division of labor, the greater the need of supervision. . . . [To each], what he has done is complete in itself. He has accepted his place in the plan about which he gives himself no anxiety. But his work is only a part, in the great plan. . . . He might acquire the knowledge, but at the expense of his efficiency in the special work he is to perform. Over him . . . stands one whose special work is to adjust the parts, make himself familiar with each, but freed from active work in any part. He is the overseer, the superintendent.[33]

Finally, military organization significantly influenced the shape of the emerging superintendency. The Civil War occurred as superintendencies first appeared around the country. Some men who later became superintendents either had served in the war or the monumental war effort had otherwise affected them. In the military, the commander demands absolute control over his subordinates, who are assigned specific duties and status in a carefully controlled hierarchical system. In 1875 this structure inspired William Payne, who had served as a superintendent before becoming a professor, to compare school superintendents to military generals: "The commanding general, who, at one glance, takes in the whole military situation, and wields his forces so as to meet the exigencies of the situation, is the natural superior of the thousands who, with powers of mind less comprehensive, merely execute the plans prescribed by their leader. . . . Superintendence is therefore not only a necessity, but is the highest and most productive form of labor."[34] Undoubtedly, some superintendents endeavored to turn their school systems into such educational armies.

Each of these four models inspired and shaped the school superintendency, and each contained gendered assumptions about control and authority. The ASSU depended heavily on the work of women volunteers who submitted to the direction of male superintendents. Other gender configurations of the organization would have been unthinkable at the time because biblical teachings required women to submit to men. The Prussian schools that inspired Horace Mann were run exclusively by men. In fact, only men worked in Prussian schools in positions ranging from teacher to headmaster. They maintained an efficient, well-regulated system of hierarchical control not unlike the similarly all-male military. Men likewise controlled industry for a number of reasons, not the least of which was that at the time industries proliferated, laws restricted women's access to economic resources that might have assisted them in starting and building even modest business ventures. Women's right to own property paled in comparison with men's, and in many states, women could not own or transfer wealth without their husband's consent; or worse, whatever they owned through their own efforts or resources belonged exclusively to their husbands or other male family members. Women did work in some industries; however, they rarely if ever enjoyed control over their own labors. Finally, the American military simply refused women admission to its ranks.

These four models share a strong hierarchical structure where few persons control the labors of many. These models were designed and implemented exclusively by a small number of men as a means of delineating social strata and lines of power. They divided men from each other, the powerful from the relatively powerless, and women existed at the bottom of these models where they existed at all. Women and many men had no direct role in the process of configuring them. Nonetheless, each of these models inspired the structure of school employment. Not everyone rejoiced, however.

Teachers sometimes complained about their declining professional independence as school systems hired administrators. David Tyack describes an Oregon teacher who protested that "by degrees there is being built in our state a machine among the 'aristocratic element of our profession that . . . will make [teachers] serfs, to be moved about at the will of a state superintendent of public instruction through his lieutenants, county superintendents."[35] Gail Hamilton, an outspoken teacher, wrote in her 1880 scathing critique of schools, *Our Common School System*, that: "The thing which a school ought not to be, the thing which our system of supervision is strenuously trying to make the school into, is a factory, with the superintendents for overseers and the teachers for workmen. . . . The superintendent is a mere modern invention for receiving a salary, whose beneficence seldom rises above harmlessness, whose activity is usually mischievous."[36] Clearly, superintendents and other supervisory personnel were not added at teachers' request. The state superintendent of Pennsylvania responded to Hamilton's attacks by defending the industrial model of schooling: "Here and there this great machine may press heavily upon one or another, yet we must have a machine in education as in everything else, and machines are good things." He quickly added: "[Her] book . . . I consider a weak book."[37]

Teachers often were better educated and more sophisticated than administrators, whom many regarded as incompetent. As teachers grew more qualified, they also became more critical of strictly hierarchical administrative practices that placed them at the bottom. These practices limited teachers' participation in school governance while reserving decision-making privileges for administrators. If an individual teacher wanted to complain, she could not appeal beyond her supervisor—which essentially left little recourse beyond resignation. The system thrived as long as women enjoyed few career alternatives, teacher training remained minimal, and teachers refrained from organizing in protest. Administrators effectively kept teachers' creative intelligence and energy from school governance.

Rather than accept these administrative practices, some women teachers suggested alternative structures based less on hierarchy and more on shared power, equality, and consensual decision-making. For example, Hamilton proposed that "teachers ought to run the schools exactly as doctors run a hospital." She continued: "The doctors do not meet in a Board a mile away and send an order into the hospital to cut off so many arms on Monday and administer so many pills on Tuesday. That is left to the men who are standing over the bedsides of the patients." [38] Essentially, she contended that control and authority in schooling should be shared among the persons performing the critical work of the institution, in this case, teaching. In such a system the teachers in multiclassroom schools should make hiring decisions, determine schedules, design and implement curricula, set standards, and group students as they deem educationally appropriate.

A few decades prior to Hamilton's published work, Catharine Beecher had proposed a similar administrative structure for teacher seminaries. She suggested that persons hired to teach in seminaries should be "supplied by the nomination of the teachers themselves, confirmed by the Trustees. The . . . teachers are to be in all respects, equal in authority and rank, and the various responsibilities and duties are to be so divided that each teacher will be responsible for certain departments." Beecher may have modeled this power configuration on Yale's then innovative program for faculty governance.[39] She compared teacher seminaries with colleges where:

Each professor is the head of his own department; and neither the president nor any of his colleagues have a right to interfere—not so much even as to give advice—much less to control. The corporation is the only body that can exercise the power of advice and control over the faculty. The president has no more power than any of his colleagues. He is only primus inter pares and acts as the presiding officer of the faculty. In some of our universities . . . the office of president is omitted entirely, as needless.[40]

Both Beecher and Hamilton maintained that the persons entrusted with the primary work of an organization should also make its administrative decisions. Just as doctors and professors decided how they should work, so too should teachers control school affairs. At the time, though, doctors and professors were men. Allowing men to control their own affairs did not challenge traditional gender expectations; however, for women to expect equivalent trust and control of a public institution presented a serious challenge to their socially approved gender roles. Middle-class women were to submit, or at the least to confine their controlling reach to the domestic sphere. Hamilton's and Beecher's models were given little if any broad consideration. As a consequence, teachers' authority in schools eroded to the same extent that sex segregation and stratification in educational employment increased.

Not only did women teachers lose ground in their professional autonomy, but they rarely moved into supervisory positions, either. Men supervised women. Whenever men taught in schools, they became lead teachers or principals, positions for which men's strength was supposedly needed. One educator explained, "One man could be placed in charge of an entire graded school of 500 students," a large school at the time. "Under his direction could be placed a number of female assistants. Females are not only adapted, but carefully trained, to fill such positions as well as or better than men, excepting the master's place, which sometimes requires a man's force."[41] A woman might be carefully trained, but her training did not necessarily point to school leadership. Instead, it led to teaching, a position for which no means of professional advancement was constructed. Essentially, men directed the activities of women, who in turn complied. By custom, women could not supervise men; so as long as even one male teacher was subordinated by a woman's potential administrative advancement, she was denied promotion. He would be promoted instead. Women generally moved into administrative positions only in all-female contexts.[42]

Some women did succeed in becoming administrators, though. A number of states west of the Mississippi allowed women to run for county superintendencies. Some of the women who waged and won campaigns for these positions took them on with great enthusiasm for proving that women could be trusted as capable community leaders. They often performed their duties quite admirably. In describing the work of women county superintendents, the *State Report* of Kansas in 1873 explained that: "As county superintendents, the verdict is that those [women] elected in this State 'have done their work faithfully and well, as well as the best and far better than many of the men.' The superintendent hopes that this new field, as well as professional chairs in high schools and colleges, will remain open to all, male and female, in fair and honorable competition."[43]

In states such as Kansas, county superintendents performed grueling, difficult, often financially unrewarding duties. The job demanded a great deal of traveling, paperwork, and supervision. Some rural county districts covered so much land and contained so many schools that even the most dedicated and diligent superintendent completed her work only with difficulty. William Chancellor, a political science professor, explained that "the average county superintendent has something like six to ten times as much to do as the average city school superintendent." When women served as county superintendents, they reportedly invested so much of themselves in their work that voting citizens often reasoned they were a better bargain than males who demanded greater pay and frequently did not give their hearts and souls to the work in the same manner. Chancellor argued that perhaps the salaries of county superintendents should be reduced to discourage men and therefore increase the number of women superintendents who were doing such excellent work. "It does not appear that the poorly paid, popularly elected school superintendents are educationally inferior to the highly paid ones. We do not wish even abler politicians as candidates. Raising salaries is not the solution of the problem of how to get real school supervision. . . . Reducing salaries might help, since it would increase the number of women school superintendents."[44] Surely this is what had already begun to happen with teaching: as women proved to be a bargain because of their cheaper salaries and their enormous personal investment in their work, men were less attracted to teaching because they had more options and could afford to be choosy.

In spite of the difficulties faced by women who pursued county superintendencies, many women eagerly supported the notion of female school leaders. Some had benefited directly from the supervision of capable and selfless women superintendents eager to prove the competence of their sex. Others simply believed that keeping women out of leadership of the profession they had come to dominate numerically was unfair.[45]

Male educators, however, tended to resist the presence of women school administrators. When Ella Flagg Young became the superintendent of Chicago schools in 1909, there was, as one of her supporters explained it, "opposition on the part of the men teachers and principals, the engineers, and the janitors, who would rather have had a man over them. They would have felt the same about any woman, no matter how efficient."[46]

Men who found themselves competing against women for superintendencies sometimes launched aggressive campaigns to denounce the administrative styles sometimes preferred by women. An opponent of a woman county superintendent candidate attacked her by claiming she spent too much time with teachers' reading circles and institutes, and did not spend enough time visiting schools.[47] He basically maintained that the superintendent should be more of a supervisor than a curriculum leader, a hierarchically separate administrator instead of a cooperative mentor. Interestingly, supervisory work could be undertaken by persons with little or no background in teaching, while curriculum leaders needed prior teaching experience. As teaching became more feminized, women superintendent candidates were more likely to have been teachers than male candidates. They also were more at ease engaging socially with women teachers. It is not surprising, then, that women superintendents' interests sometimes moved in the direction of the classroom and toward teachers. That such interest could be utilized as the basis for political attack hints at unspoken gender differences that could be exploited for political advantage among male voters of the time.

With the expansion of school administration around the country, eventually a critical mass of superintendents existed who shared similar duties, interests, and problems. At this point, a few of them arranged to meet with each other. These meetings then became regular affairs where members collectively tackled such issues as defining the superintendency, establishing normative work practices, and determining who should enter their ranks. As they individually faced contentious school boards, insufficient funding, community criticism, the slow influx of women into the previously all-male administrative realm, and indifference or even contempt from the mainly female cadre of teachers, the larger group of superintendents pulled together to buffer one another against these perceived assaults. Superintendents emerged from their unique school system contexts to unite and shape a larger, distinct, and powerful identity.

Superintendents achieved these ends in several ways during the second half of the 1800s. First, they organized themselves into formal associations of school superintendents much as male teachers had begun to form schoolmasters' clubs. Second, through these associations they established and maintained ties with government education agencies. Third, with the support of associations and governmental agencies, they endeavored to professionalize their work by describing it, developing it into a subject of academic study, and providing a new means of entrance into it by way of academic institutions reserved mainly for men. Essentially they enlisted the cooperation of university professors to create educational administration as a program of study. Finally, through their associations, agencies, and links with academia, superintendents worked to promote themselves, a promotion that conspicuously omitted the presence of women in the field of education. The net effect of these changes is that the superintendency became a formalized position, one that was increasingly male-defined and male-occupied, while being distanced from and firmly in control of the work of teachers, most of whom were women.

A number of cities established superintendencies during the nineteenth century. In August 1865, a group of male city administrators gathered to establish the National Association of School Superintendents (NASS), an organization devoted to increasing the professional prestige of education in general and the superintendency in particular. Five years later, NASS joined with two allied organizations to form the larger National Educational Association(NEA). The superintendents' group then became the Department of Superintendence of the NEA.[48]

Annual meetings of the Department of Superintendence took on several different functions. For one, they produced lively debate about the identity and role of the superintendent, as well as discussions about emerging national education issues. However, another important function was for superintendents to offer each other support. Superintendents faced many humbling problems in their daily work. Newspapers criticized school officials routinely and local politicians scored points by decrying the management of school tax dollars. To help, conference sessions offered members advice on how to handle such public attacks. Informal gatherings at meetings allowed them to share horror stories and seek solace from understanding peers.[49]

A particularly important function of the department, however, was to elevate the prestige and power of the superintendency. To this end, members worked toward building networks of influence as well as gaining expertise and funding. The department courted the support of businessmen by inviting them to attend and even address meetings. Also, a subset of the Department of Superintendence, a group that Tyack and Hansot have called the "educational trust," controlled the larger NEA for decades. This superintendent-heavy ruling clique usually selected presidents of the NEA and otherwise determined policy and the political direction of the greater organization.[50]

The Department of Superintendence also labored to forge strong links with the federal government. Henry Barnard, state school superintendent in Connecticut, believed that the government needed to collect data on the conditions of schools around the country, much as state superintendents had begun doing within their jurisdiction. He wrote to elected officials to encourage the creation of a national education office, but then the Civil War erupted, so Barnard temporarily dropped his efforts. Immediately after the war, though, he and spirited supporters resumed the project. Several of them visited Congress in 1866 to lobby politicians directly. They quickly built a useful alliance with a former schoolmaster, Representative James A. Garfield from Ohio, who later became the president of the United States. Shortly after this visit, Rep. Garfield introduced legislation "to establish a department of education for the purpose of collecting such statistics and facts as shall show the condition and progress of education."[51]

Garfield's campaign for the establishment of a department of education met with considerable resistance from fellow congressmen who wanted to spend the requested sum of $13,000 on other domestic projects. He argued in response:

> If it could be published annually from this capital through every school district of the United States that there are states in the Union that have no system of common schools; and if their records could be placed beside the records of such states . . . that have a common school system, the mere statement of the fact would rouse their energies, and compel them for shame to educate their children. It would shame out of their delinquency all the delinquent states.[52]

Garfield believed that statistical reports about education had the power to change schooling practices by exposing deficiencies and thereby tacitly assigning blame. Captivated by his pleas, Congress passed legislation in 1867 to establish a federal Department of Education. Henry Barnard became its first commissioner and thus was able to carry out his own proposal.

Some legislators believed that the creation of such a department would eventually lead to federal control of education, a fate they desperately feared. As a result, they cut Barnard's budget significantly, which had the effect of crippling his data collection and publication efforts. To manage, he relied heavily on his Department of Superintendence friends who had originally helped him lobby for the creation of the federal department. Much of the information he eventually collected came from superintendents around the country who responded to his queries.[53] In spite of limiting conditions, then, Barnard succeeded in launching the federal department with the critically important help of Department of Superintendence members.

John Eaton, the second commissioner and a former state superintendent of Tennessee, enhanced the bureau's connection with the NEA by distributing association materials with the bureau's franking privileges. County and state superintendents of the NEA in turn circulated petitions throughout the country urging Eaton's retention as commissioner.[54] Subsequent commissioners of education came from the NEA Department of Superintendence. William Torrey Harris, for instance, who served as commissioner of education from 1889 until 1906, had previously served a term as president of the NEA Department of Superintendence in 1873, then as president of the NEA in 1875. As a show of political support for the work of Commissioner Harris and his staff, the Department of Superintendence of the NEA in 1897 passed the following resolution: "The department views with great satisfaction the increasing efficiency and widening influence of the National Bureau of Education, and believes that public opinion will sustain Congress in any action looking to the placement of this bureau on a level with other bureaus of the Department of the Interior."[55]

Not everyone greeted this happy association between the Bureau of Education and the NEA, the Department of Superintendence in particular. Charles Tobin, representing numerous private and parochial schools in New York, spoke before the Congressional Committee on Education and Labor on the subject of proposed federal aid to education:

Federal aid must and does mean control, so the bill in its present language is only a subterfuge. The real purpose and plan of its proponents is as the wedge or means of entry for federalization of education. There is no public demand for the legislation, rather the entire opinion favoring the bill has been manufactured by a politico-educational machine known as the NEA, employing a high-salaried group of lobbyists whose openly expressed aims are to make education a Federal function, if legally possible, and place themselves in control of the department so created.[56]

Concerns such as Tobin's weighed heavily on the minds of legislators, who repeatedly voted down attempts to promote the Bureau of Education to federal cabinet-level status. Undaunted, the two organizations maintained and nurtured their ties.

Organized school superintendents also sought academic recognition of their work by undertaking scholarly inquiry, publishing works related to their profession, and helping establish administrative preparation programs in elite universities around the country. An important route to attaining this intellectual status was for superintendents to portray themselves as philosopher-leaders with intellectual skills that set them apart from teachers. For the most part, superintendents in the late 1800s were not particularly well educated or trained by today's standards. Those superintendents who had received a liberal arts education tended to view themselves as scholars and statesman. These leaders included William T. Harris, William Maxwell (later the New York State Commissioner of Education), John Philbrick (superintendent of Boston schools), and William Payne (later the president of Peabody Normal School).

Payne, for example, wrote *Chapters on School Supervision* (1875), the first published book about the school superintendency, while serving as a superintendent in Michigan. In this work he described the natural development of the superintendency as the process of separating the thinking person from menial laborers, the general from the troops, the superintendent-philosopher from teachers. Payne's ideal superintendent, then, produced the highest form of labor, that of thinking about and directing the actions of subordinates. The growing complexities of large schools and systems, he argued, required such an intellectual, responsible leader. He concluded that the superintendent had to be well educated and thoughtful, a background that would justify his hierarchical separation from his minions.[57]

When Charles Francis Adams challenged NEA members to welcome the scientific phase of the superintendency, he explained that philosophical inquiry and scientifically reasoned thought could produce a legitimate field of educational study of which superintendents should be masters. Soon after Adams's speech, several prominent universities accepted his challenge to develop special programs for persons aspiring to school superintendencies.[58] For example, Tyack recounts how Stanford hired Ellwood Cubberley in 1898 to build the school's education program with leadership components. The college president instructed him to make the program intellectually distinguished or else it would be discontinued. Cubberley then undertook the systematic study of education, particularly administration. He designed courses, built support among his colleagues, recruited students, and wrote textbooks. Within a few years, Cubberley had successfully managed to build a reputable program that attracted capable students into the fledgling discipline.[59]

In time, programs such as Cubberley's provided the pathway for aspiring school administrators not only to receive professional training, but also to gain access to desirable positions. Graduates of such programs often maintained their ties with their professors and formed networks of mutual support.[60] Increasingly, the process of attaining superintendencies required candidates to obtain the proper credentials without necessarily first rising through the teaching ranks. Principals held bachelor's and graduate degrees in greater numbers than they had previously. On the basis of recommendations from influential professors, school districts sometimes recruited promising university students who had little experience working in schools. Such a change effectively limited the number of women who could pursue superintendencies because many of these programs either denied women admission altogether, or they severely restricted their enrollment.

Not only was it difficult for women to gain admission to these administrative preparation programs, but professors sometimes made it difficult for the few women who were admitted to finish or receive their necessary blessing in a job search. One professor in 1926 described the type of person he believed should *not* enter such programs in the first place:

> The writer was particularly impressed with the disappointment of one graduate who majored in the field of educational administration. . . . In the fall of 1924 she enrolled in the graduate school and spent an entire year in preparing herself for a position as a school administrator. During the spring and summer of 1925 she continually sought a position as a principal or a superintendent. When schools opened in September she had not secured employment. Other students trained in the same classes under the instruction of the same professors secured very attractive positions in which they are succeeding. This indicates that students lacking qualities making for success in supervision and administration should be advised against entering classes training them for such positions.[61]

The author offered no reasons for why this applicant did not receive jobs. The only clue he included was that the applicant was female, a fact from which the reader was to infer that supervisory and administrative qualities were lacking.

Finally, superintendents sought to elevate their profession by aggressively promoting it in a favorable light. To do this, superintendents, their associations, and university professors collectively prepared exhaustive statistical studies about chief school administrators that detailed their professional preparation, social and economic backgrounds, salaries, types of duties, and other aspects of their lives and work. The weight of numerical evidence presented in these reports conveyed a scientific authority that effectively defied critical examination.[62] The positive images these reports offered clearly indicated that superintendents were highly qualified, well educated, and married more often than men in the general population.[63] Information that might portray superintendents unfavorably was minimized or eliminated. For example, in the first half of the twentieth century these reports underrepresented or ignored women's presence in the superintendency because far more surveys were sent systematically to city superintendents, virtually all of whom were men, than to county superintendents, many of whom were women. Such reports conveyed the impression that only men were or should be superintendents.

By the early decades of the twentieth century, superintendents arguably had enhanced the prestige of their position in spite of continued assaults both from outside and within the education profession. Their salaries increased significantly around the turn of the century as did the power accorded them by school boards. Wary of being saddled with an overload of administrative detail, school boards relegated greater portions of their management responsibilities to superintendents. In time they even ceded the duty most coveted by some: they allowed superintendents to oversee and to some extent control school budgets, a responsibility that essentially elevated superintendents fully to the status of business executives.

As their power increased, the social, economic, intellectual, and even physical distance between superintendents and teachers stretched and deepened. Superintendents physically isolated themselves from teachers as central offices stood ever more distant from classrooms. On a day-to-day basis, superintendents talked with male community leaders, school administrators, and persons with assumed power. They spent much less time engaging with teachers than previously. The widening gulf between teachers' and superintendents' salaries necessarily meant that occupants of these positions belonged to two distinct and potentially warring economic classes: the upper-middle and the working classes. And as superintendents sought to attend universities while simultaneously hiring normal-school-educated women for teaching positions, the enforced academic chasm between the two realms widened further still.

Across this gulf, some superintendents came to view teachers as nameless, faceless abstractions often with interests competing with their own. Worse still, teachers' annoying tendency to complain and agitate for better conditions seemed to threaten the hard-won control, stability, and homogeneity that superintendents had worked so diligently to attain. Eventually the turn-of-the-century women's movement, teachers' growing restiveness, and women's progress in attaining school administrative positions captured school officials' attention and provoked new collective strategies for maintaining superintendent authority and control.

3

OUT OF POLITICS

Ambitious women seeking school leadership positions briefly enjoyed broad-based and enthusiastic support from a powerful emerging political constituency of women. Early in the twentieth century, suffrage activism and the larger women's movement effectively propelled women into school leadership positions. During these years, hundreds of women waged successful campaigns for superintendencies, and by 1930 women accounted for nearly 28 percent of county superintendents and 11 percent of all superintendents nationwide. Activists such as Ella Flagg Young hoped that women would eventually dominate school leadership just as they had teaching. Once swept into office they believed that women would purge corrupt administrative practices, bring an elevated moral purpose to schooling, and improve public education much as they already had improved teaching. During these years women found cause for boundless optimism.

Victories would not always come easily, however. As women first won the right to vote on school-related matters in individual communities and then eventually full national suffrage, superintendent groups sought to change superintendencies from elected to appointed positions. Schools needed expert administrators, they argued; and experts could hardly be chosen in public, politically charged contests. Rather, they believed that popularly elected politicians should select superintendents from pools of qualified, well-trained experts. On the other hand, newly enfranchised women activists doubted that such an appointive system maintained the spirit of American democracy. As they eagerly prepared for their duties as voting citizens, they confronted a growing movement to take the superintendency out of politics.

The roots of the early twentieth-century women's movement extend at least as far back as Mary Wollstonecraft and her classic text, *A Vindication of the Rights of Women*, published in England in 1792. In this politically provocative book, whose first edition sold out in less than a year, Wollstonecraft outlined the ways she believed society relegated women to second-class status. She shocked some readers by offering compelling arguments for women's equality with men. Even though her critics protested against her ideas and slandered her personally for bearing a child out of wedlock, her words resonated with women who suffered daily degradation because of their sex.

To emerge from their inferior, dependent condition, Wollstonecraft argued that women needed education because it would "enable the individual to attain such habits of virtue as will render it independent."[1] By the time American women first read her work, some had begun to benefit from newly available opportunities for formal education. Though they justified this education as preparation for republican motherhood, generally they developed confidence in their own intellectual capacities as well as in their abilities to contribute to the young nation. With this increasing confidence, some women questioned the premise of a social system that denied the rights of a class of persons simply because of their sex. Yet these increasingly well-educated women, in fact all women, were systematically denied such basic rights as suffrage, full access to education at all levels, opportunities to pursue salaried work, and property ownership rights. And as women learned, read, and discussed their conditions, their uneasiness grew.

In 1845, the American Margaret Fuller gave full expression to this restlessness with the publication of her book, *Woman in the Nineteenth Century*.[2] Historian Thomas Woody in 1929 lauded Fuller's work by explaining that it "set more forcefully and clearly than any one had before, in the United States, the servitude of women and the need for their complete emancipation."[3] The book found a popular audience as successive editions quickly sold out and women patiently waited to borrow their friends' dog-eared copies. A group of New York women organized a meeting in Seneca Falls, New York, specifically to explore the social and political ramifications of Fuller's ideas; thus the women who attended this first Women's Rights Convention launched the movement of public agitation for women's rights.[4]

The 1848 Seneca Falls meeting was one of the earliest gatherings of American women to improve their own conditions as a group rather than those of others, a focus critics thought selfish. They came together to identify and explore the myriad forms of their oppression. One focus of discussion concerned women's lack of full access to institutions of higher education. Even though some academies and seminaries had opened their doors to women, most secondary and postsecondary institutions barred their admission. Ironically, as school boards hired ever greater numbers of women teachers, male students enjoyed better educational prospects than their female teachers ever would. The Declaration of Sentiments drafted from the meeting's discussions reflected this bitter situation: "The history of mankind is a history of repeated injuries and usurpations on the part of the man toward women, having in direct object the establishment of an absolute tyranny over her"; and specifically, "he has denied her the facilities for obtaining a thorough education, all colleges being closed against her."[5] Attendees insisted that women be allowed full access to all institutions and programs so that they might eventually break free of their otherwise certain dependence on men.

Clearly education weighed heavily on the minds of women at the Seneca Falls meeting. Some had attended women's educational institutions and developed a certain pride in their academic accomplishments as well as a strong faith that women's continued education would eventually bring their full independence and equality. No doubt, these women could articulate their conditions partly because they had come to enjoy formal learning; and they continued to educate themselves by reading, discussing, and writing about works such as Fuller's.

Beyond their desire for empowerment through education, however, some of the women at the Seneca Falls meeting and many of the earliest women's rights activists also were interested in education because they had been schoolteachers. At the time, teaching offered perhaps the only profession women could pursue that utilized and, in fact, required their formal education. The venerable Susan B. Anthony, for example, taught school for a few years before launching into full-time political activism.[6] Decades later, Carrie Chapman Catt, who eventually led the National American Woman Suffrage Association (NAWSA) through to the enactment of the suffrage amendment in 1920, started her public career as a teacher and then later served as superintendent of the Mason City, Iowa schools from 1883 to 1885.[7] In the years between Anthony and Catt, a host of other women educators devoted their efforts to the women's suffrage movement, including Betsey Mix Cowles, superintendent of the Canton, Ohio schools from 1850 to 1855. Cowles, who became known as "one of the most successful teachers in the State," also led the "crusade for women's rights," serving as the president of the first Ohio Women's Convention in 1850.[8] Voters in Wyoming elected Estelle Reed to be the state superintendent of instruction in 1894, which made her the first woman in the country to hold a state office. In this capacity she addressed the 1898 meeting of the NAWSA convention.[9]

Teachers generally played active roles in organizing and sustaining the suffrage movement. For example, in the 1880s five thousand

Indiana teachers signed a petition asking for women's vote.[10] Teachers formed a significant constituency of local, state, and national gatherings of suffragists. They also played key roles in the proliferation of women's rights periodicals, which offered an important forum for women to discuss the ramifications of the Seneca Falls Declaration of Sentiments. Magazines such as *The Woman Voter* effectively lent coherence as well as a sense of community to widely scattered groups of women's rights activists.[11] Of the twelve papers championing women's rights from 1849 to 1920, schoolteachers edited nine of them.[12]

Anne Firor Scott traces one of the most important links between the suffrage movement and education when she describes how the rise of female seminaries in the early 1800s eventually catalyzed the woman's rights movement. The bold, intelligent, and diligent women who founded these institutions created unique social spaces for young women to develop their academic abilities, build warm friendships with one another, draw inspiration from the model of admirable women educators, and decide that women deserved equal rights. Emma Willard, who established the Troy Female Seminary, was by all accounts a powerful, wise, and deeply compassionate person who inspired the hundreds of women with whom she worked. Willard long contended that "justice will yet be done. Women will have her rights. I see it in the course of events."[13] Graduates of the Troy Female Seminary frequently became influential teachers and leaders themselves, some even establishing their own female institutions.

Many of these women also worked for women's rights. For instance, Elizabeth Cady Stanton attended Troy, where she developed a deep admiration for Willard. Stanton later joined Susan B. Anthony in organizing the Seneca Falls meeting and providing critical leadership for the larger women's suffrage movement. The influence of Troy Seminary and other institutions like it expanded outward to touch many women indirectly. Scott concludes that "education appears to have been a major force in the spread of feminism."[14]

Not all advocates of women's education supported the movement for women's rights, however. Catharine Beecher consistently spoke out against women's suffrage, insisting that the development of teaching as woman's profession was more important than fighting for full citizenship.[15] She blasted suffragists for seeking male prerogatives where instead she believed they should aspire to developing their own inherent feminine qualities for nurturance and accommodation.[16] Beecher's position militated against suffrage because she believed that societies were civilized by the degree to which they made distinctions between the responsibilities of men and women.[17] Women therefore should not seek privileges reserved for men. Because of her views, suffragists regarded Beecher as an enemy.[18]

Advocates of women's education clearly diverged in their political views and in their willingness to agitate for women's rights. Regardless of the roiling public debates, many graduates of female educational institutions took their activism to the schools. There they labored to improve opportunities for girls by founding their own women's seminaries, or by venturing out on their own to teach in remote schoolhouses to assure that the next generation of young women would be educated. May Wright Sewall, an Indiana teacher and chair of the executive committee of the National Woman Suffrage Association (NWSA), described this sense of mission in 1885: "Naturally, so far, woman's best efforts have been given to the young of their own sex, for the educated woman's first feeling, I might almost say her primary conviction, is that her duty binds her to her own sex, that she may make to them possibilities for such training as was denied to her."[19]

As school districts began hiring women teachers in the mid-nineteenth century, women's suffrage advocates discovered important new strategies for leveraging their right to vote. First, women's increasing property ownership opened the possibility for their suffrage. Because women teachers earned salaries, low as they may have been, and because women teachers usually were single, they sometimes possessed their own property. By conventional reasoning, property owners should be entitled to vote. Therefore, women teachers who owned property should have suffrage. May Wright Sewall made this explicit argument in 1887 when she addressed the Senate:

> It is true that as respects property rights, and as respects industrial rights, the women of my own State may perhaps be the envy of all other women in the land, but, gentlemen, you have always told me that the greater their rights and the more numerous their privileges the greater their responsibilities. That is equally true of woman, and simply because our property rights are enlarged . . . because we have more women who are producers . . . , who own property in their own names, and consequently pay taxes upon that property, . . . we . . . need the power which shall emphasize our influence upon political action.[20]

Second, since communities elected school officials who in turn directed teachers' work, then teachers should have a voice in choosing school officials, the reasoning went. Male teachers could vote; however, because increasing numbers of teachers were women, and women could not vote, then many teachers effectively had no voice or control of their own working conditions or salaries. To remedy this unjust situation, a few midwestern and western communities granted women school suffrage, or the right to vote in school-related elections. Eventually entire states formalized the practice by passing legislation assuring women the right to vote on school matters. By 1910, twenty-four states had granted women school suffrage.[21]

Suffrage activists then argued that if women exercised their franchise responsibly for school-related matters, they also should be trusted with full suffrage. They further contended that because the political process could be corrupt, then women's full suffrage might lend a moral tone to democracy. Women could safeguard moral principles in the sometimes tainted political realm. In 1869, the male citizens of Wyoming concurred with this reasoning and voted to extend full suffrage to women. The chief justice of the Wyoming supreme court described the effect of this change: "The women, as a class, will not knowingly vote for incompetent, immoral, or inefficient candidates. . . . It has not marred domestic harmony. Husband and wife frequently vote opposing tickets without disturbing the peace of the home."[22] Other midwestern and western states followed suit over the next fifty years in a development that gradually offered women significant new power in civic affairs.[23] Women's work in public schooling, then, provided important justification for their eventual right to full suffrage.

Enfranchisement was not women's only means of affecting the political process, however. The citizens of some states believed that not only should women vote, but they also should be eligible for some public offices. They especially should be allowed to hold positions for which there was a shortage of competent men, such as in school supervision. U.S. Commissioner of Education John Eaton wrote in 1873: "The difficulty experienced in finding fully-educated men for the various departments of school-work has for some years past led to an engagement of women in this work . . . on the ground that cultivated women are more frequently available for the performance of such duty than equally cultivated men."[24] A number of states passed legislation permitting the employment of women in various school offices. For example, in 1888 California passed the following law: "Women over the age of 21 years, who are citizens of the United States and this state, shall be eligible to all educational offices within the state, except those from which they are excluded by the constitution." Voters in eleven counties elected women superintendents soon afterward.[25]

Occasionally women won school elections even before laws clarified their right to do so. Julia Addington's friends persuaded her to run
for a county superintendency in Iowa though she initially resisted.
When she won the seat, her opponent challenged the victory because as
a woman, she was not legally a citizen, and only citizens could hold
public offices. The state attorney general, however, issued a strong statement favoring Addington's right to hold office, and in 1876 the state
passed the following law: "No person shall be deemed ineligible, by
reason of sex, to any school office in the State of Iowa."[26]

In some cases schools needed women's leadership services so desperately that citizens sometimes elected women to offices even before
these candidates could vote for themselves. In 1879 sixteen states allowed women to hold elected school offices before granting them suffrage.[27] To protest this situation, a member of the New Hampshire
legislature in 1878 argued: "If women are capable of holding office they
are also capable of saying who shall hold it." The legislature then passed
a bill granting school suffrage to New Hampshire women.[28]

Once women could vote and then run for school offices, they
started winning. Some campaigns offered them easy victories because
previous incumbents either obviously had neglected their duties or had
succumbed to the temptation of political corruption. Even with competent and honest opponents, though, women sometimes succeeded in
their campaigns with the active help of groups of women. For instance,
in 1890 Sarah Christie Stevens won her race for the superintendency of
the Blue Earth County schools (Minnesota) because, as reporters suggested, the "ladies worked in getting out voters . . . with the energy of
male politicians."[29]

When women assumed their newly won positions, they quickly
discovered that the public held them to a higher standard of performance than men. Two years after winning the county superintendency,
Sarah Stevens lost her bid for reelection because the man who challenged her charged that she had neglected to visit every school in her
district each year. Although school visitations constituted one of the
county superintendent's most important duties, officeholders found it
exceedingly difficult to travel to each of the many remote one-room
schoolhouses, especially since the bitterly cold, long winters of the
northern prairie made rural travel impossible for months at a time. Few
county superintendents managed to visit every school annually, and
when they did, it usually only happened in small or urban counties.
Sensing that her opponent might be gaining an advantage with these attacks, Stevens appealed to the state superintendent for endorsement of
her reelection because he had witnessed the improved conditions of

schools under her leadership. He wrote back: "You asked if [women] are in every way as well qualified as men. I think not. While in most particulars I think they accomplish their work as well as men in similar positions, they are not as well able to endure exposure in the winter in riding over prairies and through the woods to visit schools." Finding little support from the state superintendent, Stevens endured the blistering attacks of her opponent, who defeated her handily. Interestingly, once in office he succeeded in visiting far fewer schools than Stevens, a shortcoming for which he was not criticized. In the end, he had won the position by exploiting the perception of women's physical frailty.[30] Even though Stevens had performed notably better than her opponent in this respect, she would have been above reproach only if her record had been flawless, a standard that he fell far short of.

Political ordeals such as Stevens's were repeated in districts around the country and contributed to women's reluctance to run for office. Carrie Chapman Catt described the problem when she wrote, "the candidate is likely to be forced to wade through mud to her victory, to make concessions to interests which nauseate her soul and to arrive at the goal with a reputation in tatters."[31] Their opponents routinely barraged women candidates for school offices with a wide range of criticisms. One minister justified this treatment when he explained: "If woman steps out of her sphere, and demands to be and to do what men do, to enter political life, to enter the professions, to wrestle with us for office and employments and gains, she must understand that she will have to take the low places as well as the high places of life. . . . If she goes to Congress, she must also go to the heavy drudgery of earth."[32]

As challenging as it sometimes was for women to win elected superintendencies, however, generally it was far more difficult for women to attain appointed positions. When the Chicago school board appointed Ella Flagg Young superintendent in 1909, this unanticipated and unlikely success heartened women's rights advocates around the country. Grace Strachan, president of the Interborough Association of Women Teachers in New York and a district superintendent in New York City, in 1910 declared: "There is absolutely no reason why women should not occupy the executive as well as other positions in the educational system. Chicago proved itself more progressive than New York, when it placed a woman at the head of its immense school system— because she was the fittest one for the place. . . . Fitness should be the only requisite of choice."[33] Left to their own preferences, however, school board members tended to appoint superintendents demographically similar to themselves, which almost invariably meant that they chose White, Protestant men. On the other hand, elected superinten-

dencies offered women better chances for school administration positions because female candidates sometimes could find enthusiastic
bases of support from local women's groups, a constituency that otherwise had little direct influence in an appointive system.

After the Civil War, women first began winning superintendencies, mainly elected county positions. They tended to invest themselves
fully in their work to prove that women could excel in positions of public responsibility; however, voters in some states regarded the employment of women school superintendents as a temporary expedient or an
experiment. Some early women superintendents faced critical evalua-
tions to determine the worthiness of their continued employment. In
1873, when Illinois first allowed women to hold school offices, ten
women won county superintendencies. At the end of their four-year
terms, the president of the state teachers association wrote an evaluation of their performance in four critical areas.

First, he explained that the women had handled the financial aspects of their work with great care and competence. "In many of these
counties the financial affairs were in the greatest confusion when the
ladies came into office, . . . strange irregularities were discovered. In
every instance . . . these crookednesses have been straightened out, the
finances put upon a surer basis, hundreds, we believe thousands, of dollars of bad debts have been collected, treasurers and directors have been
induced to keep their books with greater care and in better shape, reck-
less expenditure of school funds has been discouraged, and directors
encouraged to expend the money for things which will permanently
benefit the schools." Second, the women handled their legal concerns
with skill and diplomacy where, as he explained, "scores of controver-
sies were referred to her, and there has never been a single appeal from
her decisions." Third, because all ten of the women had been teachers,
they comfortably worked with teachers and capably offered practical
suggestions. Finally, the evaluator indicated that all the women managed the details of their work in an outstanding manner. He said, "in
looking after the details of official work, those tiresome minutiae so often left at 'loose ends,' producing endless confusion, woman has shown
great aptitude." He concluded that every woman superintendent had
doubled the efficiency of the office, and some had produced four or
even tenfold increases.[34]

Hardworking, diligent women superintendents eventually won
valuable support from a variety of places. Women in Colorado won suffrage in 1893 and within a decade women accounted for the majority of
the state's county superintendents. Many of these individual women
were hailed as "the most efficient officer we have ever had in this

county."[35] The Montana State Superintendent of Public Instruction in 1884 praised the work of the state's five women county superintendents: "School affairs in these counties are as well, and in some respects, better managed than in most of the remaining counties [managed by men]. These ladies have traveled over their large counties and accomplished work in a manner that could not have been surpassed by men."[36] The Commissioner of Education in 1880 applauded women's service to education: "Carefully considering the position of woman in the work of education, what she has done and may do as a teacher, what her nature and experience may fit her to do better than man as an officer, inspector, or superintendent, as facts have illustrated these points in this and other countries, I have favored the extension of suffrage to her in all matters relating to education and the opening of appropriate offices to her in connection with institutions and systems of instruction."[37] With such a strong endorsement from the commissioner as well as with broadening bases of support, women made rapid gains in the superintendency in the late 1800s and early 1900s. They especially won elected county positions in midwestern and western states where women had enjoyed suffrage long before their eastern sisters.

As women won increasing numbers of county superintendencies, several state superintendencies, and a few city executive positions, women's rights activists lauded these victories as harbingers of women's eventual equal rights. Enthusiastic writers filled suffrage publications with tallies of elected women school officers and other evidence of women's growing political clout. *The Blue Book* (1917) contained concise summaries of women's political victories around the country so suffrage activists could propound these speaking points at rallies, in congressional hearings, and in newsletters.[38] The 1917 *Woman Suffrage Yearbook* concluded that women accounted for half of the county superintendents in the United States, and most of them served in western equal-suffrage states. By that time seventeen different women had served as state school superintendents as well.[39] In reviewing the records of these women state officers, one suffragist noted that "Miss Permeal French has been several times re-elected as state superintendent of public instruction of Idaho. Governor Steunenburg declared her to be the best the state ever had. The same compliment by the people and by the governor was paid Mrs. Helen Grenfell, of Colorado. She had the largest vote ever cast for a candidate in the state, ran ahead of the ticket for governor, and for president of the United States."[40] Clearly, women's victories in superintendent races were a source of great pride and hope for suffragists around the country.

The overall number of women superintendents increased quickly around the turn of the century. In 1896, women held 228 county super-

intendencies, two state superintendencies, and twelve city superintendencies.[41] Just five years later, the *Report of the Commissioner of Education*
indicated that 288 women held county superintendencies for a 26 percent increase.[42] By 1913, there were 495 women county superintendents—more than doubling the 1896 figure in less than twenty years.
Also, women had won state superintendencies in Colorado, Idaho,
Washington, and Wyoming.[43]

The rapid increase in women superintendents occurred as the
women's suffrage movement moved into its most active phase in the
early decades of the twentieth century. By this time, many states west of
the Mississippi had already granted women full suffrage. Women's suffrage associations in the northeast sponsored important public demon-
strations and vigorously campaigned for national suffrage. Some
suffrage activists also wanted to elect women to public offices. Since
school superintendencies were among the first public positions for
which women were eligible, the strengthening suffrage movement effectively translated into votes for women superintendents.

Because of their clear record of excellence in handling their civic
duties in the realm of schooling, women's activists hoped that their opportunities for public service might broaden to include other government and political positions. The governor of Colorado added his voice
in support of this effort:

Since 1876 school affairs have practically been in the hands of
women. They have voted at school elections, held the office of superintendent in a majority of the counties and taught most of the
schools. In these twenty-eight years neither politics nor scandals
have impaired our public school system and in efficiency we challenge comparison with any State in the Union. What the women
have done for our schools they can do for our civic government.
They have introduced conscience into educational affairs and they
will do the same in city and State. That is the fear of those who
make politics a profession.[44]

Essentially, as women proved their leadership capabilities as school administrators, they found increasing support for transforming these
early successes into a larger acceptable role in the public sphere.

Women's suffrage was not the only focus of organized women
and their allies, though. In their exhaustive, multivolume account, *The
History of Woman Suffrage*, Susan B. Anthony and Ida Husted Harper detailed the rise of an immense variety of women's associations in the late

1800s. Noting the historical significance of this women's club movement, they wrote: "We scarcely can go back so far in history as not to
find men banded together to protect their mutual interests, but associations of women are of very modern date." They described the first societies of women, Sorosis (New York City) and the New England
Woman's Club, which were formed in 1868 "by women purely for their
own recreation and improvement." According to Anthony and Harper,
some earlier groups of women had assisted the poor or otherwise
served those in need; but because of the supposedly selfish goals of
these new societies, "they met with a storm of derision and protest from
all parts of the country, which their founders courageously ignored."
Besides these and other strictly social societies that quickly spread
throughout the country, a number of other women's groups emerged
with such diverse purposes as political reform and women's mutual education. Some groups addressed social problems like alcoholism, child
labor, and poverty, all of which plagued an increasingly industrialized
urban America. Eventually women's groups appeared in virtually
every community, and many of these were affiliated with state and national organizations. By 1900, well over a million women belonged to
clubs that comprised the National Council of Women.[45] The council,
which united sixteen of the most influential women's organizations,
first gathered in 1888 and declared:

> We, women of the United States, sincerely believing that the best
> good of our homes and the nation will be advanced by our own
> greater unity of thought, sympathy and purpose, and that an or-
> ganized movement of women will best conserve the highest good
> of the family and the State, do hereby band ourselves together in
> a confederation of workers committed to the overthrow of all
> forms of ignorance and injustice, and to the application of the
> Golden Rule to society, custom and law.[46]

Beyond the organizations represented by this umbrella group, around
3 million women belonged to other similar groups. Altogether, Anthony
and Harper estimated that well over 4 million women belonged to
women's clubs and associations in 1900, representing over one-tenth of
the 37 million females reported in the U.S. census. And women's association membership continued to climb.[47]

Women joined associations for a variety of reasons. Groups such
as the Daughters of Temperance, the National and American Woman
Suffrage Associations, the National Association of Colored Women, the
General Federation of Women's Clubs, the Women's Christian Temper-

ance Union (WCTU), Sanitary Commissions, the Woman's Loyal League, and the Freedmen's Bureau offered women the opportunity to belong to groups addressing specific social concerns. Once women joined these associations, they came to know each other, enjoy each other's company, and understand concerns uniting women generally. The club movement broke the isolation many middle-class women experienced in their daily lives and fostered connection among women beyond their circles of neighbors and kin. In addition to this social contact of club meetings, women felt enriched by the intellectual stimulation of educational programs, guest speakers, journals, and association conferences.

Women also developed important public leadership skills by participating in these groups since the growth of associations required members to understand social organizations, develop persuasive speaking and writing skills, devise strategies for political action, manage finances, and master other skills routinely required of men by their work, but generally denied women. Anthony and Harper wrote that "women displayed an unsuspected power of organization, and at its close [the Civil War] their status in many ways was completely changed and greatly advanced."[48] Historian Joan Burstyn further explains that the leadership skills developed in women's associations were not cast simply from the mold of traditional patriarchal organizations. Rather, members of women's associations tended to minimize hierarchical power configurations while instead fostering cooperation and shared power since women as a class understood what it felt like to be excluded from decision making, especially in the political and legal realms.[49]

At first, however, women hesitated to engage in political work because it seemed foreign to their experience, inappropriate, uninteresting, or even beneath the moral dignity of women. Most groups eventually discovered that they needed political power to accomplish their aims. In time, women's associations became quite powerful, adept forces on a number of political issues. Anthony and Harper elaborated:

> No other means could be so effective in convincing women that politics . . . in reality touches them at every point. They are learning that the mere personal influence which usually was sufficient to gain their ends in the household, society and the church . . . must be supplemented by political influence now that they have entered the field of public work. Women have been so long flattered by the power which they have possessed over men in social life that they are surprised and bewildered to discover that this is wholly ineffectual when brought to bear upon men in legislative

assemblies. . . . They investigate and they see that whatever may be the private opinion of these legislators, their public acts are governed by their constituents, and women alone of all classes in the community are not constituents.[50]

In the end, women's associations endeavored to become constituents so that they could attain their purposes.

Several women's associations specifically devoted their attention to supporting schools and the work of educators. The WCTU, for example, which Anthony and Harper lauded as the "most perfectly organized body of women in existence," provided quantities of literature and instructional materials to teachers around the country so classes could learn about the physiological and social problems associated with alcohol. The WCTU also campaigned for educational equality for females. The General Federation of Women's Clubs, among its many goals, worked in communities nationwide to support the appointment of women to school boards. In state and national political bodies it lobbied for legislation granting broader educational advantages for women. Members of the National Congress of Mothers, which later became the Parents and Teachers Association, advocated improved conditions in schools as well as greater representation of women on school boards.[51] Their political influence grew as their membership surged in the early decades of the twentieth century. Though the National Congress of Mothers was established only in 1897, it grew to a staggering 1.5 million members by the 1920s.[52]

A number of women's groups found they could lobby effectively for educational change by requesting cooperation from the NEA. To accommodate the interest of women's associations, in 1907 the NEA admitted several women's groups to form the Department of National Women's Organizations, which in 1909 became the Department of School Patrons.[53] The department included the General Federation of Women's Clubs, the National Congress of Mothers, the Association of Collegiate Alumnae, the Woman's Christian Temperance Union, the National Council of Jewish Women, and the Southern Association of College Women.[54]

Although women's associations initially dedicated their efforts to their specifically stated causes, by the turn of the century many of them actively supported suffrage. Because these organizations had already discovered the importance of political lobbying, they knew that women would have far more political clout if they had full enfranchisement. The WCTU, for instance, resisted championing woman's suffrage at first, but in the late 1800s members of the organization became convinced of the need for women's vote to advance their crusade. Members became tireless advocates of women's suffrage, leading Anthony and Harper to explain that "considered as a body there are no more active workers for woman suffrage [than are in the WCTU]."[55] As women's clubs and suffrage organizations increasingly joined forces, the larger women's movement became a formidable national political force in the early decades of the twentieth century.

When women first won suffrage in individual states and then full national suffrage in 1920, their power in some respects escalated to new levels. The political pressure of women's associations could no longer be dismissed as an irritating inconvenience, or as irrelevant. Women members voted and they cared. Arthur Capper, U.S. senator from Kansas, explained that "what women will do with their political power I have not the slightest doubt. It goes without saying that they are politically powerful. . . . Women's institutions must be reckoned with by all parties and all politicians."[56]

Women also frequently voted in concert. And many women were determined to bring to the polls their concerns for social improvement and moral elevation. An editorial from the Los Angeles Express captured something of the sense of moral victory as well as victory for morals represented by women's enfranchisement in California: "Those who were formerly in the habit of claiming that the ballot in the hands of woman would only multiply the number of ballots without altering the moral bearing of the ballot-box for either weal or woe were clearly mistaken. Woman has added a great moral force to the ballot in California. She has added very materially in humanizing the party platform and vitalizing the issue."[57]

Women teachers remained an active component of the larger women's movement during this time. This is not surprising because by 1910, around a half million American women worked in education in some capacity.[58] Teachers' organizations also expanded rapidly during these years as they rallied for such causes as improved classroom conditions and equal pay for women teachers. In 1893 a group of Chicago women teachers organized a club that, among other things, would "assert itself with vigor whenever woman's rights are infringed upon." They further declared:

For some reason woman has not been recognized in the club life of men. This is not wholly surprising when we recall the club characteristics of men in some lines of life, but there are supposed to be no characteristics of the man teacher's social life that inevitably exclude women. . . . There is no reason why men, as men, should not have a club to which women are not invited, but when all the club life of teachers in a given locality is masculine, the women do well to organize themselves into a club from which their brethren are excluded.[59]

Beyond women teachers' clubs and associations, publications sprouted bearing such names as *The Women's Voice and Public School Advocate*. Teachers' unions also organized in many cities and some became mighty political forces.

Not only did teachers participate actively in the women's movement, but so did women superintendents. Their records of achievement demonstrate that women superintendents typically valued their service in women's associations. Laura Joanna Ghering served as the superintendent of the Kingfisher City Schools in Oklahoma in the 1920s, and she also worked with the local Red Cross chapter and actively participated in the WCTU for twenty-five years. Bertha Palmer, state superintendent of public instruction in Minnesota, worked as a state officer of the Federation of Women's Clubs. Celestia Susannah Parrish served as one of three state superintendents of schools in Georgia (1911–18). Not only did she belong to the WCTU and the Georgia Federation of Women's Clubs, but she also founded the state's first Mothers and Teachers Cooperative Club and became its first president.[60] Betsey Mix Cowles, superintendent of Canton schools in Ohio (1850–55), worked as an organizer of various women's groups and as the principal leader of the local Female Anti-Slavery Society. Susan Dorsey, superintendent of Los Angeles City Schools (1920–29), became a charter member of the WCTU, later served on the Southern California Committee on the Cause and Cure of War, and worked as vice president of the Women's Law Observance Association. Julia Richman held a demanding New York City district superintendency early in the twentieth century, but managed to serve with the Council of Jewish Women and campaign for children's rights throughout her career.[61] Ella Flagg Young chaired a division of the General Federation of Women's Clubs during her terms as Chicago school superintendent.

Some women superintendents viewed their official duties as a means of advancing the various goals of the women's movement. One certain cause of women's activism was the elimination of political corruption. When Ella Flagg Young served as the superintendent of Chicago schools as well as president of the NEA, she endeavored to root out the ploys of dishonest officials who skimmed money from public and association coffers. In both the NEA and Chicago she met with considerable resistance from entrenched forces. Shortly after her election to the presidency of the NEA, Young discovered that a trust fund of membership dues had been invested in questionable deals by Nicholas Murray Butler, president of Columbia University and a man who "controlled" the NEA. Butler responded by hatching a campaign to overturn her election, alleging that many newly enfranchised female teachers in the association had cast votes illegally. His effort failed, but then he blocked an investigation of the trust fund. He even resorted to personal threats when he sent one of his associates to Chicago to tell Margaret Haley, the president of the Chicago Teachers Federation and Young's friend, that if Young did not back off the investigation, "they're going to kill Mrs. Young. I mean it. They're going to kill Mrs. Young." Young toned down her pressure, but within a short time, Butler resigned as trustee of the fund. Young had won this battle. However, through the rest of her career she continued to feel aftershocks from this encounter with Butler's nationwide NEA network of supporters.[62]

In Chicago, Young also faced serious opposition from members of the school board who had regularly received kickbacks from textbook publishers. Young sought to end these kickbacks and instead choose texts by their quality alone. Some board members also wanted to use school land for personal speculative business ventures rather than for school purposes. Again, Young prevented these misuses of public school properties, especially because schools needed funds desperately for teachers' salaries and other educational expenses. Her resistance to these corrupt practices eventually led the board to vote her out of office in 1913.[63]

Young was not without her resources, though. A supporter, Mrs. George Bass, recounted that one of the greatest fears of Chicago school board members was the collective power of local women's associations. Young had labored to carry the noble aspirations of the women's movement into her office, and in return for her efforts she enjoyed tremendous community support from women's associations. Bass described the situation:

[T]here was also opposition on the part of the board because of the increasing interest which the women of Chicago took in the schools over which Mrs. Young was placed and they disliked their increasingly definite knowledge of school affairs. It is true that the women of my city have followed every phase of the school situation during the past few years. A proof of their interest was seen when about two years ago, Mrs. Young was put out of her position. The women rose up, held a mass meeting, and packed the great auditorium, calling on the mayor to replace Mrs. Young.

There is no need of going through the subsequent events. It is sufficient to say that she was replaced. The bitter feeling of the board increased after this until the opposition to Mrs. Young became open on the part of some of the members who said they would like to get rid of the entire influence of the women.[64]

Because of the activism of Chicago women, led mainly by the social reformer Jane Addams, the school board reinstated Young to the superintendency later in 1913. Said one critic: "Four thousand of these teachers, bound to put Feminism and fads on top, met and mutinied and demanded that the School Board should bow down and do their will, and to rescind the election of the man and elect the woman. They squawked and screeched and threatened the Mayor and all his friends with defeat at the polls. As they had an influence on votes, the Mayor obeyed these mutineers."[65] Though she had been reinstated, by 1915 the cumulative animosity of board members had taken its toll and again Young was forced to step down, this time for good.[66]

Female superintendents found support not only from groups of women such as the one led by Jane Addams, but also from teachers and teacher organizations. For example, teachers elected Susan Dorsey president of the California Teachers' Association (southern section) before she served as the Los Angeles superintendent. During her nine years as superintendent, she maintained ties with teachers by laboring tirelessly for their higher salaries, right to sabbatical leaves, and job tenure. She deeply respected the work of teachers and maintained that "principals, supervisors, superintendents, and business managers have been added for the one and only purpose of making it more possible for the teacher to do better the essential work of teaching." She insisted that "no superintendent can administer his schools in the best fashion without advice and sometimes actual administrative assistance from teachers."[67]

Ella Flagg Young, while serving as the director of the Chicago Normal School, regularly held social and professional meetings at her house for all the teachers in her school. Once appointed superintendent, Young remained connected with teachers by campaigning for their higher salaries and greater participation in school administration. She developed strong friendships with many of the teachers in the Chicago City School system, including members of the Chicago Teachers Federation. Teachers trusted Young to the extent that at times they called on her to mediate disputes within the federation.[68]

Josephine Corliss Preston, elected to the Washington state superintendency in 1913, offered single women teachers an even more personal form of support for their work. Having been a teacher for eleven years before moving into administration, Preston understood firsthand the problems women faced in having to board around with families in the school district. She firmly believed that women needed privacy, places of their own so they could relax and think. When she became the Walla Walla County superintendent, she devised a plan for women to have their own homes, or "teacherages." Then she made sure that every teacher in her district had such a place to stay. She enlisted the help of the National Federation of Women's Clubs to expand the project to the entire state. The federation not only launched the Washington state teacherage campaign, but Women's Federations around the country also joined the effort. Women in Texas, for example, were so inspired with the idea that they "built more 'teacherages' in one year than Washington did in ten." In time, even the U.S. Commissioner of Education took up the cause so that by the early 1920s, large numbers of teacherages had been built around the country. [69]

Teacherages meant a great deal to the women who lived in them. For the first time, tens of thousands of single women could live comfortably on their own without having to board with their own or another community family. Preston regarded it as an essential part of her personal and work responsibilities to foster strong mutually supportive relationships between herself and teachers. These relationships were then fortified with the assistance of the larger community of women. Eventually teachers nationwide rewarded Preston's efforts by electing her president of the NEA. [70]

Women school administrators not only maintained close connections with teachers, but in time they also established a national association for themselves. During the 1915 NEA meeting in Oakland, California, a group of women administrators gathered to form the National Council of Administrative Women in Education. Thereafter, the group met twice a year, once during the regular NEA meeting and again during the NEA Department of Superintendence meeting. Eighteen states formed affiliates of the national group, some of them quite active. By 1932, the NEA elevated the council to department status. The council described as its purpose in the *NEA Proceedings* "to strengthen the friendly and professional relations of administrative women in educational work and to maintain high professional standards among them." [71] It avoided some contentious topics such as equal salaries for women teachers because "questions of a controversial nature . . . were being well taken care of by various teachers organizations." However, the group did take as one of its primary goals to "strive to advance the number of women in positions of leadership in education at every opportunity." [72] These efforts came when the number of women school superintendents had reached the highest point of the century. Members of the council hoped the numbers would climb higher.

School superintendencies were not the only education offices in which women scored impressive gains. In his 1927 study, *The Social Composition of Boards of Education,* George Counts explained that full national suffrage had contributed to women's phenomenal success in winning seats on city school boards; and that many communities felt out of fashion if they did not have at least one woman member. The rapid increases that he documented led him to conclude that "if this advance should continue at the same rate for a generation or two, the determination of school policy would pass definitely out of the hands of the sex which has controlled formal education in the past."[73]

Counts cautioned, however, that in spite of women's increasing representation on school boards, few boards had more than one woman member. There was little effort to have more than token representation. Even worse, while women accounted for one in six board members at the time, they served as presidents of school boards in only one case in twenty-nine. Counts also noted that women board members, like their male colleagues, were a relatively homogeneous lot. They tended to be White, Protestant, and generally from middle-class families. Three-quarters identified themselves as housewives. Teaching and social work accounted for the only other professions with any significant representation.[74]

Though women's activists were excited about the increasing women's representation on school boards, some cautioned that community elites might advance women to the ballot who had no real interest or experience in educational matters. By so promoting these women, feminists might hesitate to complain. Helen L. Grenfell, state superintendent of Colorado, explained that: "While there should be a woman on the ideal school board, it should not be merely because she is a woman. It is a great mistake for women to demand recognition of their sex rather than of themselves as individuals."[75] In spite of Grenfell's words of caution, women nationwide won school board seats after passage of the suffrage amendment. Interestingly, in spite of their quick gains and the optimism of allies such as Counts, women's representation on school boards peaked around the time his study was published in 1927 and then declined. At least another fifty years would pass before women again held more than 10 percent of school board seats.[76]

In the end, women school superintendents emerged as part of the broad-based women's movement of the late 1800s and early 1900s. The discrimination women faced as they attempted to expand their sphere of influence into public service and even school leadership was generally too great for them to conquer alone; yet the strong, supportive constituency provided by the women's movement gave many aspiring women administrators the boost they needed to win their positions. In turn, women superintendents endeavored to uphold the moral ideals of women's activism. The complex, mutually supportive relationships among women superintendents, teachers, women's association members, and suffrage activists provided the essential network for women's rise to school leadership positions. Historian Margaret Gribskov summarizes: "The rise and fall of the woman school administrator approximates the peaks and valleys of the first American feminist movement of the late 1800s and early 1900s, . . . and the feminist movement was a crucial factor in producing the large numbers of women administrators of that period."[77] After enactment of suffrage, however, the activity of women's groups continued, but much less feverishly. A steady dissipation of women's support networks presaged the eventual decline in the number of women superintendents. And new efforts to erode women's hard-won political gains would meet with little resistance.

The women's suffrage movement had sparked the emergence of women school administrators for at least two reasons. First, the quest for women's rights had triggered the larger movement of organized women's groups, many of which actively supported the candidacy of women for school offices. Second, suffrage had given women power at the ballot box, which allowed them to affect the political process directly, to become, as some had hoped, a political constituency. Once women had won full enfranchisement in all states, some suffragists then turned to the task of educating women about their new duties as citizens. The NAWSA became the League of Women Voters, which took as its primary mission the nonpartisan education of citizens for their democratic duties.[78] The league did not explicitly continue to work for women's rights, however. As Eleanor Flexner wrote in Century of Struggle, her history of the women's rights movement, "it is not at all clear whether [the League of Women Voters] may not have short-circuited the political strength of the most gifted suffragist women. Certainly it planted firmly in the minds of a goodly number of politicians the idea that 'the ladies' were not really interested in politics . . . but rather in 'reform,' which was quite another matter."[79] Regardless of the level at which organized groups of women pursued the campaign for women's rights, though, democracy as a concept as well as a practice clearly meant a great deal to newly enfranchised women.

As women cast their first ballots, however, groups of superintendents began pushing for reforms in school district governance and the superintendency that would have the effect of removing school administration from the electoral process. Threatened by suffrage-era gains in women's rights and stinging from widespread criticisms of school inefficiency, many superintendents sought to bolster their collectively sagging image. An important means of maintaining their public viability involved adopting methods like those that Taylor-inspired efficiency engineers deployed in the industries of the time. If superintendents could become clipboard- and stopwatch-toting efficiency experts and convince the public of their merit, which, incidentally, would not be determined directly by the ballot, then they might be able to deflect much criticism.[80]

The problem with experts, though, was that many superintendents believed the public could not be trusted to recognize and choose expert talent. They argued, therefore, that the superintendency should become strictly an appointed rather than an elected position for which candidates were selected based on their expert credentials. Democracy would be preserved through this system because the public would elect representatives, such as school board members or commissioners, who then would appoint superintendents. Since this strategy emerged just as women were winning suffrage and some elected school leadership positions, it is plausible that the movement toward the appointed superintendency was partly inspired by the fear of women's voting power.

Voter involvement in managing public school affairs extended back to early tax-funded school districts. The first school boards were organized so that elected citizens could oversee the use of taxpayer funds for education. Communities monitored their school board members carefully and held them accountable with periodic elections. Throughout the nineteenth century, a fascinating variety of school districts emerged with an equal variety of school-board structures and duties. Some cities that were segmented into hundreds of wards elected board members from each—which sometimes produced mammoth school boards. At these board meetings, discussions dragged on, absenteeism was high, and proceedings reportedly bordered on chaos much of the time. Other districts kept school boards small, which had the benefit of streamlining meetings, but the disadvantage of requiring more work of each member. Some communities attempted to balance the need for democratic representation with the logistical concerns of running a school district. In a few districts, though, board members were appointed by other officials, thus sidestepping direct voter accountability altogether.

Superintendents' duties and power varied with school board con-figuration, so one of the driving concerns among superintendents in the late 1800s was the reform and standardization of school board structure. Small boards were preferred for several reasons. First, superintendents typically could work more easily with small rather than large school boards because of simplified communication and management of polit-ical interests. Second, small school boards could not perform as much administrative work as large ones, leaving the superintendent with an expanded set of duties and greater power, which superintendents gen-erally wanted. Furthermore, superintendent salaries tended to increase with enlarged responsibilities. Third, if school boards shrank, each member would represent a larger segment of the population, which in turn required well-funded candidates who could afford more expensive campaigns. In districts where school board sizes were reduced, the so-cial characteristics of board members changed significantly. Wealthy members of the community replaced local candidates of more humble means. Social and economic homogeneity eventually characterized boards around the country as men from the business and professional communities and their wives increasingly became members. Superin-tendents benefited from this social change because it boosted their pres-tige to associate with these more influential community members.[81]

Superintendent groups also wanted the superintendency changed from an elected to an appointed position, a reform that they argued would take the position out of politics. Though most cities and town-ships already opted for appointed superintendencies, most county po-sitions and some local and state superintendents were elected. These elected positions were precisely the ones that women were beginning to win with the help of the suffrage movement.

Iowa, for example, granted women school suffrage in 1893, though a number of women had already been elected as superinten-dents. However, immediately after school suffrage was enacted, super-intendents began protesting. The *Journal of Education* in 1894 reported that one county superintendent said: "The principal need was that the superintendent should be a better trained *man* and should be divorced from politics. . . . There are forty-nine changes this year, and it would no doubt be better if many of these officers could have been retained."[82]

In 1893 Colorado granted women full suffrage and also first per-mitted them to run for offices such as superintendencies.[83] Women quickly established their political presence around the state, and elected officials knew this change had the potential to alter the face of politics in every locality.[84] When state superintendent Murray addressed the winter meeting of county superintendents that year, he indicated that thirty-eight out of fifty-six county superintendents had just been defeated, including "some of the best *men* of the state."[85] In response, male educators organized and devised strategies for negotiating these changes. The *Journal of Education* reported in March 1894 that the Colorado Schoolmasters' Club had been established and included the "leading educators of the state."[86] The *Journal* subsequently noted that a select committee of twenty-one persons had met with the state superintendent to consider "How to Remove the Schools from Politics," a discussion led by Aaron Gove, superintendent of Denver schools.[87] Meanwhile, women around the state voted in their first election, and their enthusiasm and high turnout led the *Journal* to explain the great excitement: "Unquestionably 'woman did it.'"[88] That same year, State Superintendent Murray—who had been concerned about the recent heavy turnover of superintendents—was defeated by a woman candidate, Mrs. A. J. Peavy, who was later succeeded by a long line of women state superintendents.[89] No doubt, the move to take the Colorado superintendency out of politics was inspired by fear of women's significant collective power at the ballot box.

In 1915 David Snedden, the commissioner of education in Massachusetts, joined male superintendents in Iowa and Colorado by offering his rationale on the need for appointed superintendents:

> The time has come when, throughout the country, educators should go on record . . . as to the fundamental soundness of the system of popular election for educational executives. . . . It should, of course, be recognized that, up to a certain level, a system of popular election may work fairly well, and yet utterly break down beyond. Few people now would argue that an engineer or a superintendent of a water supply system should be chosen by popular vote. It ought to be equally difficult to argue that an expert educational administrator should be chosen, any more than an architect or accountant.[90]

Snedden failed to mention why that particular moment was appropriate for demanding the shift from elected to appointed school administrators. Like other suffrage era critics of elected superintendencies, he neglected to discuss gender explicitly as a factor in the movement. A 1909 editorial printed in the *Fresno Republican* echoed a similar sentiment:

> If there is any public place that ought not to be elective, it is that of any sort of school superintendent. . . . But there is only one policy in regard to a school superintendent or a school teacher, and that

is to get the most competent person available, regardless of other considerations. Popular election is notoriously not the way to do that. . . . When an educational office is elective, it is always filled by a local man. Other things being reasonably equal, the local man is, of course, entitled to the preference, on account of his advantage of local knowledge. But teaching is a profession, and its largest places should be filled by its men of largest professional knowledge and tested capacity. If this happens under the elective system, it is an accident, and a rare one. Under the appointive system, it is the usual result. Our city superintendents and principals, and our university and normal school presidents and teachers, are usually the best of their kind. The exceptions are rare enough to be regarded as remarkable. Yet not one in ten of them could have got his place by election. Probably not one in three of the county superintendents could have got his place by any other process. This is the sober fact, and if we want our state and county school systems put under the leadership of the real educational leaders we must change the system.[91]

Though the author made no overt mention of women, his ideas had important implications for women superintendents. When he penned this piece, women held nearly 40 percent of county superintendencies in California (a little over "one in three"), the elected position about which he complained, and their numbers were rising. On the other hand, women held none of the thirty-three appointed city superintendencies, which he believed were filled by men who were "the best of their kind." When this piece was printed, the campaign for women's suffrage in California was well under way and would succeed two years later. Woman's suffrage clearly formed the contextual backdrop for his words. With momentum quickly building for electing women to school superintendencies, it appeared that women might take over the county superintendency just as they had in other western states.

An appointive system, however, effectively would halt women's progress into school leadership positions. Women rarely received appointments to superintendencies because they tended to be excluded from the male political networks responsible for placing most superintendent candidates. Editors of the *American School Board Journal* in 1908 lauded the networking system for identifying and recruiting superintendent candidates for appointed positions:

The method of a large middle western metropolis in selecting a superintendent of schools is progressive as well as exemplary. Instead of inviting applications broadcast, the board of education made it known that they were seeking the best man available for the place. A committee was *quietly* appointed to confer with school men in various parts of the country and select the *man* who best combined advanced scholarship, originality, tact, executive ability and general fitness for the place. . . . The method which the board pursued was correct and worthy of emulation by every school administrative body.[92]

This superintendent selection method quietly and effectively removed women from contention for school leadership opportunities. A more public means of selection or one that explicitly invoked gender as a factor would have raised the ire of organized women's groups.

Decades later, the NEA formed the Committee on the County Superintendents' Problems, which released its report in 1922, two years after enactment of the suffrage amendment. Committee members lamented that "one does not have to study the rural-school problem long until he becomes convinced that its success or failure centers in and around the office of the county superintendent." Their report concluded by strongly suggesting that future county superintendents receive academic and professional training—available to men, but rarely to women—and that the office should be removed from politics "by having him selected very much as a city superintendent is now selected . . . by a board small in number, selected especially for the purpose of conducting school affairs." Further, the committee urged the NEA to "lend its force, energy, and prestige to the support of such a campaign."[93]

As women won increasing numbers of county superintendencies, superintendent organizations came to demean and belittle the position as it existed. At the same time, organized superintendents esteemed city positions for which experts might be appointed and higher salaries paid. From the beginning, county superintendents had performed duties that were quite demanding by all accounts, though usually they were paid less than superintendents of city systems. But by the turn of the century, the county superintendency had earned a certain respectability as a challenging, but important position that Ellwood Cubberley had praised as "an office of large potential importance."[94] However, as NEA elites pushed for appointed, expert superintendents, elected county superintendents were increasingly portrayed as unskilled political hacks. These attacks usually did not offer evidence for this assessment except that county superintendents typically had not received administrative training in any of a growing number of academic programs in educational administration, which generally admitted few, if any women. The pressure for appointed county superintendencies was unmistakably clear, though; and in 1951, an NEA bulletin on the superintendency concluded that "many states have changed the traditional election [of county superintendents] by popular vote to appointment by the county board."[95]

Women's rights activists and elites in the NEA unquestionably held widely diverging views about the meaning of democracy. These differences were played out in editorial wars, in community and national meetings, at afternoon teas and in smoky cigar salons. However, one of the most dramatic and important such clashes was staged at the 1904 NEA meeting in St. Louis where Margaret Haley, president of the Chicago Teachers Federation (CTF) and Ella Flagg Young's friend, and Denver superintendent Aaron Gove addressed the gathering in a tense, much-anticipated session.

During the proceedings of the previous NEA meeting, President Nicholas Murray Butler and Haley had battled over whether teachers should be represented on the association's nominating committee. While Butler conceded little to Haley, teachers pressed him to allow Haley to address the association the following year on the topic of teacher organizations. The speech that she then wrote for the 1904 meeting, "Why Teachers Should Organize," offered a bold statement not only on the purpose of schooling, conditions of the classroom, and the need for teacher organizations, but also on the central role of democracy in America and who should control the schools. While Haley had originally wanted to debate one of the association elites, Butler instead arranged for Gove, a member of the Department of Superintendence, to prepare a response to Haley's speech, an address he entitled, "Limitations of the Superintendents' Authority and of the Teacher's Independence." Haley had been required to submit her speech in advance, but she would not be allowed to rebut any of Gove's comments.[96] Haley said:

Practical experience in meeting the responsibilities of citizenship directly, not in evading or shifting them, is the prime need of the American people. However clever or cleverly disguised the schemes for relieving the public of these responsibilities by vicarious performance of them, or however appropriate those schemes in a monarchy, they have no place in a government of the people, by the people, and for the people, and such schemes must result in defeating their object; for to the extent that they obtain they destroy in a people the capacity for self-government. . . . Misdirected

political activity in lowering the democratic ideal, reacts to lower
the educational ideal. On the other hand, a false or incomplete educational ideal fails to free the intelligence necessary for the work
of constructing a democracy out of our monarchical inheri-
tance. . . . Two ideals are struggling for supremacy in American
life today: one the industrial ideal, dominating thru the supremacy
of commercialism, which subordinates the worker to the product
and the machine; the other, the ideal of democracy, the ideal of the
educators, which places humanity above all machines, and demands that all activity shall be the expression of life. If this ideal
of the educators cannot be carried over into the industrial field,
then the ideal of industrialism will be carried over into the school.
Those two ideals can no more continue to exist in American life
than our nation could have continued half slave and half free. If
the school cannot bring joy to the work of the world, the joy must
go out of its own life, and work in the school as in the factory will
become drudgery.[97]

Aaron Gove then took the podium to describe a very different vision of democracy and school control:

In school administration a definite partition, positive and evident,
must lie between the functions of the legislative and of the executive departments. . . .

While the superintendent of schools is permitted, and it is his
duty, to participate in the councils of the legislative department,
his evident duty lies in the execution of the plans which have been
made as well by others as by himself. That part of the executive
department of a school system which relates to the teaching of
pupils is vested primarily in the superintendent; the responsibility is his, and theoretically the knowledge of the best method lies
with him. . . . The personal characteristics of the superintendent
and his method of dealing with subordinates largely modify the
character of the output. One has a right to conclude that only polite conduct shall be, but what is polite on the part of one authority is despotic on the part of another. The autocracy of the office of
the superintendent of a public-school system is necessary for the
accomplishment of his purposes, but that despotism can be
wielded with a gloved hand. A dangerous tendency exists toward
usurpation by teachers, thru organization, of powers which
should be retained by the superintendent. An apparently growing
feeling seems to exist—in truth it does exist, especially in one of

the large cities of the country [Chicago]—that the public-school system should be a democratic institution, and that the body of teachers constitute the democratic government. This is a false conception of true democracy. The truth is that the boards of education are the representative bodies of the democracy—the people—for whom they are making laws, and to whom they are responsible for their acts. A democracy of teachers for the purpose of controlling authoritatively the many hundred lines of activity connected with the administration of schools is as fatal to accomplishment as would be that of the patrolmen of the police department of a great city to organize and give directions, according to their own will, to the department in which they are placing their services.... Concerning neither administrative nor educational policies can the teaching body be intrusted with final decision....

The people are represented in the administration of a school system by a body of men and women whom they elect for that purpose. In that body rests necessarily all effective power and direction. That body selects an officer whose sole business is to execute the plans prepared by the people thru their representatives, the board of education. The instruments used for that execution, namely the teachers, are furnished to this executive officer, who is instructed to use them in the performance of his duties, he having the knowledge and skill and ability to select given instruments for given purposes in order to obtain the results....

An organization of teachers for legislative purposes or for directive purposes is comparable to an organization on the line of the younger part of a large family for the control of the parents' efforts. I know such conditions do sometimes exist in domestic affairs. It is not rare to find the sons and daughters directing the affairs of the household in opposition to the opinion of the parents. The fact of the existence of this condition occasionally, however, will scarcely justify us in commending it....

The teacher's independence ... is the independence of the free American citizen who has entered upon the performance of a duty definitely and positively outlined at the outset.... The teacher has independence and can have independence like that of the man in the shoe factory who is told tomorrow morning to make a pair of No. 6 boots. The independence of that workman consists in the fact that he can sew four stitches in a minute or forty, can work rapidly or slowly, as he chooses or as he is able; but his dependence is that the boots must be made and made exactly, according to the order both in size and quality and execution.[98]

Gove in essence argued that teachers should have little power in school administration; superintendents should have absolute authority; and teachers should not complain because they could appeal to school board members, their elected representatives. In 1904, however, only some women could vote for school board members because national suffrage had not yet been enacted. Nonenfranchised women could only influence elected board members through indirect persuasion rather than through direct vote. Also, while Gove explained that school board members should be the democratically elected representatives in school administration, the Department of Superintendence, of which Gove was an active member, had been working to eliminate elected boards and replace them with appointed ones. Previously he, himself, had addressed Colorado county superintendents on the topic of removing the schools from politics just as the state's women prepared to cast their first votes. Gove's notion of democracy, then, entailed that a class of persons who could not vote should appeal to elected representatives whose existence he and his colleagues rejected. Interestingly, Gove was voted out of office that year by his school board.[99]

4

A Change in Fashion

The early-twentieth-century women's movement galvanized the energies of millions of women and their allies as they fought to expand women's acceptable roles in American society. The movement gained impressive momentum and at times some dared hope that women finally would win equal political, economic, social, and intellectual status with men. The movement had many enemies, though. Even as women's organizations scored significant political victories around the country, a potent backlash movement brewed that threatened to reverse any gains.

Foes of the women's movement used a variety of means to undermine women's expanding public roles. A particularly powerful weapon involved questioning the femininity of independent, well-educated women. Louis Dublin, an avid eugenicist and a statistician for Metropolitan Life, in 1921 explained that: "The education of women is today a disgenic influence. It is leading women away from matrimony and childbearing. . . . There must be a change in fashion which will make it unapproved for healthy and self-sustaining men or women to remain unmarried."[1] Educated women who stood outside conventional roles as wives and mothers therefore threatened the population with what eugenicists called "race suicide," or White, middle-class women's refusal to reproduce their own race. This threat, combined with the fact that divorce rates increased and childbirth rates declined in the early twentieth century, led to what Joe Dubbert has labeled a "masculinity crisis" where some men worried about retaining their traditional control over reproduction, the economy, and the public sphere.[2] To resolve this crisis, traditionalists created a new class of socially suspect persons who then were stigmatized to the point that anyone falling within the bounds of the suspect category suffered severe social and economic consequences. Since many women's activists had chosen to pursue their education, to stand outside conventional marriage, to refrain from motherhood, to support themselves through work such as teaching, and to build supportive social networks among themselves, critics initiated a powerful backlash that essentially accused single, educated women of neglecting their feminine duties to their families, or worse, of deviance.

These attacks were particularly effective when aimed at school-teachers because by the 1920s and 1930s, teaching had enjoyed more than a half-century legacy as a profession primarily for single women. By 1900, women held 70 percent of all teaching positions and around 95 percent of them were single, widowed, or divorced.[3] In the fifteen years following World War II, however, two dramatic changes occurred in women's educational employment. First, the percentage of single women teachers dropped precipitously.[4] Second, the number and percentage of women superintendents also declined rapidly. (See table A.1 and figure 1.1.) While many factors contributed to these shifts, this chapter explores one that traditionally has been overlooked: the practice of sexually stigmatizing women (and men) who defy narrowly defined gender roles. This stigmatization has taken the forms of labeling individuals as sexually deviant, creating environments where so-called deviant persons are not tolerated, and punishing such individuals through social, legal, and economic means.

In the mid-1800s, Catharine Beecher argued that women were well suited for teaching because of their natural maternal skills. Single women, she maintained, made particularly good choices for teachers because market forces supported their lower wages; thus they were cheaper to hire than men who might have families to support. She explained that single women would only work until they got married; once married, they would be occupied taking care of their homes and families. Until such time, teaching would serve as preparation for marriage and motherhood rather than as a substitute for them.[5] On the other hand, Beecher left open the option for women to choose celibacy over marriage when she wrote that marriages built upon necessity rather than "pure affection" were "productive of much of the unhappiness of married women, of many sorrows, sickness, and premature decay and death."[6] Beecher remained single herself. Inspired by the possibility of economic independence, many women took advantage of the opportunity to choose teaching and to avoid marriage by default. School administrators expected women who opted for marriage to leave the classroom unless critical teacher shortages necessitated their employment.[7]

As the number of single women teachers climbed through the nineteenth century, the public came to accept their celibacy as a respectable life choice; nevertheless, some questioned why so many teachers remained single.[8] Catherine Goggin, president of the Chicago Teachers Federation, explained in 1899 that because of the independence of schoolteachers, a large percentage of them chose to remain spinsters because a female teacher "learns to govern, not to be governed. . . . Her ways become fixed and set; she cannot be molded to suit any man. Her individuality has become too strongly developed."[9] Commenting on her own refusal to marry, she said that she simply could not face having a man call her "Ducky," a pet name that would have connoted her subordinate household status.[10]

From the Civil War through World War II, single women served as readily available and relatively inexpensive school employees. School boards and administrators offered a variety of public rationales for hiring them instead of married women teachers. For example, an Ohio school board described its preference for single women teachers: "Why should we allow two-income families when there are single women without jobs?"[11] Grace Strachan, New York City district school superintendent and a married woman, explained: "A woman teacher who marries and who retains her position as teacher, assumes obligations to two masters, and, I agree with St. Luke's gospel, which says: 'No servant can serve two masters: for he will hate the one and love the other; or else he will hold the one and despise the other.'"[12] Some school systems preferred single women simply because, as one superintendent explained, "I know that the married woman teacher is a source of friction."[13] For reasons such as these, the practice of hiring single women teachers proved quite popular.[14]

While school boards typically preferred hiring single rather than married women, high unemployment rates during the Great Depression induced them to formalize the practice and to issue policies barring married women from the classroom. Married women did not need the jobs, boards reasoned, because their husbands, theoretically, could support them. In 1928, the NEA surveyed 1,532 cities with populations above 2,500 and found that 29 percent required the instant resignation of women who married. An additional 25 percent of city school systems dropped women at the end of the year of betrothal. The same survey also found that over 50 percent of cities with populations over 100,000 required married women to resign immediately. These marriage bars spread quickly during the Depression, leading historian Howard Beale to explain in 1936 that "many young schoolma'ams have refused to consider marriage. . . . New school rules [have] appeared to keep school teaching a spinster's profession."[15]

During the golden age of women school administrators, women in school leadership positions frequently were bound by policies against marriage as were teachers. For example, in 1903 the New York Board of Education instituted the following policy:

> No woman principal, woman head of department, or woman member of the . . . supervising staff shall marry while in the service. It shall be the duty of a District Superintendent to bring to the notice of the Board of Superintendents the marriage of any such person in his district, and such fact shall be reported to the Board of Education, which may direct charges to be preferred against such teacher by reason of marriage.[16]

Many women administrators either refused to marry or assumed their duties once their marriages ended. Ella Flagg Young's husband, for example, died soon after their marriage. She then pursued her teaching career, rising quickly in the Chicago system until she became superintendent in 1909. Shortly after Susan Dorsey bore a son, her husband, a minister, abandoned her, taking their son with him. Dorsey eventually entered school administration, becoming the superintendent of the Los Angeles schools in 1922. Other women superintendents, such as Mildred Doyle (superintendent of schools in Knoxville, Tennessee, 1946–76), Julia Richman (New York City district superintendent, 1903–12), and Ira Jarrell (superintendent of Atlanta, Georgia, 1944–60) chose to remain single throughout their lives.[17]

As with teachers, policies aimed at banning administrators from marrying did not apply to men. Men were held to an informally enforced, opposite standard. School boards expected to hire only married male administrators. This employment practice originated before the Civil War, when school boards first selected school superintendents, and has continued through modern times.[18] One superintendent wrote in the mid-1800s:

> A broad-minded, judicious, and cultivated gentleman is needed at the head of every large school. . . . To secure and retain this increased number of men of this excellence, it would be necessary to pay them liberally . . . for men of right character and ambition for the work they are to do will have families which they must support.[19]

Men of "right character" were assumed to be married. Periodic surveys of the superintendency produced by the NEA Department of Superintendence, later the American Association of School Administrators (AASA), have regularly demonstrated that virtually all of the men who have served as school superintendents during this century have been married.[20] A member of the Duluth, Minnesota board of education simply explained in 1963 that "We would like to have a man who is married, with a family."[21] Generally, in education, a profession numerically dominated by women, male superintendents have demonstrated their character by marrying in significantly greater percentages than the general population of men. Thus they have affirmed their authority in the private realm where women traditionally have been expected to obey while receiving economic support in return.[22]

From the 1920s to the 1940s, the nearly unquestioned acceptance of the single woman educator began to erode, despite policies that supported their presence in schools. These years witnessed what Joe Dubbert calls a "masculinity crisis," or a perception that men were losing their traditional places of power in a gender-stratified society. He argues that such social phenomena as declining marriage and birth rates among educated, middle-class White women, the challenges posed to masculine gender roles by the suffrage-era women's movement, and the popular perception that women were taking control of such social institutions as the schools all fueled this crisis.[23] A virulent backlash movement soon emerged that took aim at economically independent and educationally privileged women, including teachers.

Critics followed several lines of attack. First, they portrayed single women teachers as threats to the masculinity of male students and educators. Second, they accused spinster teachers of contributing to the demise of the (White) race. Their third and perhaps most powerful attack conflated spinsterhood with lesbianism, thus creating a climate where single women teachers seemed socially dangerous.[24]

From the late 1800s until the middle of the twentieth century, single women constituted the majority of schoolteachers. Fearful of being identified with a profession dominated by women, however, a Massachusetts superintendent complained: "What we need is more of strong manly character in our schools. . . . In the development of character, the influence of woman is indispensable; but she alone would make boys womanish and girls not altogether womanly." Another observer in 1903 described the American schoolboy as having a "highly-strung nervous system, a want of power of concentration, and often an effeminate appearance."[25] Critics found receptive audiences when they created the specter of effeminate, public-school-educated boys.

Other critics used the opposite approach, worrying that because women worked in schools as teachers and increasingly as administrators, they were becoming masculine. Said one critic, "by the very act of working, something has happened to her. . . . She has become, in important psychological elements, a man. Most significantly they absorb, with their jobs, the masculine attitude toward sex."[26]

For male educators, however, the chief threat to masculinity was to their own. G. Stanley Hall, psychologist and perennial member of the NEA's ruling power clique early in the century, wrote in his widely read book, *Adolescence:*

> The progressive feminization of secondary education works its subtle demoralization on the male teachers who remain [in the schools]. . . . It is hard, too, for male principals of schools with only female teachers not to suffer some deterioration in the moral tone of their virility and to lose in the power to cope successfully with men. Not only is this often confessed and deplored, but the incessant compromises the best male teachers of mixed classes must make with their pedagogic convictions in both teaching and discipline make the profession less attractive to manly men of large caliber and of sound fiber.[27]

Hall argued that male teachers would lose their virility if they worked alongside female teachers. The existence of large numbers of women who stood beyond the reach of heterosexual marriage certainly must have exacerbated the threat to the masculinity of these men. Some male teachers responded by leaving education, while others worked their way into positions viewed as more "manly," such as newly created vocational education programs, school athletic programs, or school administration. Around the turn of the century, schools added vocational and varsity athletic programs, in part to keep adolescent boys from dropping out.[28] These programs also served the purpose of attracting "manly" men into school work in areas that completely excluded women. Said one man about school vocational programs: "The establishment of industrial and trade schools will, we think, bring a considerable number of men back into the teaching profession. The curriculum of these schools will, by its nature, require the total exclusion of women."[29]

A particularly effective attack on educated, single women involved implicating them in "race suicide." Critics charged that White, middle-class women were abandoning their responsibilities to marry and reproduce the (White) race. Edward Thorndike explained that "the . . . harm done by the present use of educational funds to hire women rather than men lies in the prevention of gifted and devoted women from having and rearing children of their own flesh and blood."[30] Statistician Louis Dublin lobbed an attack at the International Congress of Eugenics in 1921:

I am trying to find out why educated women do not marry. . . . There is the curriculum, which is clearly not developing an inclination on the part of young women to marry early, if at all. The courses educate girls away from matrimony rather than toward it. . . . There is relatively little opportunity for meeting young men and, in many cases, especially among the girls of strong personality, there is developed a desire to make good in a career. . . . She would try out her wings at teaching. . . . Her whole enthusiasm during these vital years is for making good in her chosen work. Her friendships with men suffer because of her preoccupation. . . . By the time they realize that marriage is desirable, they have lost their attractiveness and cannot compete successfully with the younger and fresher girls who are willing to take the step without so many reservations. The whole situation is crystallizing in the impression on the part of many men that college women do not make desirable wives.[31]

Dublin's statements are typical of public commentary at this time. He begins rhetorically, asking to understand why many women remain single. He then offers as a reason that these women are lacking in attractiveness as mates, and are remiss in maintaining their appeal to men.[32]

Other critics employed psychological theories as support for their contentions. For example, in 1916 Walter Gallichan wrote *The Great Unmarried*, a collection of essays about the social problems caused by the existence of large numbers of single persons. He cautioned that "typical celibate women, approaching the neuter order, are becoming more common in the middle and better-educated classes. . . . A large number enter the teaching profession. . . . The repressed life of the celibate school-mistress is an instance of the general effect of enforced celibacy upon women. . . . They have specific difficulties, trials, and bodily and nervous maladies. Upon many celibacy is compulsory." Gallichan continued, referring to single women as psychologically deficient because "they pass the greater part of their lives in a feminine community, segregated, and debarred from frequent intellectual association with the opposite sex. . . . Love, conjugality, and maternity, with their deep emotions, their felicities, pains, and disciplines, are beyond the limited boundary of their experience. A species of psychic sclerosis may be diagnosed in these cases."[33]

Other critics were more overt, linking gender to illness and, in turn, to character and temperament. A writer for the *Eugenics Review* in 1919 stressed that "unmarried female teachers are the worst tempered and spiteful individuals of all mankind, chronically suffering generally from anaemia, neurasthenia, hysterics, neurosis of all kinds, rheumatism, stomach and bowel trouble, and more or less sexual diseases. It is due to the 'Zolibat' [celibate] condition of this class of women, which is highly injurious to their health. Every married woman with another occupation can freely exercise it in her leisure time when her economical circumstances demand it, but a schoolmistress is not permitted."[34] Clearly, for women to be kind-spirited and physically healthy, they should have regular sex with men. Although the author did not explicitly draw the connections between personality traits, physical health, and heterosexual activity, he believed women who positioned themselves outside conventional heterosexual practice not only suffered disproportionately from serious maladies, but also were somehow suspect.

After the enactment of suffrage and as the eugenics movement gained in popularity, two concurrent developments in the understanding of human sexuality filtered into American popular culture. First, translations of Freud's groundbreaking theories on the relationship between repressed sexuality and neuroses, as well as his extensive analyses of women's sexuality, stirred great public interest.[35] Second, Havelock Ellis and Krafft-Ebbing published their theories suggesting that women were capable of sexual response and were not the asexual persons previously believed. Even more titillating, or perhaps troubling, was the revelation that women could experience sexual relationships with other women.[36] To many, this notion seemed beyond possibility, because women generally had been regarded as passionless and lacking in sexual energy, and therefore unable to find sexual satisfaction with other women. Yet with the "morbidification" of these relationships, which essentially equated them with disease, the public perception of single women shifted. This shift eventually affected women educators greatly.[37]

That single women educators experienced sexual relationships with other women was documented by the noted sex researcher, Katharine Bement Davis, in her pioneering investigation printed in 1929, *Factors in the Sex Life of Twenty-Two Hundred Women*. Davis, a single woman who had taught school for much of her early professional career, later became an esteemed social activist as well as a researcher for the Bureau of Social Hygiene. The League of Women Voters sponsored a poll in 1922 that named her one of the twelve greatest living American women.[38] For her study, Davis surveyed 1,200 unmarried college-educated women to determine patterns in their sexual experiences. Teachers and superintendents accounted for 52 percent of the sample. Almost half of the single women educators reported having experienced one of the following: (1) "intense emotional relations with women unassociated with consciousness of a sex experience and unaccompanied by physical expression other than hugging and kissing" (22 percent); and (2) experiences of a sexual nature defined by Davis as either "intense relationships accompanied by mutual masturbation, contact of genital organs, or other physical expressions recognized as sexual in character," or "intense relations recognized at the time as sexual in character, but without expression other than hugging and kissing" (25 percent). Finally, 53 percent of the women in this study group indicated that they had never had "intense emotional relations with another girl or woman," thus accounting for all the single women educators' mutually exclusive choices.[39]

The public recognition that some spinster teachers may have experienced same-sex sexual desires and relationships transformed older visions of single women educators as virtuous, selfless, asexual pillars of morality into those of sexual and mannish deviants. Attacks aimed at these women who stood outside heterosexuality eventually became implied or overt broadsides against lesbianism. As such, many came to view spinster educators as dangerous threats to the social order.

Scholars, policymakers, and public figures offered three main reasons for regarding single teachers with suspicion. First, sexually ambiguous persons or those who seemed to flout gender-appropriate behavior were regarded as deviant, yet influential role models for children developing gender and sexual identities. The eminent sociologist Willard Waller explained in his classic 1932 text, *The Sociology of Teaching*, that "there remains a large and pitiful group of those whose sex life is thwarted or perverse. The members of this group, often consciously and usually with the best of intentions, carry sex problems into the schools, and transmit abnormal attitudes to their pupils because they have no other attitudes." Students under the tutelage of these persons might then grow up with abnormal gender qualities. Boys might develop effeminate characteristics and behaviors or girls masculine ones.[40]

The second threat posed by single teachers included the possibility that they might influence future generations to pursue a similar vocation and lifestyle. Spinster teachers were viewed as recruiters of their successors. In order for young women to be educated in the direction of marriage and motherhood, feminine teachers were needed. In 1932, one writer warned:

We think we can ignore these women [spinsters] when we are the safely married ones, happy in our children. We cannot. For some of them are teaching our daughters. They are responsible for the next generation of mothers. . . . The influence of home is strong, but that of school is more authoritative. Do we quite understand what school is doing to the young girl? Can womanhood be taught by women who, in the main, have grown old in a bewilderment of sterility, who have not themselves been trained to face and acknowledge the despair that is on them, who communicate through the very air of their schools a disillusion that is still half a dream? Can it be taught by those who consistently belittle the feminine mind-stuff of their pupils? . . .

This belittlement we have all sensed. It is chiefly noticeable in the insistence that a promising child should become a teacher and in the unconscious drop-by-drop poison of suggestion that marriage is a flippant and accidental thief of useful women. "We had such hopes of her . . . but—she married."[41]

The image of the influential and not altogether heterosexual teacher was popularly portrayed in the critically acclaimed 1931 German movie, *Maedchen in Uniform*. *Maedchen*, which depicted a lonely girl's crush on her female teacher at a boarding school, was initially banned in the United States because of its homoerotic content. Eleanor Roosevelt intervened to help lift the ban, but several versions of the film were censored. In spite of these problems, the *New York Times* called *Maedchen* the best film of the year and audiences packed movie houses around the country.[42] In the end, the movie and others inspired by it further sensitized Americans to the possibility of homosexuality in school settings. To some, this realization was enough to evoke repugnance.

Perhaps the greatest fear that many expressed was that sexually suspect teachers might prey on children and cause them to become homosexual. Without evidence, yet receiving wide and uncritical acceptance at the time, Waller contended that "nothing seems more certain than that homosexuality is contagious." Homosexual teachers would create homosexual students; it followed that it was a matter of public concern that teachers be carefully selected. Waller believed that screening candidates was essential and that "one technique would probably depend . . . upon such personality traits as carriage, mannerisms, voice, speech, etc." With this screening technique, women and men who betrayed traits commonly ascribed to the other gender would likely be stricken from the application process. Waller summarized: "If the schools ever decide to take their task of character education seriously, they will need to set it up as one of their major objectives to produce individuals normally heterosexual." Clearly, there was mounting concern about offering students proper heterosexual role modeling by teachers.[43]

The growing criticism of teachers who crossed traditional gender lines provoked closer scrutiny of teachers' personal lives. Lifestyles among single women educators, which a generation earlier had been accepted and respected, now were perceived as deviant. For example, around the turn of the century, single working women commonly lived together in "Boston marriages," or long-term, romantic relationships between two women. Historian Lillian Faderman explains that these female relationships made sense: "They afforded a woman companionship, nurturance, a communion of kindred spirits, romance (and undoubtedly, in some but not all such relationships, sex)—all the advantages of having a 'significant other' in one's life and none of the burdens that were concomitant with heterosexuality, which would have made her life as a pioneering career woman impossible."[44] Blanche Wiesen Cook has argued that the single, strong, independent women who led many of the early century social reforms maintained close, supportive relationships with other women, sometimes including lesbian relationships.[45]

Chicago school superintendent Ella Flagg Young maintained a longtime relationship with Laura Brayton, a woman who had once worked as a teacher under Young, then later served as her personal secretary. The two lived together for many years, traveled together, and when Young died in 1918, she left Brayton the then huge sum of $12,000. The public viewed Young as an upstanding, pure, selfless, and dedicated educator who had served not only as the Chicago superintendent, but also as the first woman president of the NEA. Prominent women educators living a similar lifestyle only a generation later would likely have been severely criticized. In a climate of suspected deviance, though, single women faced the challenge of carefully managing their images, living in the shadow of suspicion, altering their personal lives, or leaving the profession.[46]

Directly or indirectly, the public responded to the newly created deviant image of single women educators. School systems dropped their marriage bars for women teachers during and after World War II. The NEA encouraged this practice by arguing that married women should be hired as teachers because "marriage and parenthood are likely to enrich a teacher's understanding of childhood and family life and thus will help her to be a better teacher." Ironically, this argument inverted Catharine Beecher's contention a century earlier that teaching would provide single women with excellent preparation for marriage and motherhood. The NEA also argued that "to abolish the celibacy rule . . . would do much over a period of years to remove the 'old-maid school teacher' cliché which is so distasteful to many teachers and so injurious to the morale of many of the younger members of the profession."[47] A Kentucky school bulletin in 1937 bluntly offered its assessment of single teachers: "The attractive woman who finds it easy to marry and establish a home is the kind of woman that the schools need and cannot secure or retain under regulations against marriage. . . . Married women tend to have a saner view on sex, and are less likely to become 'queer.'"[48] Essentially because of the new stigma attached to single women teachers, school districts increasingly were willing to forego the benefits of hiring them to avoid appearing to promote deviance.

Many school systems resisted dropping their marriage bans, however. Some systems refused to hire married women teachers as long as the effects of the depression lingered and two-incomes families were thought unfair. The social premium placed on employment during these years, when 11 million remained jobless, left married women with little clout in arguing for their places in schools. Besides, as one superintendent explained, the "non-employment of married women is excellent socially . . . and [unmarried women] make less trouble than married teachers."[49] Other systems sought to maintain their marriage bars because they feared, at least in part, that their schools would become "dumping grounds for married women."[50] The NEA countered this argument by explaining that because the percentage of unmarried women teachers was almost the same as that for women "professionals and technicians," the proportion of married women teachers would likely remain unchanged if marriage bars were removed.[51]

When the United States entered World War II, however, perceptions as well as realities changed. Millions of men abandoned their civilian jobs to join the military effort, leaving vacancies in numerous sectors of the economy. Under these conditions, single women enjoyed relatively lucrative employment opportunities they could not have imagined earlier. Many teachers left the classroom for higher wage jobs in war-related and other industries. The ensuing shortage of teachers meant that some resistant school systems had to drop their marriage bars or face disruption and even closure.

When the war ended in 1945, school systems did not tend to reinstate marriage bars. First, the postwar baby boom soon produced swollen school enrollments and the need for more teachers. Second, women's opportunities in other employment areas widened during and after the war. Despite government advertising campaigns urging women to leave their wartime jobs to make room for returning male veterans, newly created feminized vocations such as clerical work provided women with alternatives to teaching. Third, marriage rates increased during these years, creating a smaller pool of single women. Fourth, school boards and administrators around the country eventually agreed with arguments made against marriage bars and came to regard them as impractical, if not unfair. Finally, the stigmatization of single women made them less desirable teaching candidates than married ones, especially for a profession eager to shed its reputation for producing spinsters.[52] In the best-selling 1947 book, *Modern Woman: The Lost Sex*, authors Ferdinand Lundberg and Marynia Farnham went so far as to argue "that all spinsters be barred by law from having anything to do with the teaching of children."[53]

For these reasons, the percentages of single women teachers plummeted. Where single women had accounted for 69 percent of women teachers in 1940 (76 percent if widowed and divorced women are included), they held fewer than 30 percent of these positions just two decades later (42 percent with widowed and divorced women). While the NEA had speculated in 1942 that lifting marriage bars would not cause the number of married women teachers to rise, within only two decades the percentage of married women in teaching was double the percentage of married women in the work force. Teaching had changed from a single to a married woman's profession.

The percentage of married women superintendents also increased after school districts lifted marriage bars. While definitive statistics have not been compiled for superintendents as they have for teachers, the marital status changes of women superintendents in Kansas might suggest national trends. Between 1943 and 1962, the percentage of women county superintendents listed in *Patterson's American Education* with "Mrs." in front of their names (indicating marriage, widowhood, or divorce) increased from 23 percent (13 out of 57 women) to 77 percent (53 out of 69 women). While this percentage is not generalizable, it suggests that marriage rates among women superintendents might have paralleled those of teachers.[54]

From these data it is plausible to suggest that married women long had sought school positions and, with the lifting of the marriage bars, they finally enjoyed a fair chance at such employment. The supply of qualified married women simply may have filled the available vacuum. It is also reasonable to posit that married women might have sought employment in schools over other sectors because the hours and nature of the work were considered more compatible with family responsibilities. However, these factors alone fail to explain sufficiently why married women not only came to dominate the ranks of educators, but also to double the percentages of married women in the U.S. labor force over such a short period, especially since by that time teaching had enjoyed a century-long legacy of celibate female practitioners. Arguably, other factors were at work to reverse the marital status characteristics of women educators.

TABLE 4.1

Married Women in the Labor Force Compared with Single, Widowed or
Divorced, and Married Women Teachers, 1920–1960

Year	Married Women in U.S. Labor Force (%)	Married Women Teachers (%)	Single Women Teachers (%)	Widowed or Divorced Women Teachers (%)
1920	9[a]	10	86	5
1930	12[a]	18	77	5
1940	17[a]	25	69	7
1950	25[a]	47	43	9
1960	31[b]	59	29	13

Note: Statistics derived from Folger and Nam, *Education of the American Population*, p. 81, unless otherwise noted.

a. Lynn Weinner, *From Working Girl to Working Mother* (Chapel Hill: University of North Carolina Press, 1985), 89, cited in Nancy Cott, *The Grounding of Modern Feminism* (New Haven, CT: Yale University Press, 1987), 183.

b. U.S. Department of Labor, Bureau of Labor Statistics, *Labor Force Statistics Derived from the Current Population Survey: A Data Book, Vol. 1 (September 1982), Bulletin 2096, table C-11; 1985: BLS News Release, USDL 85–381 (September 19, 1985), table 1; total from unpublished tabulations.*

While single women educators had already suffered damage to their employability during the years of the spinster/lesbian "threat," the damage escalated to unprecedented heights after the release of what proved to be a popular and important study on human sexuality. The year 1948 saw the publication of Alfred Kinsey's *Sexual Behavior in the Human Male*, a remarkably detailed, careful, and what was considered surprisingly candid study for the time. The book quickly sold out of several printings and remained on the *New York Times* bestseller list for months. So widely influential was the book that George Gallup estimated one of every five Americans had read or heard about it.[55] Academics, professionals, and media figures actively discussed this study, which was joined in 1953 by Kinsey's companion volume, *Sexual Behavior in the Human Female*. To complete these volumes, Kinsey and his staff collected the sexual histories of 12,000 men and women from every state, but primarily from residents of the northeastern quarter of the country. He indicated that "the ultimate sample shall represent a cross-section of the entire population."[56]

FIGURE 4.1

Married Women in the Labor Force Compared with Single, Widowed or
Divorced, and Married Women Teachers, 1920–1960

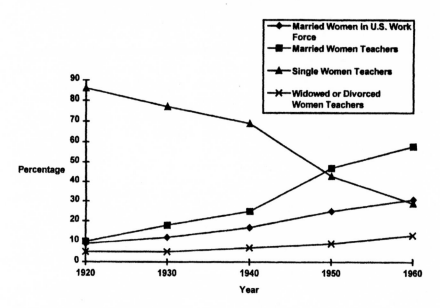

One of the most unexpected and shocking revelations in these
works concerned the incidence of homosexuality among men. Kinsey
reported that a full 50 percent of all males admitted having some attraction to other men; over a third had experienced at least one orgasm
through homosexual contact; and 4 percent engaged in homosexual relationships exclusively. Kinsey explained that these experiences did not
occur within segregated portions of the population, but rather that "persons with homosexual histories are to be found in every age group, in
every social level, in every conceivable occupation, in cities and on
farms, and in the most remote areas of the country."[57]

Kinsey's studies encouraged significant open public discussion
about sexuality, a discussion for which Americans were enthusiastic
and ready. While his work was widely applauded, incensed critics accused him of everything from improper research methods to aiding
communism.[58] Politicians used his results for purposes beyond those he
had intended. They hailed the unexpectedly large figures on the incidence of homosexuality as proof that the homosexual menace in society
loomed larger than anyone had feared and that something needed to be

done to remedy the situation. Shortly after the publication of the volume on male sexuality, the search for the perpetrators of supposedly rampant and immoral sexuality in society began.[59]

The military, in the midst of its efforts to downsize after the war, became one of the first institutions to hunt for homosexuals, launching investigations to rid the rank and file of all homosexual activity.[60] By 1950, reports emerged in Congress that cells of homosexuals had infiltrated all areas of the U.S. government, not just the military, and that they posed serious threats to national security and integrity. "One homosexual can pollute a Government office," one congressman warned.[61] To demonstrate congressional commitment to the elimination of this peril, the *Congressional Record* printed counts of homosexuals in each government department along with the numbers investigated and purged.[62] Organizations and businesses working with the government were encouraged to follow suit. Eventually, the hunt for homosexuals extended to all segments of the population as the FBI, the Post Office, local police forces, and other agencies conducted investigations to identify and turn them in.[63] It is estimated that thousands lost their jobs in these investigations and many thousands more adjusted to lifestyles filled with profound terror at the prospect of the total economic and social ruin that usually followed such actions.[64]

Schools were not spared. *New York Daily Mirror* columnist Lee Mortimer claimed that homosexuals were organizing in high schools to recruit young students.[65] In response to this threat, school systems around the country began formal and informal means of identifying and purging anyone rumored to be homosexual. For example, the state of Florida recommended in a 1964 report that personnel in the Teacher Certification Division of the State Department of Education should handle charges of homosexuality among teachers. Anyone suspected of homosexuality would lose their teaching certificate.[66] In addition, some local systems hired investigators to gather evidence on allegations of homosexuality among teachers.[67] Changes in Florida and California state penal codes in the early 1950s allowed school boards to use illegally obtained information to fire suspected homosexuals.[68]

Many teachers lost their jobs in these orchestrated sweeps. When named in such campaigns, teachers had little recourse, regardless of the veracity or relevance of the charges.[69] Teachers suspected of homosexuality also were often dismissed on other grounds to avoid publicity and, as Karen Harbeck explains, to protect school boards "from costly litigation concerning burden of proof, defamation, and discrimination."[70] The personal punishment exacted on these teachers is difficult to fathom, so damaged were their reputations, relationships with their families, support networks, and means of economic survival, along with their hope and self-esteem.

Teachers who remained in their positions also paid a price. In an atmosphere of fear and intimidation, teachers felt they had to stay in line. Administrators and the public at large expected them to do so. A 1970 study funded by the National Institute of Mental Health reported that 77 percent of Americans believed that homosexuals should not be allowed to teach.[71] School districts sometimes dismissed teachers who were merely rumored to be homosexual or who did not fit stereotypes of masculinity or femininity. It is likely that to avoid these and other possible dangers, teachers endeavored to portray gender-appropriate behaviors at work, to live beyond the shadow of suspicion. Women accentuated their femininity by crafting a soft, "womanly" appearance, maintaining a submissive countenance, pretending to have active heterosexual relationships, and sometimes marrying for the sake of appearance.[72] They avoided curricular areas that would raise eyebrows such as high school physical education or coaching, and some resisted efforts toward advancement into male domains. Male teachers gravitated toward instructional areas regarded as appropriately masculine, feigned interest in sports, and carefully guarded their manner so as not to betray any effeminacy. The homosexual menace in schools essentially provoked educators to maintain consciousness of their own and others' gender-appropriate appearances and behaviors.[73] Essentially, this heightened awareness and the justifiable fear that held it in place created an atmosphere where gender role identities became deeply polarized.

This increased gender polarization affected jobs in schooling differently. Women pursued gender-appropriate work when they taught in classrooms, worked with children, and took orders from their superiors. On the other hand, women who desired to move into school administration found that their ambitions could be viewed as masculine, aggressive, ambitious, and inappropriate. Women administrative aspirants, then, increasingly contended with gender role conflicts.[74]

Some women resolved these conflicts by dismissing any interest they may have had in seeking careers in the male-dominated administrative realm. Some women pursued these opportunities anyway, but adjusted their wardrobes and behaviors to seem more feminine and therefore less threatening and gender role deviant. Women who were or had been married seemed safer because marriage was regarded as proof of heterosexuality, an important facet of appropriately feminine character. One expert, commenting in the 1960s on women administrators, particularly elementary school principals, explained that "some of the important psychological characteristics of administrators. . . are the ability to work cooperatively with people, a love of children, a factor of flexibility. . . [which are the] ideal psychological characteristics of. . . the ideal mate, and in the case of a woman, the ideal wife. Women who possess these characteristics have a strong urge to marry to become part of a family."[75]

Women who pursued administrative advancement and yet did not carefully manage their femininity usually faced covert as well as overt resistance, sometimes even hostility.[76] Single women could not as readily prove their heterosexuality as married women and therefore seemed sexually suspect. One administrative aspirant stated the problem succinctly: "The image of an administrator in this state is of a married person."[77] As a result of this increased scrutiny of women's sexuality, fewer single women succeeded in attaining administrative positions. Even as recently as 1988, a study on the superintendency published by the National Center for Education Information noted that proportionately more male and female administrators were married than the overall population. "While fifty-seven percent of all households in this country are married-couple households, ninety-four percent of superintendents and eighty-seven percent of public school principals are married."[78]

Women who attained administrative positions found their work riddled with conflicts. On one hand, the nature of administrative work had undergone structural changes after the war to favor men even more than previously. For example, the longer hours and heavy responsibilities increasingly required that administrators have a helpmate at home.[79] In 1963 the *School Board Journal* published an article explaining,

> When a board of education employs a school administrator, it is also bringing the man's wife and family into the community. . . . [T]he executive's wife must adapt her life pattern in the best interests of her husband, her children, and the community. . . . She must be a competent homemaker and family partner aiming her attention toward the rearing of her children and supplying both practical and emotional support to her husband. . . . Her contribution to the educational program is indirect but important in that she frees her husband from the minor details of home and family management.[80]

An at-home spouse was an expectation for male administrative candidates, but a problem for women whose male partners usually worked full-time and customarily shared few of the family responsibilities. Women who resolved this problem by choosing a female partner suffered the perception of deviance. Mildred Doyle, who enjoyed a long and distinguished career as the superintendent of Knoxville schools, was finally defeated for reelection in 1976 after some political miscalculations and the anonymous circulation of a letter questioning the nature of her relationship with her female, longtime companion.[81] To avoid this fate, women tended to marry and work double shifts by putting in long days at administrative work and then assuming family maintenance responsibilities at night.[82] A number of women endured this double burden quietly while finding themselves passed over for promotion in favor of men.[83]

The numbers of women who held school superintendencies declined rapidly from 1950 to 1970, the steepest drop of any point in this century. The percentage of women who held all types of superintendencies declined from 9 percent to just over 3 percent. Several conditions affected this decline, such as the consolidation of schools and the newly instituted requirement for administrative credentials from university schools of education that often kept low quotas on the number of women admitted (changes that, arguably, were intended to increase the masculine appeal of the work).[84] However, the profound gender role polarization of school employment that occurred during these years of the "homosexual menace" pervaded nearly every aspect of the school context and undoubtedly also influenced the decline of the woman superintendent.

When women entered the teaching profession in the early days of common schooling, they widened their sphere of activity beyond the hearth, risking criticism from those who would have had them maintain their traditional roles. The economic advantages of hiring women for teaching positions soon became obvious even to their critics, however. But when women quickly dominated the ranks of teachers and demonstrated the promise of assuming widespread leadership, both at a time when women were gradually winning suffrage, marrying less frequently, divorcing more often, and bearing fewer children than previously, traditionalists reacted to these presumed threats. Psychologists, sexologists, educators, and social critics invested considerable energy in the effort to produce scientifically derived definitions of acceptable White, middle-class femininity. During and after World War II, when school systems ceased to enjoy either the economic benefits of hiring single women as women's employment opportunities expanded, or the administrative benefits of employing women without troublesome husbands, mounting opposition to spinster teachers found full expression. Politicians and governmental organizations labored to rid the public workforce of suspected homosexuals. Gender divisions became increasingly starkly delineated, and those who defied the conventions suffered the burdens of deviance and ostracism.[85]

5

THE WAY OF THE BUFFALO

Mary Dawson, the editor of *The National Elementary Principal*, decided to feature an article in 1966 about the recent decline of women school administrators. The topic was hot. Only a year before, the National Council of Administrative Women in Education had released a widely publicized report portraying a shockingly rapid drop in the number of women school administrators nationwide. The council contended that while women had held a dominating 56 percent of elementary principalships in 1950, only ten years later their numbers had dropped to a scant 4 percent. They similarly described the demise of women superintendents, reporting that while 765 women had served as school superintendents in 1939, a mere 222 did so in 1962, representing a 70 percent decline in twenty-three years.[1] Because the council had been organized in part to spur an increase in the number of women school administrators, it faced the twin horrors of seeing its membership decimated and women's administrative influence in public schools minimized. In response, Dawson arranged to cover the matter in *The National Elementary Principal*. She convened a panel of experts—four male professors in the Administration and Higher Education program at Michigan State University and one woman who had recently served as an elementary school principal. Dawson asked the panel to figure out why, as the article later expressed it, women school administrators were "going the way of the buffalo."[2]

The panelists took turns speculating about the decline of women administrators, particularly elementary principals. Most blamed women for their lack of professionalism. One suggested that the job had grown too complex for women, while another indicated that women's career transience due to pregnancies and childrearing made them poor candidates for principalships compared with their more reliable and ambitious male colleagues. Panelists blamed the structure of schooling insofar as consolidated schools had produced larger, more lucrative administrative positions to which men were more likely to aspire. Since, as they concluded, women were largely responsible for their lack of ambition and professionalism, then the topic of their diminishing numbers "deserve[d], at best, a footnote." The introduction to the edited transcript clarified this attitude of indifference: "Amidst the clamor and bedlam which accompanies change, relatively minor problems frequently get lost in the backwash of innovation . . . [such as] the problem of employment opportunities for women interested in educational administration." In particular, the matter of sex equity among elementary school principals is "minor in the frenzy of today's educational changes."[3]

In spite of the dismissive tone of the piece, some people did care about women's leadership influence in education. But in the midst of a frantic national effort to reach for the moon, defeat a ubiquitous Cold War enemy, and perpetuate the nation's image as the most powerful on earth, most school administrators preferred to focus instead on headline-grabbing issues. Only a few scattered accounts disrupted the otherwise notable absence of discussion about women's decline in school administration. If topics published in journals, newsletters, proceedings, and books reveal something of the consciousness of a profession, then school administrators seemed remarkably uninterested in questioning the mechanisms by which women's suffrage–era gains in educational leadership had diminished.

Even the most cursory investigation would have revealed that indeed, as the council's report had indicated, women had lost substantial administrative ground after World War II. My statistical study of the superintendency indicates that in 1950, 716 women served as county or intermediate superintendents, a number that dropped by half in twenty years to 373. Where five women held state superintendencies in 1950, only one served in 1970. (See table A.1.) Yet even with these disturbingly rapid changes, the organizations vested with the power to confirm these figures and study them over time chose to focus instead on other research matters, particularly the ways in which the superintendency could be elevated closer to the status of such professionals as scientists, lawyers, doctors, and corporate executives.

The matter received little attention other than this published panel discussion in which a solitary woman was teamed with four men holding doctoral degrees. Her arguments bolstered those of her fellow panelists; yet as a woman, she was poised to speak from a "woman's perspective" and lend credence to the notion expressed elsewhere in the journal that "I guess it's a man's world after all. Time to go, old girl."[4] Clare Broadhead herself had moved out of her elementary principalship and into a consulting position by the time of the panel discussion. In the end, one panelist concluded that "our task is not to worry about the vanishing buffalo," of whom Broadhead was one, but rather to figure out

how to get more men into teaching.[5] The panelists regarded gender balance in school employment as unimportant, then, unless male influence
was in decline.

Although the turn-of-the-century women's movement had created enormous momentum favoring the ascent of women into school
administration, a massive cultural shift extending from the economic
depression of the 1930s through the Cold War effectively reversed the
trend. Several factors contributed to the shift. First, the women's movement, which had been instrumental in propelling women into leadership positions, lost its focus and faded in the decades after passage of
the suffrage amendment. A quietly brewing, yet powerful backlash
movement further eroded organized efforts of women's groups. This
backlash stigmatized women (and men) who crossed gender-appropriate lines of behavior. Beyond these means of discrediting women, however, were significant efforts on the part of school administrators,
university professors, and government and private funding agencies to
promote school administration as respectable work for hundreds of
thousands of unemployed war veterans seeking civilian careers. In the
end, then, perhaps the single greatest contributor to the climate change
for women school administrators was World War II and the social up-
heaval that followed in its wake.

World War II transformed social and economic conditions during
America's direct military engagement as well as in the decades immediately following. The war effort created starkly delineated gender
roles for Americans as the military recruited millions of men for active
duty, but relegated most service-minded women to clerical duties or
otherwise encouraged them to assume private sector jobs vacated by
men. Women best served the country when they, like Rosie the Riveter,
constructed weapons of war, stitched uniforms, or prepared food ra-
tions. Military men, on the other hand, learned to issue commands, to
uphold the orders of their superiors in the rigidly hierarchical military
system, and to ridicule any evidence of effeminacy or perceived weakness among their peers. Physical separation further heightened the differences between men's and women's worlds during the war. Men
served on military bases in large, same-sex communities with a pervasive culture of masculinity; women mostly labored back in the United
States, and often in communities of women who had migrated to industrial centers.

Although jubilant about the Allied victory in 1945, soldiers returning from military duty faced an array of new stresses and adjustments.

Veterans who had endured the traumas of combat undoubtedly wrestled with horrible memories after their return. Beyond the psychic toll of combat, veterans suddenly found themselves in competition with millions of other servicemen for jobs and housing. Soon after the war, for example, five million men could not find housing and were forced to sleep in cars or small, crowded dwellings. Some lived temporarily in makeshift Quonset hut villages until they could make other arrangements. Chicago advertised old streetcars for sale as possible homes. Public service messages encouraged Americans to do what they could to assist veterans down on their luck, perhaps by offering them a lift to the next town, providing them with work, or temporarily opening homes to them. Lower peacetime industrial production levels and sharply higher unemployment greatly exacerbated these conditions.[6]

To avoid a collapse of the economy, the federal government instituted a number of measures designed to ease veterans' adjustment back into civilian life. Veterans Preference Programs, for instance, gave former soldiers preferential consideration for federal jobs. One of the most ambitious of the postwar programs, the G.I. Bill of Rights (the Servicemen's Readjustment Act of 1944), provided grants of up to $500 a year for scholastic expenses and a monthly allowance of $50 for any veteran to attend college for four years. This program was intended not only to help veterans prepare for new careers, but also to reduce the number actively seeking employment in the years following the war.[7] Higher education effectively staggered the return of these men to the workforce, which allowed the economy to accommodate them better. By 1960, nearly four million men had used these funds to pursue college degrees.[8] Women also received G.I. Bill benefits, but because of their limited service, only a few hundred thousand women were even eligible.

With federal support in hand, men enrolled in colleges and universities during the years following the war, driving enrollments sharply up beyond wartime levels. This new wave of students completely altered previous student demographic characteristics. Veterans tended to be older than traditional students. They were frequently from lower-middle-class, working-class, or poor families rather than from the upper-middle- or proprietary-class families customarily served by institutions of higher education. These new students were men, which altered a suffrage-era increase in women's access to higher education. Also, during the war, colleges and universities had faced the frightening prospect of plummeting enrollments as young men headed for military service. To survive, many institutions recruited women to fill vacant slots. These efforts succeeded in attracting large numbers of women students, women anxious for the rare opportunity to receive instruction in prestigious programs previously accessible mainly or only to men. When men returned from service with their G.I. Bill benefits in hand, however, higher education institutions that had survived the war with women's enrollment then reversed their strategies and encouraged women to withdraw to make room for veterans.[9] As a result, the percentages of women college graduates severely declined after the war while the percentages of men increased. (See table 5.1 and figure 5.1.)

During the war, some male teachers abandoned the classroom to join the military effort. Many women also left teaching; however, they tended to venture into higher-paying wartime industries instead. When the war ended, teacher shortages developed as baby-boom children made their way to grade school. To make matters worse, teacher wages had not risen during the war and the postwar economic downturn made the prospects for salary increases grim. As a result, few persons found teaching an attractive occupation, a situation that made the teacher shortage even more acute.[10]

To alleviate the shortage and to help returning veterans find jobs, government agencies and local school systems launched initiatives to encourage men to teach. This encouragement met with little resistance and, in fact, was often celebrated.[11] Raymond Callahan, in his account of the efficiency movement in twentieth-century educational administration, *Education and the Cult of Efficiency* (1962), wrote that "after a careful study . . . we might decide that it was essential for America's future to get our most intelligent and socially responsible young men into the teaching profession and then work out ways and means of achieving this goal."[12] Recruiting men into education was not easy, though, because

TABLE 5.1

College Graduates by Sex, 1900–1990

Year	Number of Men	Men	Number of Women	Women	Total Number
1900	22,173	81%	5,237	19%	27,410
1910	28,762	77%	8,437	23%	37,199
1920	31,980	66%	16,642	34%	48,622
1929-30	73,615	60%	48,869	40%	122,484
1939-40	109,546	59%	76,954	41%	186,500
1949-50	328,841	76%	103,217	24%	434,058
1959-60	254,063	65%	138,377	35%	392,440
1969-70	484,174	59%	343,060	41%	827,234
1979-80	526,327	53%	473,221	47%	999,548
1989-90	485,000	47%	558,000	53%	1,043,000

Source: Department of Education, Center for Education Statistics.

FIGURE 5.1

College Graduates by Sex, 1900–1990

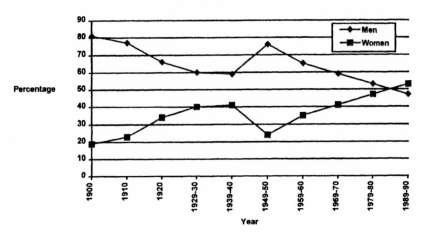

most regarded it as women's work and therefore demeaning to their battle-molded sense of masculine place. One way school districts attempted to achieve Callahan's goal was to make up for relatively low teacher salaries by promising young men "that a promotion to the elementary-school principalship will be rapid." Writer Alice Barter explained in 1959 that "in order to attract or retain these men, some school systems have weighted opportunities for administrative advancement strongly in their favor."[13] While some school districts resisted increasing teacher salaries, they did offer substantially higher salaries to administrators.

Men answered these recruiting efforts and became teachers. While men held 17 percent of all teaching positions in 1945, their numbers increased to 27 percent ten years later, and reached almost 32 percent in 1965.[14] At the same time, the proportion of women teachers obviously declined. In addition, the percentage of women principals fell by nearly half during the same period. Essentially, school systems had lured men into education with promises of rapid advancement even at the expense of the women who had previously served as principals. [15]

Men discovered other incentives for teaching as well. Some who had received extensive technical and scientific training during military service easily found jobs as high school math and science teachers. At the time, high school teaching positions sometimes paid higher salaries than those in elementary schools. Besides the promise of high school work, some men were lured into teaching to coach.[16] Coaching positions held appeal for at least two reasons: they allowed men to enter a largely feminized profession by working in a clearly male-identified niche, thus their masculinity was not called into question; and coaches usually earned salary supplements for their afterschool work with athletic teams. Some coaches received sizable supplements.[17] Beyond the matter of pay supplements, coaching eventually became an important prerequisite duty for persons aspiring to administrative positions. Experts speculated that "because of athletic publicity, the coach is better known around the community than any other teacher, and because of this familiarity with the community power figures as well as the general public, he is more likely to be promoted."[18] An AASA report published in 1971 indicated that 80 percent of all superintendents at the time had coached school sports before moving into administrative work.[19]

Even without these enticements, the 1960s brought another compelling reason for young men to consider teaching as a career. With the draft threatening to press them into service for the Vietnam War, college men pursued teaching, a draftproof profession. Said one man, "I decided to go into teaching to stay out of the army." One study on the motivations of men and women for entering teaching clearly found that males taught so they could avoid the draft.[20]

With increased numbers of men teaching in all grades, the 1950s and 1960s presented easy opportunities for them to move into administrative positions. To simplify matters further, some thought that school administrators should be recruited even without prerequisite teaching experience. Roald F. Campbell, professor of educational administration at the University of Chicago and later Ohio State University, wrote that school administrators should be hired with minimal, if any teaching experience "in the hope of tapping a new population for administrative work."[21] Since women accounted for the overwhelming majority of schoolteachers at the time, arguably men constituted the new population he had in mind.

Ultimately, the postwar decades witnessed men's increased presence in the classroom. Not surprisingly, men also outstripped women in attaining superintendencies. With men's greater representation in the teaching ranks, there was a larger pool of them from which administrative candidates might be chosen. Since school systems generally preferred men for administrative work, and since some men had been recruited specifically for later promotion, their odds of advancement were greater.

Administrative candidates also increasingly needed advanced certificates to be considered for promotion. No longer could individuals simply rise through the ranks. To obtain certificates, administrative aspirants needed to take courses in educational administration at colleges and universities. Many of these programs set low quotas on the number of women who could enroll, some allowing no more than 2 percent of available slots to go to women.[22] This situation did not change for some institutions until enactment of Title IX in 1972. For those who could be admitted, graduate coursework cost money and took time that normally would have deterred all but the most diligent or financially able. The federal government, however, had generously provided essentially free college education for millions of men, some of whom used their G.I. Bill benefits to obtain administrative credentials. The 1971 AASA report explained that "the so-called 'G.I. Bill' . . . appeared to be the largest single source of assistance to superintendents pursuing graduate study." Around 74 percent of superintendents surveyed that year reported having pursued a master's degree while receiving these funds. Of the superintendents who had undertaken doctoral study, nearly 39 percent had used veterans' benefits to complete their work. Overall, the G.I. Bill had assisted nearly 70 percent of all superintendents who served in 1971. Not only had men been enticed into education, but they also had been tracked into leadership positions at the expense of women's opportunities and often with federal government support.[23]

Interestingly, a century earlier men left teaching at least in part because of the increased certification requirements that entailed longer preparation and summer training. However, after World War II when states instituted certification requirements for school administrators, men eagerly complied. A clear difference between the case of male teachers and that of male administrators was the promise for the latter of monetary rewards and greater social status. Teachers in the mid-1800s were required to prepare for teaching at their own expense, to forego opportunities for supplemental summer income, and then to receive ever-shrinking salaries, salaries so low that arguably they were intended to increase the number of women. When men left teaching, women filled the available positions. On the other hand, in the mid-twentieth century when states required certificates and advanced study for school administration positions, the federal government largely underwrote the training with G.I. Bill funding. In addition, school districts promised administrative candidates attractive promotions with rewarding salaries. Essentially, administration was made an appealing enough job that men chose it; yet in the mid-1800s, teaching became unattractive to men, so they abandoned it.

In her impressive theoretical work on occupational sex segregation, Myra Strober argues that "by and large, women move into only those jobs that men leave for them. When occupations become sex stratified, it is usually when men choose the plum positions, leaving the remainder to women. . . . [W]omen's opportunities for choice are . . . overshadowed by men's actions."[24] It appears that large numbers of men chose plum school administrative positions in the postwar years.

Schools suffered from critical shortages of funding after the war.[25] They also struggled to hire enough teachers and other staff to keep schools running smoothly. These difficulties, in conjunction with the nation's massive postwar social and economic problems, left schools far short of public expectations. As the baby-boom children made their way to school, many people perceived decrepit conditions in public education. A number of books appeared in the 1940s and 1950s that condemned various shortcomings in schools, particularly what some considered the anti-intellectual tone of instruction as well as the undemocratic methods of administration and instruction. Some critics disliked what they considered the intellectually weak influences of progressive education.[26] Others feared that communists threatened to infiltrate schools and corrupt the values of the nation's youth. Some school critics focused their attacks on the people running schools. A report issued by the AASA in 1952 explained that "school superintendents never appeared more expendable than at this mid-century." They were, the report concluded, forced to leave their positions and sometimes suffer physical breakdowns.[27] With the different complaints lodged against the schools, a writer for *McCall's* in 1951 concluded that "public education in America is under the heaviest attack in its history. This attack is not aimed at the improvement of free education. It is aimed at its destruction."[28]

One criticism aimed at superintendents was that they tended toward cronyism by promoting each other and closing ranks against outsiders, keeping educational control tightly contained. This made them vulnerable to the charge of promotion through political connections rather than proven administrative skill. In response to this accusation, the Committee on the Certification of Superintendents of Schools of the AASA began working to eliminate the system of political favoritism and instead to promote the profession toward greater respectability. They sought the creation of rigorous university training programs based on scientific methods applied to the newly emerging social sciences. They also planned to devise a program of certification so that superintendents as a group could monitor their own professional quality.[29]

After the war, several events converged to produce a strong renewed effort toward upgrading the status of the superintendency. In 1947 the National Conference of Professors of Educational Administration

(NCPEA) was formed to assess the status of theory and practice in administrative training.[30] Sociologists and psychologists developed theories regarding social organizations, group dynamics, and human behavior, all of which informed school administration. Wartime military experiments in leadership and personnel training influenced administrators, especially those who were veterans.[31] The Kellogg Foundation, which had shown growing interest in school administration, served as the catalyst for these developments by investing substantial sums of money to initiate reforms in school administration. As a result, the Cooperative Program in Educational Administration (CPEA) was launched, a project aimed mainly at improving graduate programs in school administration as well as increasing university collaboration with administrators in the field.[32]

The CPEA became a joint venture of the Kellogg Foundation, the American Association of School Administrators (AASA), the National Council of Chief State School Officers, the County and Rural Education Division of the NEA, and seventeen North American university sites. The executive secretary of AASA could not contain his enthusiasm in describing the new program: "I look upon the CPEA as the most important action the association has taken during the years I have known it. . . . We are moving toward a self-disciplining profession we can all be proud of." By "self-disciplining" he meant that the AASA would play an integral role in determining the course of preparation in college credentialing programs. What is more important, though, he believed that school administrators had the "right and duty of a profession to police itself to ensure a high selectivity of people who enter it and a rigorous program of education for those who practice it."[33] Through these efforts, school administrators would have a greater opportunity to determine who would join their ranks as well as how they would practice.

With major funding behind the project as well as the positive media attention it generated, school administrators around the country eagerly awaited their chance to participate in the new professionalization movement and to obtain official credentials. Membership in the AASA nearly doubled in a ten-year period, representing greater growth than in the previous ninety years. The number of colleges and universities offering administrative preparation programs expanded rapidly so that by 1960, over three hundred existed.[34] Truly, the postwar effort to reform school administration had effected a monumental transformation.

Although initially research had not been a vital component of the CPEA, it grew in importance as research conducted at cooperating university sites received increased professional attention. The Kellogg Foundation then encouraged the formation of a new group in 1956, the

University Council for Education Administration (UCEA), which, besides seeking to improve the training of school administrators, also worked to stimulate and conduct research, and to distribute the results. The organization launched the *Educational Administration Quarterly* and *Educational Administration Abstracts,* two journals that eventually became important defining forces in the field of educational administration.[35]

The bulk of the research produced by the UCEA revolved around behavioral psychology, sociology, and other empirical social sciences. These seemed especially fitting avenues for many UCEA projects in part because the American military had begun to explore and utilize research in these areas during World War II and many UCEA participants had served in the war effort. Also Herbert Simon's influential book, *Administrative Behavior* (1947), nudged the field of educational administration closer to the behavioral sciences. Simon asserted in this work that through scientific analysis, administrative decision making could proceed through consistent, logical, linear processes. This formalist, functionalist approach assumed that there always existed a best means for handling any situation that a manager might encounter. By following procedures such as those outlined by Simon, the best means supposedly could be determined objectively. As a result of this influential work, researchers at UCEA institutions mainly concentrated on such leadership behaviors as decision making, goal accomplishment, goal setting, and activity directing. Generally, researchers tended to posit linear, causal models of leadership. They attempted to create a replicable science of school administration.[36]

Contemporary feminists have argued that these studies of leadership behavior have presented problems for women generally because the scientific, positivist underpinnings of such works are inherently gender-biased. Feminist philosopher of science Evelyn Fox Keller explains that science is not a discipline defined only "by the exigencies of logical proof and experimental verification," but rather is a socially constructed body of knowledge and set of practices. The research generated by early UCEA projects was largely conducted by, for, and about men, even though researchers couched their work in value-neutral terms and undoubtedly would have taken offense at charges of gender bias. Nevertheless, this body of research effectively excluded women's voices and experiences.[37]

Early UCEA research presented other problems for women en route to administrative positions. Women increasingly found that to become school administrators, they needed to attend credentialing programs steeped in these views rather than rising through the teaching ranks as they had in the past.[38] As the body of empirical research findings on educational leadership grew, the training of school administrators in the resulting methods increasingly became a requirement for employment and professional development. Since women enjoyed limited access to these programs and since they were not financially supported as well in pursuing this training as men, credentialing programs built on male-biased empirical research purveyed in predominantly male graduate programs effectively reduced women's administrative opportunities.

As late as 1971–72, the UCEA reported that 98 percent of educational administration faculty were male, and 2 percent female. Female students in these programs were represented slightly more frequently. Around that time, only 8 percent of educational administration degree recipients were female.[39] Although the UCEA and CPEA had labored to improve the training of school administrators and to create a body of knowledge with which to train them, in the end few women attended these programs and proportionally even fewer taught in them or wrote related books and articles. Although program organizers may not have intended consciously to discriminate against women, the changes made in administrative preparation programs after the war effectively contributed to women's declining numbers.[40] In his history of the UCEA, *Building Bridges*, Jack Culbertson frankly describes some of the difficulties the organization confronted in attempting to improve gender equity in school administration preparation, problems that included personal resistance, failure of administrators to adopt promising materials developed by the UCEA, and lack of effective support networks for persons of color and women.[41]

As the community of school administrators, educational administration professors, and their allies gained in stature through conducting scientific and theoretical research and establishing credentialing standards, they called for other reforms as well. In particular, they launched a concerted effort to consolidate school districts around the country. With consolidation would come greater administrative power and responsibility as well as more centralized authority. Roald Campbell explained that larger districts were essential "if the superintendency of each district is to attract a professional executive." Presumably larger districts enjoyed greater tax bases than smaller, unconsolidated ones; they therefore could afford to pay higher salaries for chief school officers. Rural areas, though, were likely to resist consolidation because of a distrust of "experts" and a desire to keep control of schools in local hands. However, Campbell indicated that "these dispositions are subject to some alleviation, and continuing efforts in that direction are needed."[42] The mechanisms of "alleviation" and "continuing effort" are not clear from his discussion.

During the push for school consolidation, women were far more likely to superintend small rural or intermediate school districts than other types of systems. (See table A.1 and figure A.1.) These systems tended to pay superintendents significantly less than large city school systems, which made rural positions generally unattractive to some men. As small school districts consolidated into larger ones, women superintendents tended to lose their jobs. The 1971 AASA study dismissed this decline in the number of women superintendents:

> [This study confirms] what all previous studies have concluded: namely, that the superintendency is a man's world. . . . Previous studies revealed that of the few female superintendents in the United States, most were in rural areas. . . . Perhaps the significant reduction in the number of rural school superintendencies and the replacement of county superintendencies with the revitalized intermediate unit of school administration may help to explain the continuing decline in the percentage of public school superintendents who are women.[43]

The author of this study did not attempt to explain why women were not sought for superintendencies in large school districts, nor did he demonstrate the need for consolidation. He simply implied that women led small districts and small districts suffered the costs of consolidation; therefore the number of women superintendents declined. The author did not find this decline problematic.

Consolidation also affected elementary principals. One of the panelists who participated in 1966 *The National Elementary Principal* discussion of women administrators' "going the way of the buffalo" explained that consolidation probably played an important role in the decreasing numbers of women elementary principals. Consolidation effectively had resulted in larger schools with principalships that held greater appeal to men. He said that "consolidation is making a school large enough to hold positions that are attractive to males."[44]

In the end, states and school districts heeded the call for consolidation. The National Commission on School District Reorganization reported in 1947 that 104,000 local districts existed in the United States, though only a fraction employed superintendents. Fifty-nine thousand operated by 1956, and by 1980 fewer than 16,000 school districts existed around the country. Some states also eliminated the position of county superintendents in favor of smaller local units, or much larger regional units. In Kansas, for example, women accounted for 73 out of 104 county superintendents, or 70 percent in 1950; however, when the state eliminated the county superintendency, only two women superintendents of any district type remained by 1970 (see Appendix). The call by educational administrators for the reorganization of school districts, then, was in the end one designed to increase the stature of the profession. As the prestige and salaries of superintendents increased, the number of women superintendents declined.

From the late 1800s through the mid-1900s, the NEA portrayed itself as the main professional organization for all people involved with public education. Teachers, administrators, deans, club women, and a number of other groups with a range of educational interests, joined under the umbrella of this larger organization. In spite of the apparent unity evoked by a single organization name, a relatively small group of superintendents and college presidents controlled the NEA over this period, often to the chagrin of teachers. During these years very few teachers were elected president of the organization. The first teacher to serve as NEA president was not chosen until 1928 and only a few were elected through the 1960s. The 1952 AASA report explained this control: "The school superintendent has a unique responsibility for developing greater strength and unity of purpose and action in the organized teaching profession" with responsibilities "far greater than their relative numbers indicate."[45] Willard Ellsbree in 1939 speculated that superintendents' disproportionate power in the organization was in part due to their flexible schedules and higher salaries that made conference attendance much easier than it was for teachers. However, he also contended that "teachers have been untrained, transient, and frequently indifferent toward professional matters outside their own bailiwick" and that "it is not to be wondered at, then, that the leadership in the associations has rested largely in the hands of administrators."[46] In 1946 William Spalding, superintendent of schools in Portland, explained that: "Administrators are more adept in political activity than are teachers. They are more forceful persons. They have had experience as leaders. This enables them to obtain control of teachers' organizations when they wish to do so. It enables them to influence policy greatly out of proportion to their number. It puts them in places of authority within the organization even when they are not actively seeking these places."[47] Most of the NEA presidents had been superintendents and much of the power of the larger organization emanated from the Department of Superintendence, which later became the AASA.

This mostly male group assumed for itself the responsibilities of safeguarding the education profession and establishing standards of professionalism. When school administrators spoke about the need for educational professionalism, they often meant different things in different situations. When administrative organizations called for greater "administrative professionalism," they generally implied that the standards for administrators should be rigorous, carefully defined, monitored, and controlled by school administrators themselves. They modeled this notion of professionalism after law and medicine, where practitioners formed associations for self-regulation. When superintendents and other administrators spoke of the need for "teacher professionalism," however, they usually meant that educators throughout the hierarchy of school employment should pull together to support public education against attacks from outside; that teachers should endeavor to upgrade their skills; and perhaps most important, that teachers should cooperate with their leaders. In this sense, professionalism customarily entailed belonging to the NEA, a broad-based association of educators that had long been controlled by superintendents at the local and national levels. To insure professionalism throughout the ranks, superintendents believed they should foster "loyalty to state and national education associations." Superintendents, then, monopolized the process of defining professionalism for public school educators. When teachers sought to define professionalism for themselves, administrators called them militant unionists disloyal to the cause of public education; such teachers therefore were deemed "unprofessional."

The monolithic control of the NEA would not last, however. Some seeds for its demise were planted in 1935, when passage of the National Labor Relations Act brought a legal framework to employer-employee relations in the private sector. Although this legislation did not specifically protect public school educators, states soon passed legislation mandating that school districts negotiate with teachers. After World War II, teacher bargaining took on new dimensions, expanding from basic welfare issues to including curriculum and management matters. Superintendents in the AASA recognized that negotiation with teachers was consistent with postwar notions of democratic education: to educate for democracy, educators must practice democracy. However, superintendents maintained that negotiations should be conducted within bounds, which they alone should delineate. The 1952 AASA report explained, "the right to band together for the advancement of common interests is not only considered compatible with the general welfare but is believed to be basic. The right to strike against vital public services such as schools, fire protection, or police protection cannot be tolerated."[48]

Within a decade of this statement, however, teachers not only had begun to organize successfully and bargain for higher salaries and better working conditions, but they had also launched their first strikes. The American Federation of Teachers (AFT) led the charge with victories in New York City. The NEA, though, was divided on the matter. Even though school administrators in the NEA denounced militant bargaining tactics, NEA teachers noticed the AFT victories and pushed for more aggressive tactics themselves. Advocates of collective bargaining, grievance procedures, and strikes eventually prevailed in the NEA by 1968.[49]

Teachers gained power and better salaries with these strategies; however, the inevitable confrontations with administrators produced wounds that never healed.[50] Adversarial relationships between teachers and administrators became the norm as teachers fought for improved working conditions and benefits, while administrators sought to uphold their own authority. Teachers and superintendents found their mutual trust diminished to the extent that by 1973, the AASA announced its decision to sever ties with the NEA and to become an independent organization.[51]

At that point, superintendents no longer found themselves towering over a united education profession. Where once they had dominated the leadership and control of the NEA, they now stood outside teachers' organizations. Rather than viewing this change as a step toward the empowerment of teachers, most superintendents mourned the loss of "professional unity," that is, with superintendents in control. In many ways the power and authority of teachers had increased with the breakup of the NEA and the rise of collective bargaining. However, since superintendents previously had enjoyed the power to define professionalism in education, some deemed changes that undermined their authority as unprofessional.

Women superintendents may have suffered an additional loss with the increased antagonism between teachers and administrators. Over the previous century, many women superintendents had enjoyed their greatest support from primarily female groups of teachers, not from male school administration organizations. A number of women became superintendents through the active campaigning and support of teacher groups. In return, these superintendents often looked after the welfare of teachers, working incessantly for higher teacher wages and improved working conditions. During the years of growing antagonism between superintendents and teachers, however, it is possible that the cleavage between the two groups may have disconnected women superintendents from one of their bases of support.

The changes in the structure of public education and school administration after World War II clearly made school administrative work more favorable for men than it had been previously. Interestingly, administrative work also became less amenable to women's participation, especially given the heightened social expectations for women's domesticity following the war. If postwar America accentuated men's traditional roles as career workers outside the home, then middle-class women's roles increasingly became those of homebound wives and mothers. During and immediately following the war, higher percentages of women married than had previously, and they did so at younger ages than their parents. They also bore more children than their mothers. Many couples conceived children at the war's end: in 1946, the nation's birth rate increased 20 percent over 1945 levels. That year, Benjamin Spock published *The Common Sense Book of Baby and Child Care*, a book that eventually sold millions of copies. The national explosion of women's domesticity had begun.

Not all women eagerly chose homemaking, though. Some women who had obtained heavy industrial jobs during the war expected to continue with their new, relatively high-wage careers. At the war's end, however, industries encouraged women to leave to make room for returning male veterans. When some women resisted leaving their jobs voluntarily, supervisors fired them. In 1945, for example, a Detroit auto factory laid off women hired during the war. Rather than leaving passively, these women organized a march to "Stop Discrimination because of Sex," but in the end they could not have their wartime jobs back. These women faced the grim prospect of competing with male veterans for available jobs. When men consistently won the more favorable positions, women confronted the choice of unemployment or low-wage, dead-end jobs that men would not accept, such as the new "pink collar" jobs of secretarial work. In the end, the war actually boosted women's employment permanently, but it also brought a sharper sexual division of labor.[52]

Rather than accept jobs newly defined as female-appropriate, many women instead chose to marry and maintain households while their husbands worked outside the home. In 1946 the marriage rate reached a high of 118 per 1,000 women, almost 50 percent higher than the 79 out 1000 women who married in 1926.[53] To ease women's adjustment into domesticity, magazines offered helpful household and family point-ers, and books described women's new roles.[54] For instance, in the best-selling 1947 book *Modern Woman: The Lost Sex*, Ferdinand Lundburg and Marynia Farnham suggested that women should regard a return to the home as a natural means of restoring balance, a change with impli-cations as far-reaching as contributing to world peace. Further, they argued that "[a woman must] accept herself fully as a woman [and] know . . . she is dependent on a man. There is no fantasy in her mind about being an independent woman, a contradiction in terms."[55]

Some women wanted to have both a career and a family. Because most school systems dropped their marriage bars after the war, married women had the new option of pursuing teaching careers while raising a family. Married women constituted a distinctly different group of teach-ers from single women, however. They operated within entirely differ-ent sets of social definitions and constraints. Single women enjoyed some flexibility in their job choices. Society expected married women, on the other hand, to put their husbands' careers first. This usually meant quitting work when children were born so husbands could maintain their jobs without child-care responsibilities. Women also were expected to pack up and move whenever husbands accepted jobs elsewhere. Being good wives and mothers also meant that women generally needed to put their families' needs before their own. These expectations tended to limit married women's career possibilities outside the home because school boards and administrators held married women's family duties against them when considering candidates for promotion.

It was during these social changes that men displaced women school administrators. The majority of women educators who served in the 1950s and 1960s were married women who customarily made their careers secondary to their husbands'. Simultaneously, administrative positions like the superintendency increasingly required credentialing, graduate coursework, longer hours, and career trajectories that were difficult for women, given these accentuated gender-role definitions.

Throughout the ranks of school administration, women quietly slipped away, or perhaps were pushed out. The phenomenon was scarcely mentioned at meetings of superintendents and other adminis-trators. For the most part, the professional literature about school ad-ministration also ignored the vanishing woman administrator. The National Council of Administrative Women in Education attempted to alert the public to the trend, as did a few women who published isolated pieces during these years. Otherwise, when women's administrative decline was noted, the authors tended to offer a few perfunctory expla-nations, while treating the whole matter as a trivial curiosity. For the most part, women were blamed for their lack of professionalism, which was then defined in a variety of ways.

In 1966 one writer, Harris Taylor, claimed that women seemed to be less motivated by money than men generally; thus they entered school administration less frequently. He claimed that since women teachers tended to have working husbands, they did not need the money as much as men who bore the main responsibility for supporting their families. Also, because NEA figures showed that male teachers held second jobs much more frequently than women, they clearly were more motivated to make higher salaries and therefore would be enticed into administration. Women, lacking that incentive, would decline advancement. He concluded, "it is apparent that women teachers do not have, or need to have, the strong drive for additional income that characterizes their male colleagues."[56] Taylor neglected to mention that in part schools had been consolidated and administrative salaries raised with the specific hope of recruiting men.

In a second argument for women's lack of professionalism, Taylor contended that women moved too frequently to be considered as viable administrative candidates. An NEA study he cited found that 45 percent of men and only 31 percent of women had taught in just one system. He concluded that "since school districts tend to give preference to teachers with tenure when filling administrative positions, men have a decided advantage." What Taylor failed to explain is that during these decades married women were expected to move as their husbands' jobs dictated, but husbands were not required to reciprocate. Objections to women raised on these grounds amounted to clear gender discrimination.[57]

Taylor explained that women tended to interrupt their careers with leaves more often than did men and thus were viewed as less professional and less committed to career advancement: "The teaching careers of women show a long record of leaves and temporary retirements for one reason or another. Two-thirds of the married teachers . . . have taken at least one extended absence from teaching," he explained.[58] Women's career interruptions usually occurred during pregnancies. When women teacher became pregnant, school board policies usually forced them to quit their jobs by the fifth month at the latest. Expectant women typically had no choice about temporarily leaving teaching—until the early 1970s when court action upheld women's right to work throughout their pregnancies. By Taylor's logic, though, women who bore children and temporarily left their teaching positions were not considered professional enough for administrative advancement. Since teaching had become a married women's occupation during the baby boom, fewer women were likely to maintain Taylor's standards of profession-alism than when teaching had been the domain of single women.[59]

Taylor also contended that women did not prepare themselves professionally as often or as well as men. He said that in 1962, less than 16 percent of women held two college degrees while 40 percent of male administrators did; men also held doctoral degrees four times as often as women. Since women at this time did not receive federal funding for education to the same extent as men, since it was customary for women to put their husbands through college but not the other way around, since women had been closed out of many institutions of higher educa-tion to make room for veterans, and since many educational adminis-tration credentialing programs did not admit many if any females, women had significantly less opportunity to pursue graduate degrees than men. Taylor essentially blamed women for not availing themselves of minimal or nonexistent opportunities.[60]

Increasingly through the 1950s and 1960s, the path to school ad-ministrative work proceeded by way of internships. Teaching became less of an administrative prerequisite as administrative internships grew more important. One writer explained, however, that internships served as a disincentive to women because they generally did not ex-press interest in pursuing them.[61] Administrative interns needed to work closely with mentors who tended to be men. Presumably women's hesitance in entering these mentoring relationships stemmed in part from social mores of the time that viewed with suspicion men and women who worked closely together in similar positions.

Some school districts even maintained written policies favoring men for administrative promotions over women. One writer, who de-scribed a policy study of eighteen school systems, found that there was no institutional discrimination against women even though one-third of those systems had clear policies preferring male administrators.[62]

In the end, the persons who discussed women's declining admin-istrative influence in schools tended to offer a variety of explanations that all essentially faulted women for failing to meet the criteria for se-lection. Therefore discrimination was not the culprit, they asserted, but rather "women's choices and family commitments" were to blame.[63] Further, they argued that the trend would continue since that was the price women paid for choosing to be wives and mothers. The 1966 *National Elementary Principal* panel discussion concluded with the opinion that "the continued desire to mix professional careers with personal family responsibilities will hamper the woman as long as the social milieu of the United States continues to stress the fundamental role of the woman as mother, wife, and companion."[64]

The standards and expectations for persons pursuing school administration had not always been as they were in the mid-1960s. After the war, school administrators seeking to make school leadership a higher-status occupation endeavored to transform the professional nature of school administration and simultaneously increase its appeal to men. Many of the enacted changes effectively placed school administration beyond the reach of most women, especially married women teachers with family obligations. At the same time, education changed from a profession primarily consisting of single women to one made up mainly of married women. This dramatic change in women teachers' marriage rates largely went unnoticed among education writers and scholars of the time. Most operated within the ahistorical assumption that teaching was a career for married women—ignoring or perhaps denying the long-standing tradition of single women teachers that stretched from the common school era through the years immediately after World War II. Ironically, single women educators, who could have maintained the new professional standards more readily than married women, were stigmatized precisely for not being as feminine as married women, who in turn were considered unprofessional. Educational administration, then, had become a profession that held all women in a double bind from which advancement into the male-defined and dominated administrative hierarchy was improbable.

In the late 1960s, several education journal articles and research projects emerged that moved beyond merely noting and explaining away the decline in woman school administrators. Some offered women tips on how to advance into administrative work. Sanford Reitman, for example, found that women tended to be more passive than men and therefore needed to labor to become more assertive to get ahead.[65]

In a significant change of direction, however, some researchers sought to locate the cause of the demise of women administrators outside women. A number of these researchers were women who identified with the efforts of the fledgling modern women's movement. Increasingly some hailed sex discrimination as the chief reason for the decline. Suzanne Taylor in 1971 described her own research:

My study showed that all other things being equal, superintendents were not likely to hire women as administrators. Half of the school systems studied did not encourage women to train or apply for administrative positions. Moreover, even though there were no written policies precluding women from administrative appointments and very few school systems acknowledged unwritten policies, women were still not likely to be appointed principals or superintendents. In fact, analysis of the data revealed that the only factor which appeared to have any significance on the hiring process was that of sex.[66]

Other studies cited women's outstanding abilities as administrators, usually rating them ahead of men. One study concluded that "nothing in our studies has convinced us that males are inherently superior to females as educational administrators and we view the de facto discrimination as totally unjustifiable."[67]

The views of these newly visible researchers provoked widespread debate in the education community about where to fix the blame for the low numbers of women administrators. School administrators and professors of educational administration tended to deny that widespread discrimination against women existed because "it does not seem to be a widespread, official policy. Even a casual review of the policy handbooks of school districts reveals no such sanctions."[68] However, women and women's advocates, emboldened by the rapidly growing and influential women's rights movement, disputed these denials of discrimination. By the early 1970s, the debate had become public and heated, fueled by growing bodies of research upholding each contention. Women's rights supporters eagerly reentered the fray to create systemic changes that would lead to greater roles for women in educational leadership.

6

Is This All?

Betty Friedan felt restless and dissatisfied. A middle-class, White, well-educated woman, Friedan had devoted her adult life to living the popularly depicted image of female domestic bliss as a suburban housewife; however, something did not quite seem right to her. She described the sense in the opening page of what became her best-selling and controversial book, *The Feminine Mystique* (1963): "The problem lay buried, unspoken, for many years in the minds of American women . . . a strange stirring, a sense of dissatisfaction, a yearning that . . . each suburban wife struggled with . . . alone. . . . [S]he was afraid to ask even of herself the silent question—'Is this all?'"[1]

Middle-class women around the country wondered the same question as Friedan's words tapped a powerful, shared sense of emptiness and frustration. The book quickly sold over a million copies and fueled a passionate national discussion of women's "proper place" in American society. Newspapers and magazines ran stories exploring the condition of women's discontent. Friedan, it seems, had touched a sensitive part of the national psyche. On one hand, *The Feminine Mystique* provoked anger and active dissent among some women who asserted publicly that they were happy and satisfied in striving to fulfill their household duties as wives and mothers.[2] However, Friedan's thoughts resonated with other women who acted on their quiet frustration by forming discussion groups and anxiously awaiting opportunities to do more. Within a few years, organizations such as the National Organization for Women (NOW), Women's Equity Action League (WEAL), the National Women's Political Caucus (NWPC), and other groups rallied in what became the groundswell of the modern women's movement. Much like their suffrage-era forebearers, women's activists and liberationists alike turned their attention toward questioning rigidly defined women's roles in the home, the workplace, and society at large. A difference in their strategy, though, was that while suffrage-era activists lobbied to advance a range of social causes through political and social activism, the modern women's movement also utilized the legal system as a principal tool in its fight for women's rights. Inevitably the women's movement turned some of its organized energy toward public education, including the roles of women administrators.

In the early 1960s, President Kennedy established the President's Commission on the Status of Women as a return favor for the political help of several prominent women. He appointed Eleanor Roosevelt as the commission's first head and directed the group to study and compile information regarding women's domestic, economic, and legal status. Although the commission maintained a careful commitment to women's traditional roles, it highlighted some troubling social inequalities between the sexes. In 1963, it published a report that carefully documented pervasive inequities between men and women. Kennedy then issued an order requiring that the civil service hire "solely on the basis of ability to meet the requirements of the position, and without regard to sex." Also that year Congress passed the Equal Pay Act prohibiting private employers from paying men and women different wages for equal work. Many states around the country joined in the spirit of reform by establishing their own commissions on the status of women to gather data on sex discrimination.[3]

Growing social awareness of sex discrimination followed the civil rights movement that for years had employed civil disobedience and other public actions aimed at dismantling racial barriers and injustices in American culture. The slow, grudging social and political victories won by the civil rights movement inspired women eager to fight for their rights as a group. When Congress debated Title VII of the 1964 Civil Rights Act, which had been introduced to protect against employment discrimination based on race, creed, and national origin, one congressman pushed to include sex among protected classes—a segregationist tactic aimed mainly at killing the bill. When the bill survived this challenge and passed, it quickly became an important legal tool for women who faced job discrimination. Through the Equal Employment Opportunity Commission (EEOC), the agency charged with implementing Title VII, women for the first time availed themselves of federal assistance in filing sex discrimination grievances.[4]

Women soon discovered that the EEOC and the private sector generally did not take sex discrimination grievances seriously, however. Women's resulting frustration, in combination with the momentum generated by state commissions on the status of women and the inspiration of Friedan's *Mystique*, provoked a small group of women to form the National Organization for Women (NOW) in 1966. NOW, organized and headed by Betty Friedan, consisted mainly of women who had worked on state women's commissions. NOW assumed as its purpose: "To take action to bring women into full participation in the mainstream of American society now, assuming all the privileges and responsibilities thereof in truly equal partnership with men." Generally the organization sought to bring women's advocacy to Washington and to work for powerful laws assuring women's rights, especially in the face of anemic government efforts to that point. Other organizations soon appeared that pushed for the liberation of women in different arenas. The Women's Equity Action League, for example, focused on women's economic and legal issues.[5]

Shortly after the emergence of the modern women's movement, women across the country began rallying for women's rights and the end of sex discrimination. Feminists succeeded in drawing massive attention to the newly invigorated movement by staging elaborate and flashy public events. Women's marches and rallies drew large crowds and throngs of reporters. Liberationists who publicly burned their bras became media icons of "feminist extremism." By the early 1970s, the women's rights movement had become such an important part of the American cultural landscape that a cover story in the *New York Times* acknowledged, "the walls of economic and psychological discrimination against women in the American job market are beginning to crack under the pressures of the Federal government, the women's liberation movement, and the efforts of thousands of individual women themselves."[6]

While women across the country celebrated their new organizations, camaraderie, and growing political power, their adversaries predicted that the women's liberation movement would not last long. When the women's movement magazine, *Ms.*, began publication in 1972, ABC news anchor Harry Reasoner gave it six months to exhaust its message. The editors at *Education Digest* proclaimed in 1973 that "women's lib is dead." While fatalistic predictions were intended to demean organized efforts for women's rights, instead they often ended up fueling the efforts of women eager to change their lot in society.[7]

In spite of the gloomy predictions, women fought for and won some concessions in the workplace as well as in governmental services. Some women's organizers decided that a particularly effective strategy for eliminating sex discrimination was to target the nation's schools as sites of both discriminatory indoctrination and hiring practices, especially in school administration. Women's groups lobbied politicians and powerful education organizations for reforms. They wrote articles, editorial pieces, or books demanding the end of sexism as did Betty Friedan and Anne West in 1971 when they wrote in *The American School Board*

Journal: "The new feminist consciousness will not be eclipsed—neither by the public schools nor by any of the other great institutions of our society. . . . Whether they realize it yet, school board members and school administrators across the country are being thrust into the front lines of this new struggle for equality, just as they have been in the movement for racial justice."[8] And even though schools may have been thrust into the front lines of the battle to end sex discrimination, long-standing traditions of according women second-class status in school employment would be difficult to change. Entrenched political forces would, with enormous tenacity, resist relinquishing their power.

When women's rights activists discovered that the process of voluntary change would come slowly if at all, they turned to the legal system as the tool of choice in the campaign for nondiscriminatory schools. After all, the National Association for the Advancement of Colored People (NAACP) had pioneered successful legal challenges for civil rights in landmark cases such as *Brown v. Board of Education* (1954). These victories occurred against overwhelming odds and unfathomable social resistance. For women as a class to begin using legal means of seeking redress for an endless list of discrimination grievances, however, a great deal of work first needed to be done to identify or create legal tools with which women could fight.

The U.S. Constitution, a document drafted by men, mentions "women" only once. Until the 1970s, constitutional law denied women many rights that men customarily took for granted. Women could not necessarily attend any publicly supported school, serve on juries, be tried by a jury of their peers, work in state or federal offices, collect the same salary as their male peers, choose their own home, or even decide their own name.[9] By the early 1970s, though, women's advocates had begun to win favorable legislation from Congress and rulings from the Supreme Court, each of which chipped away at the Constitution's neglect of women's rights. A brief detour through the history of legal and legislative precedents concerning American women is in order, then, to better contextualize the events of the 1970s.

Coverture

In the eighteenth century John Adams and the other founders of this country relied heavily on Lockean philosophy and the English legal system as guides for their legal ideologies. The *Commentaries* of Sir William Blackstone, an eighteenth-century English jurist, provided an essential base for drafting American legal documents, especially those concerning property, matrimony, and rights. Blackstone wrote that "by marriage, the husband and wife are one person in law; the very being of legal existence of the woman is suspended during the marriage, or at least is incorporated and consolidated into that of the husband; under whose wing, protection and cover, she performs everything."[10] Coverture, the term for this relationship, meant that women's legal identities were essentially the same as their husbands'. They had no separate civil existence. Women therefore had no right to enter into contracts, own property or wealth, or even protect themselves from husbands who legally could beat them or impose sexual intercourse against their will.[11] The common acceptance of this ideology effectively handicapped women who might have pursued education, public careers, or leadership because women essentially had no public existence in a legal sense. Coverture supported men's right to control their wives completely and all of their property. It is not coincidental that during the early years of the republic when the ideology of coverture prevailed, property ownership among women declined significantly from pre-Constitution levels.[12]

Separate Spheres Ideology

In the mid-1800s women began protesting their general lack of rights, a movement epitomized by the Seneca Falls Declaration of Sentiments. Largely because of this public agitation, the legal system eventually discarded coverture as a workable legal doctrine. Gradually individual states established married women's property acts that removed the most egregious liabilities. In the place of coverture, however, the new doctrine of separate spheres emerged. On one hand, separate spheres acknowledged women's legal existence, but on the other it relegated them to a distinctly different place from their husbands before the law.[13] This theory, which emerged from middle- and proprietary-class perspectives, held that husbands should represent couples in the public world as breadwinners while wives should govern the private world of the home. With the separate spheres ideology, women at least assumed a role of some distinct legal importance rather than having to live invisibly in their husbands' shadows. However, this ideology clearly constrained women in their acceptable avenues of public service.

In 1873 Myra Bradwell, a talented legal authority in her day, tested the separate spheres ideology by applying for admission to the Illinois state bar. She and her attorney decided to use one of the new Civil War amendments as a vehicle for her case. The Thirteenth, Fourteenth, and Fifteenth Amendments were designed to protect individual rights, especially those of former slaves, against arbitrary exercise of power by states. The Fourteenth Amendment, in particular, was written to address the right to due process and to provide equal protection under the law. Hoping to capitalize on latitude implied in the Fourteenth Amendment, Bradwell's attorney argued that this newly enacted amendment protected her right as a citizen to practice law.[14] The Supreme Court held, however, that states could determine who should have the privilege of practicing law and further that this privilege "in no sense depends on citizenship of the United States."[15] Justice Bradley also issued the opinion that

> [t]he civil law, as well as nature herself, has always recognized a wide difference in the respective spheres and destinies of man and woman. . . . The natural and proper timidity and delicacy which belongs to the female sex evidently unfits it for many of the occupations of civil life. The constitution of the family organization, which is founded in the divine ordinance, as well as in the nature of things, indicates the domestic sphere as that which properly belongs to the domain and functions of womanhood.[16]

Since married women had no legal existence beyond the home apart from their husbands, the Court ruled Bradwell, herself a married woman, "incompetent to perform the duties and trusts that belong to the office of an attorney and counselor."[17] With this opinion Justice Bradley dismissed the notion that the law was created by a particular class of persons with interests to protect. Instead he described civil law as something omniscient and larger than social concerns. By attributing separate spheres ideology to nature, he avoided wrestling with the social conditions that had created separate social spheres for men and women.

As a result of the Bradwell decision women could only practice law or hold public positions in states that granted them the right to do so. States west of the Mississippi sometimes offered this opportunity as they granted women a few basic rights such as suffrage in the late 1800s. Also, since the vast western territory desperately needed workers to build the economy and infrastructure, out of necessity women performed a few public services in which men had little interest. Elected officials created laws benefiting women; however, they did only when enfranchised members of the public perceived the necessity for doing so. Otherwise, women who worked in the public sphere tended to assume roles that resembled those of the private sphere. In education, women taught behind the closed doors of the classroom, while men maintained a public presence in school administration. Legal doctrine supported and enforced this sex-based configuration.

The Demise of Separate Spheres Ideology

Nearly a century after enactment of the Civil War amendments, the modern women's movement fought for legal reforms to end sex discrimination. The Supreme Court discarded separate spheres doctrine piecemeal as it began examining sex-related cases with a stricter standard of review. *Seidenberg v. McSorleys' Old Ale House, Inc.*, a 1970 federal district court case, offered the first evidence of this new standard. For over one hundred years, McSorleys' had prided itself as an establishment catering exclusively to men. To challenge this social exclusion, two women sought and were denied service there. They brought suit. The Supreme Court concluded that the women could be denied admission to the club only if such exclusion bore a rational connection to the permissible purpose of the exclusion. The Court dismissed arguments that male customers did not want women, that mixing men and women was immoral, or that the cost of upgrading bathrooms might be steep.[18]

In a related case, *Sail'er Inn, Inc. v. Kirby (1971)*, the California Supreme Court unanimously overturned a statute disallowing all women from bartending, including bar owners. The court found that sex "is an immutable trait, a status into which the class members are locked by the accident of birth." As in the Seidenberg case, the court found that sex bore no relation to ability to contribute to society. Additionally, the court also concluded that "sexual classifications are properly treated as suspect."[19]

These cases and many others that followed in quick succession demolished much of the old separate spheres ideology grounded in the breadwinner-homemaker dichotomy. In essence, justices recognized social changes in the world around them and assumed responsibility for setting legal precedents within the courtroom. Justice Brennan perhaps best summed up the dominant thinking that produced these changes: "Laws which disable women from full participation in the political, business and economic arenas are often characterized as 'protective' and beneficial. . . . The pedestal upon which women have been placed has all too often, upon closer inspection, been revealed as a cage."[20]

The dismantling of separate spheres ideology prepared the way for legal activism on behalf of women seeking equity in educational employment. Court decisions and legislative initiatives that have been particularly influential over the past several decades include:

Title VII

With the passage of the Civil Rights Act of 1964 and Title VII pertaining to women's employment rights, for the first time women were able to file grievances for sex-based job discrimination. The government created the EEOC "to administer Title VII and to assure equal treatment for all in employment." Women soon discovered, however, that the EEOC frequently failed to press sex discrimination cases vigorously.

Numerous loopholes in the legislation permitted and continue to allow discriminatory hiring practices. For example, to comply with Title VII provisions, employers only need to assure that jobs are open to everyone regardless of sex.[21] Actual discriminatory hiring practices are not necessarily covered. Also, employers are required to institute advertising avoiding mention of sex, devise sex-neutral interviewing and testing processes, and eliminate job descriptions based on sexual stereotypes. These conditions are easy to circumvent, however, because employers only need to drop overt mention of the sex-specificity of jobs.

In spite of these significant limitations, though, Title VII occasionally has served as a useful legal tool for pressing sex discrimination cases. Although the time and expense of bringing Title VII claims has frustrated most women, some who have sought educational administration positions have successfully challenged their employers. In *Spears v. Board of Education of Pike County, Kentucky*, a woman proved that she had been denied promotion because of her sex. To win this case, however, her situation needed to be overwhelmingly obvious. Since she could demonstrate that the school system had promoted nine men with inferior qualifications while she waited, she won her case.[22] Even though relatively few women have won employment discrimination cases through Title VII, the amendment has served to make employers and employees alike aware of the possibility of legal redress for unfair employment practices. The legislation has also helped inspire women's groups and legislators through the years to press for more powerful legal means of fighting sex discrimination, such as Title IX.

Title IX

When Congress added Title VII to the 1964 Civil Rights Act, the language did not specifically address educational or employment discrimination. Congress later drafted Title IX of the Education Amendments of 1972 to provide more inclusive coverage against discrimination. It reads: "No person in the United States shall, on the basis of sex, be excluded from participation in, be denied the benefits of, or be subjected to discrimination under any education program or activity receiving Federal financial assistance."[23] To enforce this legislation the government stipulated that any institution receiving federal money could be denied those funds should institutional practices be found in violation of Title IX. Because of these financially compelling punitive measures, schools and systems around the country moved with haste to comply when Title IX was enacted. In contrast, when Title VII was passed, employers tended to move slowly and only enough to avoid legal entanglements.

Several important changes occurred after enactment of Title IX. First, graduate and professional schools dropped quotas limiting the number of women admitted to their programs. Before passage of this act, schools of education frequently limited the number of women who could enroll in administrative credentialing programs, sometimes to as few as 2 percent; yet after Title IX, women flooded into these programs. In 1972, the year Title IX was passed, women earned only 11 percent of all doctoral degrees awarded in educational administration; but by 1981–82, a decade later, they accounted for around 40 percent of these degrees, representing nearly a 400 percent increase.[24]

In their 1987 work, *A History of Thought and Practice in Educational Administration*, Campbell, Fleming, Newell, and Bennion explain the increase in the numbers of women in educational administration programs differently: "The women's movement had helped to raise aspirations and furnish opportunities; many who had been teachers before bearing children and raising their families returned at mid-career to seek doctorates in administration. . . . This academic field was at the forefront of an important social movement."[25] What they failed to explain is that until Title IX forced graduate programs to drop their quotas on women, women simply did not have the same access to credentialing programs as men. The women's movement not only made women aware of opportunities, but it also destroyed some of the barriers that kept women from career advancement.

Along with opening graduate educational opportunities to women, Title IX also precipitated an increase in the percentages of women in undergraduate programs. The trend toward greater enrollments of women continued after enactment of Title IX so that by the early eighties the overall number of women college graduates exceeded that of men. (See table 5.1 and figure 5.1.)

Women's participation in sports programs increased dramatically shortly after 1972 as well. In 1971, the year before enactment of Title IX, one girl participated in high school sports for roughly every twelve boys. Five years later, however, one girl participated on high school athletic teams for every two boys, a ratio that has continued through the present.[26]

The success of Title IX in opening athletic opportunities to young women has not always extended past team membership, though. Since coaching has traditionally served as a stepping-stone position for persons seeking school administration promotions, the increase in the numbers of girls in high school sports around the country should have allowed large numbers of women to gain coaching experience and then be well poised for career advancement. However, once the federal government mandated equality of girls' sports with boys', it also required that coaches of girls' teams be paid comparable supplements to boys' coaches. Women generally coached girls' teams before Title IX and they usually received no pay for their work. When Title IX attached money to positions for girls' coaches, men quickly took these roles and pushed women out in the process.[27]

In spite of the early Title IX victories for students, many women have found that enforcement of the legislation in cases of sex discrimination in school employment has been weak at best.[28] Even though the federal government initially threatened to withhold funding from noncompliant institutions, it has resisted enforcement on behalf of women bringing employment discrimination cases. In the 1980s the situation further deteriorated as the Reagan administration pushed for a limited interpretation of the law and essentially ceased any enforcement actions.[29] To make matters worse, the Supreme Court dealt Title IX a nearly fatal blow when it ruled in the 1984 *Grove City College v. Bell* decision against enforcement of the legislation. Congress, however, reversed this Supreme Court ruling in 1988 with the Civil Rights Restoration Act, but the effectiveness of this legislation in assisting women in education with job-related sex discrimination claims remains to be seen.

Sexual Harassment

Sexual harassment has long served as a means for those with sex-associated social and positional power to demean and oppress others. With the enactment of Title VII, for the first time redress could be sought for this type of workplace oppression. The amendment prohibits sexual harassment of employees because such behavior creates a hostile and abusive work environment that serves mainly to disadvantage women. In the early days of harassment cases, courts tended to view the harasser as one who merely possessed certain proclivities. Recovery in these cases was possible only if the harassed person suffered tangible loss such as a firing. In 1986, however, the Supreme Court unanimously ruled that harassment is actionable even when there is no financial loss. Since then courts have applied a more stringent test by determining whether the advances were welcomed by the complainant. Specifically, the EEOC defines sexual harassment as "unwelcome sexual advances, requests for sexual favors, and other verbal or physical conduct of a sexual nature, occurring under any of three conditions: when submission is either explicitly or implicitly a term or condition of employment, when submission or rejection of the conduct is the basis for employment decisions affecting the individual, or when the conduct has either the purpose or effect of substantially interfering with the individual's work performance or creating an intimidating, hostile or offensive working environment."[30]

An important new development in sexual harassment law occurred when the Supreme Court ruled in the spring of 1992 that a female student who was sexually harassed and abused by a male teacher in Gwinnett County, Georgia, could also sue under Title IX for compensatory damages, a far more severe penalty to the school system than court injunctions alone.[31] The implications of this ruling for female employees of school systems have yet to be clarified; however, sexual harassment complainants may now be able to seek legal remedies and thus inspire faster reform by school boards and systems.

Mandatory Leave

In the 1974 case *Cleveland Board of Education v. LaFleur*, the Supreme Court found that school systems could not insist upon mandatory unpaid leave for pregnant teachers. The Cleveland school system had wanted a pregnant teacher to take a leave of absence. Attorneys for the system argued that such leave would help smooth transitions between academic terms as well as to help protect the health of the mother and unborn child. The Court rejected these arguments, saying that such a line of reasoning presumed the pregnant woman to be physically incompetent.[32] Justice Rehnquist, however, disagreed. In his dissent he argued that such individualized legal treatment as this woman received was "in the last analysis nothing less than an attack upon the very notion of lawmaking itself."[33] In spite of his sweeping objection, this ruling moved mothers a step in the direction of having their employment rights protected and of ending overt discrimination based on motherhood.

Male-Only Groups

Ever since school administrators began controlling schools in this country, male administrators have enhanced their power in communities by joining all-male service, social, and political organizations. Because of the importance of these connections in the management of school district affairs, school board members and administrators have argued through the years in favor of hiring only men for superintendencies. Beyond community-level connections, some of the prestigious national honorary education organizations long maintained policies excluding women members. For example, Phi Delta Kappa, the education honorary society, did not admit women until the 1970s. In attaining the

full benefit of community and professional support, male superintendents enjoyed a clear advantage over women with their access to such
male-only organizations.[34]

In 1984, the Supreme Court delivered a crippling blow to such established sex-exclusive social groups. In *Roberts v. United States Jaycees*,
the Court ruled that chapters of the Jaycees were subject to public ac-
commodations laws and therefore had to admit women as well as men.
Although this ruling has opened the doors for women to enter these organizations, it remains to be seen if they will be admitted in large numbers or whether women's membership will allow them to make the
connections they need to move into positions of school district leadership as it is now configured.[35]

Veterans' Benefits

For over a hundred years, U.S. veterans' benefits programs have
granted scholarships, loans, preferential hiring, and other benefits to
persons who have served in wars. However, since military services in
the past have imposed quotas of 2 percent on the number of women
who could serve in the military, these benefits have gone primarily to
men. In 1979, a female, long-time civil servant in Massachusetts challenged such a program after she had repeatedly been passed over for
promotion in favor of less-qualified males. The Supreme Court ruled
against her claim by arguing that "classification by veterans is gender
neutral because the class of non-veterans includes many males, and the
class of veterans a few females." The majority opinion went on to explain that because there was no motive to discriminate against women,
the case had no merit. Justice Marshall dissented by saying that "in
practice, this . . . has created a gender-based civil service hierarchy, with
women occupying low grade clerical and secretarial jobs and men holding more responsible and remunerative positions."[36] For example, since
in 1971 around 70 percent of school superintendents surveyed by the
AASA had received higher education and administrative credentials
with G.I. Bill benefits, and since at the time women constituted only a
small portion of the eligible benefits recipients, clearly these programs
disproportionately benefited men in administrative advancement. This
legal decision is one of the modern women's movement–era cases that
did not favor women's social, political, and economic advancement.

Women's Educational Equity Act of 1974

Following Title IX came the enactment of Section 408 of P.L. 93-380,
also known as the Women's Educational Equity Act of 1974. This legislation earmarked federal funds for numerous projects designed to dis-

mantle sex-based inequities throughout the nation's educational system. Included among the authorized activities were research, training, education, evaluation, and information distribution.[37]

Significantly, WEEA provided federal funding for research to be conducted on women's employment opportunities in education. Until this time, relatively few funded studies had explored discrimination against women seeking school leadership positions because organizations that could have afforded to sponsor such work regarded the topic as unimportant. In the vacuum of sex-equity research, school boards and professional organizations easily ignored pressure from women's groups to expand women's employment opportunities in education. WEEA essentially provided important momentum and funding for the development of a new field of scholarship and research. As a result, the volume of education-related sex-equity research increased significantly after 1974. In more recent years, though, federal funding for this research has declined.

Even though women have succeeded in winning sex-discrimination lawsuits against some school systems and educational organizations, women still have not come close to attaining equitable representation in school administration the way it is now structured. The data presented in the appendix shows that in 1990 women accounted for around 5 percent of all school superintendents in the country (see table A.1), even though educational administration credentialing programs graduated nearly equal numbers of men and women that year. Clearly, women aspire to administrative advancement, yet somehow they are not attaining these positions. Perhaps in frustration, Edna Manning, president of the Women's Caucus of the AASA, suggested in 1984 that "litigation is the only sure way to gain widespread change."[38]

Pressing for legal action is a difficult tactic for a number of reasons, however. First, filing a legal complaint is a complex process. Also, individual women must first be aware that they face discrimination, a situation that some would rather deny. Then they must substantiate this patterned behavior. Some who successfully compile convincing evidence then hesitate to follow through because they fear being branded as troublemakers, a label for which women may be punished or denied consideration for promotion in any district.[39] Sakre Kennington Edson documented these and a range of other problems faced by women seeking educational administrative positions in her longitudinal qualitative study, *Pushing the Limits: The Female Administrative Aspirant* (1988). One assistant principal she interviewed explained: "If you go to the civil rights committee, honey, you probably won't ever get a good administrative position. Oh, you could win the case, but they can make life unbearable for you by giving you the worst school in the city. If you didn't have a hard time from then on, I'd be very, very surprised."[40]

In spite of the threat of retaliation, Edson found in her five-year study of women administrative aspirants that increasing numbers of women were contemplating legal action for relief against the persistent discrimination they experienced. They considered such measures because they found that without legal action, they were continually frustrated in their efforts for promotion. Regardless of the disadvantages, she noted that women were beginning to believe that they could prosecute, win, and possibly benefit from such an undertaking. Edson described study participants as hopeful that the courts may be changing enough to rule more favorably for women than in previous years. Finally, she noted that women may be sensing that political and legal power can be attained by those who take hold of the process—even if individual women must endure great resistance and antagonism from the educational structures they seek to lead.[41]

Typically in the 1970s and 1980s, school administrators and their allies insisted that sex discrimination in educational administration was a negligible problem even though women's participation in positions such as superintendencies was significantly below that of men.[42] Many have resented the intrusion of legal authority into the school administrative decision-making process and have, as a result, effected only the changes necessary to avoid court cases.[43] To this end a number of articles have appeared in education journals advising school administrators and boards of the tactics needed to avoid law suits.[44] Some have complained about the extra work needed to bring school systems into compliance with equity legislation. Occasionally, organizations have worked to undercut the process of ending sex discrimination in educational employment as Fishel and Pottker maintain that the Council of Chief State School Officers did when it lobbied the government to avoid collecting data on the superintendency by sex.[45]

As legal reform has begun to affect school systems around the country, a common response from persons in positions of leadership has been to agree ostensibly with the principles of sex equity in educational employment while at the same time engaging in conscious or unconscious discriminatory practices. A 1979 survey conducted by WEEA revealed that superintendents and school board presidents agreed: "Men and women should be given equal opportunity for participation in management training programs, . . . society should regard work by female administrators as being just as valuable as work by male administrators, . . . the educational community should someday accept women in key administrative positions, . . . it is acceptable for women to compete with men for top positions in educational administration, . . . [and] women have the capability to acquire the necessary skills to be successful administrators." Yet, in spite of these positive sentiments about women's potential for educational leadership, respondents also indicated that prejudice against women runs deep. For example, while 70 percent of the women surveyed agreed that "the possibility of pregnancy does not make women less desirable administrators than men," significantly fewer men agreed (44 percent of male superintendents and 41 percent of male school board presidents). Similar discrepancies in attitudes existed on statements about menstruation and the necessity for mothers to stay home to take care of children, both of which were thought to affect women's work performance. Apparently some have accepted equity in principle, but not when job candidates are demographically different from those who create, define, and control the positions. In sum, 43 percent of the school board presidents and 29 percent of the superintendents agreed that "some jobs . . . should remain men's jobs and other jobs should remain women's jobs."[46]

In spite of great public attention to issues of sex equity in employment and some legislative and judicial changes supporting women's chances in male-dominated fields, opinion on the necessity for these changes has been far from unanimous. In the late 1970s, for example, when many women believed their gains were mounting impressively, a powerful conservative backlash movement was quietly gaining strength. In the 1980 political season this movement demonstrated considerable clout and effectiveness in demolishing many of the advances of the women's movement. A conservative president was elected. Governmental agencies charged with enforcing equity legislation brought these efforts to a halt. The Family Protection Act, introduced in Congress in 1980, was aimed at discouraging teaching about women in "nontraditional" roles. In the face of growing attack on the feminist cause, even the founder of NOW, Betty Friedan, softened her position when she remarked in 1981, "I do not think women's rights are the most urgent business for American women."[47]

As I write this volume, women have begun attaining mid-level school administrative positions in impressive numbers. Slowly, they are also assuming more school superintendencies. This gradual change is not an accident, but rather is the result of persistent, courageous, collective efforts by activists determined to see equitable distribution of power in school employment. It is also a tribute to the women and men who have mentored and encouraged women onward. Beyond the efforts of key individuals, several organizations are devoted specifically to assisting women aspiring to school leadership. The AASA sponsors the Women's Caucus; the Women's Advisory Council, which publishes research related to women administrators and enjoys a growing social and political presence within the larger association; and the Women Administrators' Conference, an annual meeting that offers support for women either serving as administrators or seeking such positions. Patricia Schmuck points out that in recent years a large number of other regional and state organizations of women administrators have emerged to advocate women's continued active presence in school administration.[48]

Research on women school administrators has blossomed since the mid-eighties as well. Through the dedicated lobbying of women scholars, the American Educational Research Association has included sessions and symposia related to women administrators. Professional journals such as *Educational Administration Quarterly* have begun to devote greater attention to women administrators and the larger issue of sex equity in school employment. A number of important scholarly books have been published in the past two decades that explore the intersections of gender and traditions of school administration. Among them are such notable works as Charol Shakeshaft's *Women in Educational Administration* (1987, 1989), Catherine Marshall's *The Assistant Principal* (1992), Patricia Schmuck's *Sex Differentials in Public School Administration* (1975), Susan Chase's *Ambiguous Empowerment* (1995), Sari Knopp Biklen and Marilyn Brannigan's *Women and Educational Leadership* (1980), Meg Grogan's *Voices of Women Aspiring to the Superintendency* (1996), Sandra Gupton's *Highly Successful Women Administrators* (1996), Neal Gross and Anne Trask's *The Sex Factor and the Management of Schools* (1976), and numerous others.

Because of this and other recent research on equity in school administration, accounts describing the experiences of persons of color in school leadership are beginning to emerge—and these important projects are overdue. Long hidden in far greater obscurity than women school leaders in general, the very few persons of color who have led school districts have performed amazing feats of leadership, political skill, and management of the office in the face of deep racism in our society—all while aiming to improve the educational conditions of students in their districts. For example, Amie Revere describes Velma Ashley, who held the superintendency of the Boley, Oklahoma schools from 1944 to 1956. As an African American woman, Ashley's name and legacy have largely been overlooked. Revere also reports that by the early 1970s, three more African American women assumed superintendencies: Edith Gaines (Hartford, CT), Margaret Labat (Evanston, IL), and Barbara Sizemore (Washington, DC)—and in the 1984–85 school year, twenty-nine African American women held this office.[49] Nancy Arnez describes some of the women who held the office in the early 1980s, including Ruth Love, general superintendent of the Chicago schools.[50] As recently as 1996, however, Kofi Lomotey laments that we still know very little about African American educational leaders generally.[51] This breathtaking silence speaks volumes about the intractable problem of racism and the inequitable distribution of power in school leadership. The particular mechanisms of racism and sexism are quite different, although the net effect in school administration is similar in the sense that both persons of color and women are systematically discouraged from possessing at least a representative share of formally structured power in schools. The achievement of female superintendents of color is particularly striking because they have faced the dual oppressions of sexism and racism, making their ascent into school administration all the more difficult.

In an important effort to report the numbers of persons of color and women in school superintendencies, Effie Jones and Xenia Montenegro began tracking the demographics of these officeholders in the 1980s—with the sponsorship of the AASA. Montenegro's 1993 report indicates that persons of color accounted for only 3.5 percent of all superintendents that year, which is minimally higher than the 1981 figure of 2.2 percent. This meager growth rate invites detailed study and analysis. The same study reports that women's representation in the superintendency had grown faster—evidencing a linear increase from around 1 percent in 1980 to over 7 percent in 1993.[52]

Beyond the numbers, other studies indicate that persons of color and women are screened out of positions such as principalships of large high schools or superintendencies because these appointments are contingent upon attaining and successfully navigating through a series of intermediate administrative positions. Charles Moody describes systems of sponsorship into school administration that Whites take for granted, but that Blacks are often denied.[53] Catherine Marshall argues that the assistant principalship in particular serves as a gatekeeping position. Certain individuals are permitted access to assistant principalships, which may then allow them to rise in the administrative hierarchy. Others are sorted into dead-end administrative positions.[54] White males tend to receive the most effective mentoring, which allows them to move ahead in their careers, while persons of color and women are slotted into relatively difficult assignments, which often turn into long-term positions with little chance of promotion.

Even though there are many qualified women candidates for superintendencies, school boards, the organizations charged with filling these positions, evidently are not ready to select significant numbers of women for their educational leaders. School boards have themselves been composed mainly of men.[55] When the screening process for positions begins, boards tend to eliminate females from the pool of applicants except for token representation. School boards typically set criteria that minimize the viability of female candidates, such as requiring several years of superintendent experience. This is particularly difficult for women because they are underrepresented in this position from the start. When women candidates pass the initial screening and are invited for interviews, they find that school board members can put them in the uncomfortable position of asking illegal questions about family and personal business. Women who report violations are unlikely to receive appointments. Women who refuse to answer such inquiries are viewed as uncooperative. Women who choose to answer these questions candidly may find that their personal obligations are held against them while men are not similarly penalized.[56]

Even before the job-screening process begins, school boards usually show little initiative in identifying talented female applicants. Groups and associations that might be able to recommend potential women candidates are not consulted. Instead, school boards rely heavily on the services of executive head hunters to identify candidates for superintendencies. Some commercial organizations provide this service for a fee. State school board associations and educational administration professors at leading universities generally offer this service as a convenience for school boards. Commercial and state school board associations tend to compile pools of applicants for positions that include a token representation of women. When school boards choose male candidates, they defend their actions by asserting that they had considered at least one woman applicant. Such a practice helps school boards avoid losing legal battles involving Title VII, which requires that searches be open regardless of sex; yet it does little for increasing women's representation in superintendencies because there is no stipulation that school districts actually need to hire female candidates.[57]

In recent years, though, slightly greater numbers of women and persons of color have been appointed to superintendencies of large urban school systems; but arguably some of these systems are economically distressed and plagued with a host of problems. Only in desperate situations do school boards seem willing to hire women or persons of color for superintendencies. When school boards hire them, these school administrators face a range of subtle and overt forms of discrimination that make their work exceedingly difficult. Increased attention must be paid not only to equitable hiring, then, but also to creating conditions that foster the success and retention of superintendents once hired.[58] However, because these superintendents face insurmountable difficulties and sometimes fail, boards may feel justified in future discriminatory hiring practices—which essentially amounts to another double bind.

In some cases women simply are uninterested in pursuing superintendencies because the work is too far removed from the classroom and contact with students and teachers, or what they regard as the real work of education. The superintendency as it is configured holds little appeal for some women. Besides, when men are promoted, they advance into a primarily male realm where they are welcomed. When women are promoted, they often feel as though they have lost contact with their friends, many of whom are teachers—and teaching is still a profession numerically dominated by women.

Since the rise of the modern women's movement, women have used the political and legal systems to fight for some measure of access to power in public schools, at least to the extent that power inheres in positions of school administration; yet women's representation in these positions is still far short of their proportion in the teaching force. What must happen to make the distribution of power in schools more representative of individual school communities and the pool of educational workers as a whole?

7

CONCLUSION

During my senior year of high school, the last thing I wanted to do was teach. I had given some of my teachers fits and knew that it would be no fun on the receiving end of other adolescents' mood swings and social experiments. However, I had devoted myself to academic achievement and a wide variety of extracurricular activities throughout high school in part because I knew that without scholarships, I could not afford college. So I assumed important leadership roles in several activities; and in academic work I benefited from a few extraordinary teachers. Yet in spite of these outstanding high school experiences, I often felt frustrated with the inadequacies of our school, in how students were treated, and in the insulting layers of trivial, mind-numbing rules that students and teachers alike were expected to observe. What many regarded as a good, rural, Appalachian school seemed bleak and discouraging to me at times. In a fit of anger and idealistic passion, I decided in the last month of my senior year that I would become a teacher so I might somehow play a role in improving things.

As class president, I got to cut class one day to talk with our principal about some pending senior class graduation business. I had missed many classes over the years to work with this man on a variety of school-related projects. Sometimes I talked with him because I had been a troublemaker (I had edited the student newspaper and co-edited an issue of the underground newspaper at the same time); but sometimes I had served as a peacemaker (as the band drum major, I had mediated conflicts between the band and the administration). We knew each other well, and in spite of our differences, I respected this towering man in the school-color green leisure suit and enough turquoise jewelry to trigger metal detectors from a distance.

On this day, we quickly digressed from discussing business to reflecting on the events of the previous four years, and we did so while walking through the halls during class. It was then that I told him my of plan to become a teacher. Just as I had hoped, he beamed and expressed great pride in my career choice; however, he wanted to know why I wanted to teach because by then I had gotten my scholarship and theoretically could pursue other careers. I explained that there was much about schooling in general that needed improvement. I wanted to do what I could. For that reason, I hoped to teach, then become a principal, and later a superintendent—because it seemed from my vantage point that school administrators had the greatest flexibility and power to create the changes obviously needed. But what happened next is frozen in time for me.

He stopped in his tracks, stroked his chin a couple of times and then said, "You know, you can change things by staying in the classroom." I paused because this statement confused me. He might have been telling me that teaching is the most important work in schools and is where I should direct my efforts. However, he himself had chosen to leave the classroom for the principalship. Maybe he was implying that my potential for school leadership was inadequate. This interpretation did not seem likely, though, because he had praised my leadership frequently in public. Had he lied? Or he may have meant that teachers have more power than I perceived, and if I intended to be a reformer, the classroom would be the best place for my efforts. Or perhaps he meant that principals and superintendents do not have much power compared with teachers and therefore such aspirations would be a waste of my time. The latter two interpretations hardly seemed likely since he spent much time telling teachers exactly what he expected of them—and he rarely countenanced any discussion, let alone disagreement. Our conversation quickly ended as the last bell for the day rang. I walked away feeling deeply disappointed because I valued his opinion, which in this case I interpreted as a lack of confidence in me *as an individual.* It was not until I began my dissertation research that I realized he probably meant that I *as a woman* should not pursue school administration.

A few years after this conversation, I began my education career when I accepted a position as a physics teacher in a southern, economically depressed, industrial town. My first physics class had eleven young men and three women. Within a few years I managed to build a program of around seventy physics students with equal male and female representation. I devised a number of interesting, if not downright bizarre class activities and lessons—and I loved this work! Truly it seemed I had chosen the perfect job. Things would change, however.

Just before the start of my fourth and final year of teaching, the outgoing president of our local NEA affiliate called me. She explained that she had been unable to find anyone willing to serve as president for the upcoming year, and if I did not take the position, then the organization would fold. After recovering from the multiple shocks buried in this message, I told her that I felt utterly incompetent to assume this duty—I barely knew how to teach, much less to lead an organization of my more capable and mature peers. When she refused to take "no" for an answer, I reluctantly agreed.

That was a tough year to serve, too, because many teachers throughout the district had encountered difficulties with the relatively new district administration, thus there were misgivings among teachers about the local NEA unit. First, in a school system where students of color and White students accounted for roughly equal percentages, teachers of color had virtually disappeared. Some Black teachers had been harassed or fired. That year in response, we gathered statistics to document this phenomenon, but we had to do so by pooling the collective memories of teachers at each school because the district administration refused to gather this data. We reached the shocking conclusion that over the previous three years, teachers of color had declined from 28 to 11 percent. We announced these figures in a public forum, after which the district administration launched an ambitious recruiting initiative for teachers of color. This experience taught me important lessons about the persistence of institutional racism and the political value of demographic information.

Second, a number of male and female teachers who seemed even vaguely outside conventional heterosexuality were refused promotion, transferred against their will, demoted, or punished for unrelated reasons. There was little legal support for defending these teachers outright because our state, with a notoriously homophobic senator, had no laws to protect teachers, or anyone else, against discrimination based on real or perceived differences in sexual orientation.

And finally, during those years I repeatedly saw extremely talented, intelligent, and capable women denied promotions to principalships and the superintendency. One school board member even told a female candidate for the superintendency: "We're just not ready for a woman around here." She knew that if she brought a suit based on this discriminatory comment, she would never get another administrative position. I wondered if I would ever stand a chance myself.

I became a social activist that year. Well-intentioned colleagues told me that if I aspired to a career in school administration, I might as well forget it because word of my efforts would follow me around the state. So I went to graduate school hoping that I might somehow make sense of what had happened to my dream of improving schools.

As I began researching this project for my dissertation, I came to understand that I was only one of many persons through the decades who have been frustrated in their efforts to improve the schools. In particular, I realized that gender discrimination played an inescapable role in shaping my experiences in public schools—both as a student and teacher. Teachers have little structural support for devising their own curricula, determining their own schedules, deciding who should be accepted into their ranks, and otherwise controlling the terms and conditions of their work and environment. These decisions usually are made by school or system-level administrators, most of whom are men. Over the past century, women have been systematically restricted in their access to these administrative positions. Women, then, essentially have little formally structured control over the purposes or conditions of the profession they dominate numerically.

In the early 1990s when I started this project, this phenomenon seemed particularly odd to me because women were making rapid progress in the legal, medical, religious, and business professions, even though they had not yet cracked the upper strata in significant numbers. Educational employment, in contrast, seemed to be moving forward disturbingly slowly. Initially, I simply had assumed that women had never wielded any meaningful power in education, but that assumption kept me from asking deeper questions about how that state of affairs had evolved. As I began to question my own assumptions, this research started to emerge.

Why do women have so little formal power in public schooling? This question seems to deserve a simple, clear answer that structures the messiness of human events into a geometrically flawless theory. The difficulty, though, is that much of the story defies a unitary understanding or grand explanatory narrative. Whenever I am tempted to describe the historical flow of complex events with a neat model, I quickly discover the profound limitations of such an approach. This story, like any other, is rich and varied, and the events of one context never translate precisely into clear lessons for another. Though I refrain from offering an overarching, summarizing theory, I will explore a few ideas discussed in this work.

First, not all men and women have accepted the strictly gendered division of roles and power in school employment. For example, in spite of their limited social, political, and economic resources, some women have exercised extraordinary agency in shaping the course of public schooling. Before common schools first appeared, women sought formal education, and when that was denied them because it supposedly expanded their gender-appropriate sphere too far, Catharine Beecher forwarded the argument that women would perform more effectively in their designated domestic sphere if they could be educated. Women such as Emma Willard set up exemplary institutions devoted to women's education. Then to broaden women's sphere of influence further, women sought a profession, or work outside the home that justified their receiving education. Beecher and others proposed that women should teach—which was essentially a natural extension of their domestic duties as wives and mothers. In enormous numbers women took up their "first public profession." Though women still had few legal rights, women's activists were able to leverage their work as teachers into a broad campaign for women's rights, especially suffrage. With the turn-of-the-century women's movement, women moved into positions of power in public school employment. When they sought fully equal power and status with men in running schools, however, the broad organizational clout of the women's movement met its match in the subtle, pervasive, and powerful will of a few men eager to preserve their own power. After a period of retrenchment, the modern women's movement utilized the legal system to win professional advancement in educational employment and access to power. Even more recently, women aspiring to administrative positions and their allies have begun to organize among themselves, distribute information, lobby for reform, publish research and information that exposes injustices of the system, and provide moral support and social networks. Little by little, women's representation in positions of formal power in education is in fact increasing.

Women, then, have not been powerless victims. Over the past century and a half, individuals and organized groups of women have exercised impressive power in dismantling millennia of Western patriarchal tradition. Women's resistance has taken varied forms. In some cases they have squarely confronted their oppression and oppressors. At other times, they have worked within narrow parameters to maneuver for greater influence, essentially turning a position of weakness into strength. For instance, although separate spheres ideology should have confined middle-class women to their homes, to bear children, and never to veer into the world of public concerns, these women managed to exploit the limitations of the ideology to expand their roles and power. If women were to raise children, then they should have dominion over childrearing even outside the home. Dualistic ideologies can be played both ways.

Catharine Beecher cleverly capitalized on the limitations of separate spheres ideology in this manner. However, by continuing to operate within this dualistic belief system, she and others risked backlash and unanticipated new forms of oppression because binary logic can tolerate only so much deviation. Even though women claimed teaching as their own distinctive profession that allowed them legitimately to work outside the domestic sphere, the implicit limitation of this development was that men would need to create a parallel profession from which they could exert controlling influence, much as they did in the home. Where women complied with the wishes of their husbands and fathers, in schools they acquiesced to male supervisors and superintendents—even when these men otherwise had little educational experience or expertise to offer teachers.

Historian Linda Kerber has suggested that a potentially fruitful means of analyzing separate spheres ideology in women's history is to examine men's and women's separate spheres literally, that is, to study the physical spaces they each have inhabited and controlled.[1] It is noteworthy that when women first assumed duties as schoolteachers, they usually worked in areas distinct from those used by men. Multiclassroom schools in cities tended to place the schoolmaster upstairs with older students, while women tutored younger students downstairs. Later when "egg crate" schools became popular, women teachers managed individual classrooms arranged along corridors with a principal's office placed in the most central, commanding position. Women teachers of one-room schoolhouses in rural areas managed their class spaces on a day-to-day basis, yielding to occasional visits by roving male superintendents who otherwise maintained separate administrative offices among the male-owned businesses of the community. Outside school activity, single women teachers spent their primary time living with neighborhood families who provided them with room and board (and usually a measure of scrutiny), renting space at a boarding house (frequently under the community's watchful eye), or staying at home with their kin (to whom they were legally responsible). In each of these cases, women enjoyed little if any privacy because they had to accommodate the needs and schedules of their hosts. Women teachers generally had few physical spaces they could control.

Interestingly, one-room schoolhouses provided women with a space where they could be independent much of the time. They set up and maintained these schools and even dictated who could access the space. Occasionally women even inhabited these schoolhouses, representing a remarkable shift in women's possibilities because in these cases women not only controlled their workspace, but also their living space. They nearly became independent of men in their day-to-day lives. When Josephine Preston spearheaded the effort to build teacherages for single women teachers in the early decades of the twentieth century, even greater numbers of women had the luxury of controlling their own private spaces. In some cases, teacherages hosted several women teachers and thus became separate communities of women. However, administrators provided some official oversight to keep women's independence from going too far.

At the same time, male school administrators also enjoyed control over their own workspaces. They socialized primarily with a closed group of men in their communities, and participated in all-male or primarily male professional education associations. Male administrators did not socialize with female teachers, in part to avoid scandal, but also by all accounts, they seemed to prefer the social company of other males. Besides, many men believed that close professional association with women diminished their stature.

In some ways, contemporary schooling maintains the tradition of gender-segregated spaces and gender-specific control. Administration, primarily a male realm, is physically removed from teaching, a primarily female domain. The chasm between the superintendency and the classroom has widened. Superintendents in medium to large systems rarely visit classrooms or teachers in a meaningful, ongoing manner except for ceremonial occasions or to make public gestures. Otherwise, teachers with business to conduct with administrators usually must break away from teaching duties to go to a remote downtown location. Not only is there physical separation between these realms, but the matter of who controls the space is still relevant. The contemporary classroom provides teachers little of the independence of the one-room schoolhouse. Classrooms are subject to the constant supervision of building level administrators who monitor furniture arrangements, physical conditions, curricular mandates, and classroom conduct, but otherwise provide little instructional assistance. Teachers rarely may deviate in their use or control of classroom space. Teachers have little power to control their own working conditions.

What makes segregated physical space particularly relevant to this volume is that as superintendents and teachers have become increasingly physically removed, there has been a corresponding decline in meaningful dialogue. The dialogue that exists tends to be formal, artificially dualistic, and often antagonistic. Such is usually the consequence of separation. When administrators insist on physical segregation, metaphorical and literal barriers are effectively erected that perpetuate an unequal distribution of power. These barriers make it more difficult for teachers to share institutional power with administrators.

Yet this tidy analysis of the problems inherent in a dualistic model of "men's space" and "women's space" is more complex than it may at first seem. Although sex stratification and segregation have gone hand-in-hand to produce a system where women generally have little significant power or controlling influence on the shape of public schooling, at times the separation has worked to women's modest advantage. In the early decades of this century when men and women arguably were segregated most in public school employment—because women accounted for 86 percent of all teachers and men held around 89 percent of all superintendencies—women created powerful organizations that included teachers unions and a variety of women's associations. Within these segregated social networks, women amassed important power. Historian Estelle Freedman argues that women's separate communities and organizations have at times provided valuable spaces for women to create strength and establish mutual support that might not have been possible otherwise.[2] Certainly some men have consolidated their power through connections with all-male networks. Sex segregation has offered single-sex communities bases of social support. The problem here, though, is that men's groups have had far more power to begin with—and when they have closed ranks, they have in effect kept women from sharing power, especially when it has seemed as though women might be making extraordinary political, social, and economic gains.

Sex has not been the only dimension of social segregation in public school employment. When persons of diverse racial, cultural, and ethnic groups, as well as different economic classes, have constituted growing portions of the overall population, superintendents as a group have safeguarded their homogeneity as White, Protestant men of European descent. It is as though social diversity has inspired efforts to consolidate control more completely in the hands of established power groups. For instance, when teachers unions organized and gained power in the early decades of the twentieth century, superintendents collectively aimed to dismantle them. They simultaneously endeavored to enhance their own reputations as professionals removed from the laboring classes, including teachers. As persons of color and diverse cultural backgrounds have accounted for growing portions of the overall population, school leadership has remained firmly in the hands of Whites. Rhetoric calling for uniformity and efficiency conveniently masks what amounts to institutional racism, fear of cultural diversity, or desperate concern about class conflict.

Recently a friend asked me a simple, yet critically important question that left me stumbling and grasping for a worthy answer. "What should we do about women's relative lack of formal power in public schools?" In that moment I was reminded of my short-lived work as a teacher/social activist. Then I wondered: Is it appropriate for an academic to prescribe a specific course for change? Many academics stop short of this because it borders on political activism, and the academic tradition requires maintaining the appearance of impartiality. I am not impartial, however. I adamantly want to see greater sex and gender equity in the negotiation of educational power.

To some it may seem that the most obvious solution to women's lack of power in public schooling is to recruit more women for superintendencies. This simple solution is inadequate for several reasons, however. First, it unquestioningly accepts the notion that the superintendency and school administration are appropriate structures for distributing power in public schools. While there is no doubt that school administrators often provide valuable services to students, teachers, and school communities, I wish to suggest that the present configuration of school administration is inextricably woven with traditional gender definitions that are premised on males controlling females. Unless that tradition and the resulting administrative structures are carefully deconstructed, a reliance on the present structure risks perpetuating the same power inequities, but perhaps cut along different social dimensions.

Second, the tactic of reversing a tradition of gender inequity by putting more women into superintendencies effectively ignores the complexity of how power is constructed. Surely women's movement activists thought they would gain much more power in controlling public schools when they campaigned for and won the right to vote in school elections. However, just as women won suffrage, school administrators around the country lobbied to take the superintendency out of politics—which had the effect of denying women the full voice and power they had sought. To make one simple change in a structure without also considering the persons who comprise the structure, how they interact, how they fit into the larger culture, and what their experiences are as individuals, is to risk creating a rigid structure that might just as soon be used against women as for them. This has happened repeatedly over the past 150 years.

Third, cynics easily can manipulate to their advantage the simple solution of hiring more women superintendents. To them, the only effort needed to dampen women's complaints is to provide a superficial, easily measured solution—that is, to increase the numbers of women school administrators without also altering the deep structure of schooling.

Fourth, some women's activists seem to assume that women invariably provide good school leadership while men do not. Obviously, this is not true. Some women provide less than stellar leadership, all other things being equal; conversely, some men offer outstanding, sensitive leadership. To say that women should be school administrators simply because of their sex is just as dangerous as the time-honored practice of insisting that only men be leaders because of their sex.

Finally, the practice of simply promoting women into superintendencies avoids questioning and analyzing the deeper, more troubling, and sacred issue of who has power to shape and control schools. The superintendency is one manifestation of formal power in public schooling, and sometimes a highly symbolic one at that; but a broad array of other individuals and constituencies also have power in schools, including school boards, teachers organizations, local politicians, moneyed interests, well-organized community groups, media, corporations with educational interests, governmental organizations, and a host of others. For a deeper analysis of the structure of power, these constituencies, individual persons, and larger social forces must all be understood in their infinitely complex patterns of interaction. The superintendency, then, is not a neat center of power in public schooling.

And besides, even if one were to accept the superintendency as the main seat of structured power in schools, and therefore the site for correcting past inequities, many women simply do not aspire to the superintendency as it is currently configured. Does this mean that women do not tend to want power? Through the years some analysts have blamed women for their lack of ambition or desire for power in schools. Women, however, have had little if any role in defining and shaping the structure of public schools and the superintendency in particular. Some men have constructed it as a position that would appeal to a narrow class of men, to elevate their status in a profession of women. Why would large numbers of women suddenly desire a position that was created largely by and for a few men? Are many women simply limiting themselves by not aspiring to the superintendency as it is now configured? Or is it perhaps that as persons who still do not enjoy fully equal rights with men, they intimately understand the mechanisms of oppression and wish to avoid perpetuating the same on others?

Regardless of how some women differ from men or why, many women explain that they do not aspire to administrative advancement for reasons such as: "I don't want to leave my students—that's where my heart is"; "In administration, you're totally isolated from the people you care about"; "It's all politics and gamesmanship"; "You work so many hours that you never have any time for your family or what you care about"; or perhaps very simply, "That work just doesn't appeal to me."

Let me break each of these statements down a bit. When women indicate that they do not want to leave the classroom, their contact with students, other teachers, or the community, those holding a patriarchal worldview might believe that such women lack ambition. However, schools could just as easily have been configured so that administrators worked more closely with teachers and students. School districts could have remained small instead of growing into consolidated, monstrous bureaucracies with large tax bases for paying high enough administrative salaries to attract men seeking executive compensation and status— as well as distance from the female cadre of teachers. Administration also could have emerged to serve, rather than control, the work of teachers. Through much of this century, medical and legal administrators have served doctors and attorneys in facilitating the logistics and business aspects of the work; however, most doctors and lawyers despise administrators' dictating the terms of their legal and medical practice, or questioning their professional judgment. In contrast, school administration, especially the superintendency, has been configured to exist in a remote location from the classroom and to exert a controlling influence on the work of teachers. If women and men value the work of teaching, why should they have to leave it to "move up"? I argue that the present configuration of school administration and the lack of a self-defined promotional system for teachers have their roots in the gender-segregated and stratified legacy of tax-supported schooling.

When women say that they do not want to leave the persons and the work they care about, there are several issues to consider. There is an implicit assumption in the hierarchical structure of schooling that teachers are among those with the least value. Their salaries are relatively low; their sanction to control their own working conditions is limited compared with others higher in the hierarchy; and they must obey the wishes of administrators above them. Even though some school leaders might employ public language praising the fine and valuable work of teachers, teachers are not generally valued in the actual structure of schooling. Hierarchies impose differential value: those at the top are more valuable to the system than those at the bottom. In defiance of this value system, however, many teachers, both male and female, believe that teaching truly is the most important work in the schools and regard a move away from students as counterproductive. Besides, many persons enter teaching to create relationships with students, to develop and foster caring, intellectually stimulating connections that help students grow, but that also are personally rewarding to teachers. Administrative work, as it is now structured, is remarkably cut off from these social possibilities.

When school administrators, especially superintendents, manage to maintain caring relationships with people in their school communities, it is a testament to the resilience and persistence of a particular individual who perseveres in spite of the system, because the structure of the office itself makes caring and the maintenance of relationships difficult. Administrators are physically removed. The distribution of power among superintendents, school employees, students, and the school community is profoundly lopsided and renders attempts at true collegiality and connection difficult at best.[3] Yet many superintendents in the past lobbied diligently to have broad powers, physical separation, and reduced connections with school employees, most of whom were women. Such changes made the work more appealing and respectable to the few men who measured their masculinity by their professional and social association with other men—and distance from women.

When women complain that school administration is "all politics and gamesmanship," they might mean that it is conducted from a distance, essentially in an abstract, gamelike structure where power is constantly negotiated, shifting imperceptibly with each potentially bungled policy or victorious reform; where one interest persistently strives to dominate another; where cumulative scores are kept and winners rule. The game often becomes more important and real than individuals, and the game is quite removed from the immediacy of personal connection and relationship—where rules and policies serve as guides rather than tools of control.

When women indicate that administration holds little appeal because it demands long hours so that there is little time for family, they may be revealing a great deal about gender-role differences in family structures. In spite of significant social change over the past century, women still perform most of the work of raising children and managing their households, whether they are married and have traditional nuclear families or not, and whether they hold full-time jobs or not. Women employed in the public sector usually clock their forty plus hours and then assume full-time duties as mothers and/or partners on top of that. Though men now contribute more to the domestic workload than they used to, women still perform the bulk of the work.[4] School administration, especially in the post-World War II years, became a job that demanded longer hours and heavy work-related social obligations. These demands increasingly required that administrators have devoted partners willing to handle domestic chores. School administration journals even published articles advising administrator's wives of the special duties expected of them. Such administrative expansion effectively made the work much more difficult for women who, even when they served as superintendents, found that they still bore primary responsibility for raising children and taking care of the home.

Should women simply cast off socially defined constraints requiring them to assume the bulk of domestic work? Again, a solution is not easy. Women and men must be able to negotiate their roles without having default imperatives thrust upon them. To insist that women discard their socially defined roles is to expect them to bear the brunt of all social change without also providing any support—especially in dealing with inevitable backlash. The work of the superintendency has been structured to fit better with conventional gender-role expectations for males than for females. And persons who cross their gender-associated roles, such as men who desire female-associated duties or women who seek male-associated ones, are stigmatized and usually discouraged or prevented from attaining desired positions. Women and men who defy traditional gender roles are labeled as deviant, perhaps as gay or lesbian. Women who assert their heterosexuality and otherwise test the limits of gender-role scripting are known as aggressive, ruthless—or worse.

In sum, the solution is not simply to get more women into superintendencies, but rather there must be a larger reconceptualization of how power is structured in public schooling. In that process it is imperative to consider whether social structures systematically deny power to individuals or groups. What certainly confounds efforts at reconceptualizing power in schools is that our larger society itself is structured quite unequally. Persons who are White, moneyed, male, Christian, well-educated, and from geographically privileged regions of the country have significantly more power by default than other individuals. Within this larger context, it is difficult to create a haven of equity and social fairness, with active, though sometimes painful deliberation; yet I believe this is precisely what must occur. After all, what happens in schools influences what happens in society and vice versa.

Any discussion of power in public schooling must include teachers, both as participants in the process as well as in the distribution of power. Perhaps as much as women have been denied power in public school employment, I also argue that teachers as a class have been kept from power, except when they have organized and demanded it. Since teachers forfeited much of their independence and decision-making authority when the profession shifted from men to women, which is when male administrators were added, then clearly the discrepancy in power in educational employment is embedded in traditional gender-role definitions. Even today, men are not as likely to take up the work of teaching as women because currently it is configured with little power, and therefore is work that some men (and women) regard as beneath their dignity.

For power to be distributed more equitably in public schooling, those who currently have a disproportionate share must be willing to relinquish it. That usually does not happen in a vacuum, however, but instead occurs when groups with relatively little power organize and force the matter, when law or public policy requires an open process of power negotiation, or when positions of power become so unpalatable that persons privileged with choice regard them as undesirable. Arguably this final condition may be occurring already in some economically distressed urban school districts. It is in these districts that persons of color and women are beginning to attain administrative positions with some regularity.

Those who must consent to relinquishing some of their power must also be willing for others to have more. Teachers perform the staggering bulk of formally educating our nation's youth. Yet they have been cut out of power, bit by bit, especially in school governance. With each successive administrative layer added to the bureaucratic hierarchy, teachers' decision-making authority has been reduced and replaced with administrative dictates, commands, a series of prescribed steps, lessons, and methods that teachers must implement with mindless precision. Teachers usually begin their careers with lofty goals and dreams of "making a difference" to young people and their communities, but they often end up feeling beaten down, discouraged from thinking and trying things, and utterly burned out in a system that makes little provision for their intelligence or creativity. Besides, when schools fail to capitalize on the gifts of their primary workers, a vast reservoir of innovation and passion remains untapped. And ultimately teachers grow weary, feel like automatons, and then pass on their sense of bitterness and drudgery to their students.

In this century, school administrators often have labored to control teachers, or they have treated teachers like abstract enemies, embattled opponents who need to be reminded where power resides. This antagonism, I argue, is born of separation between teachers and administrators, separation in power, social relationship, race and ethnicity, culture, economic class, physical space, sex, and gender. If power truly is to be renegotiated, teachers and administrators must be willing to bridge these differences.

Perhaps no one has explained this process better than Ella Flagg Young. Young, as has been noted throughout this volume, provided remarkable leadership of the enormously complex Chicago Schools as well as the NEA. She also served as an important symbol to suffrage-era women of their hopes and possibilities. Less well noted in the historical record is that she also was a gifted theorist. She studied with John Dewey at the University of Chicago where he supervised her doctoral studies. There, she edited a series of books with him, and together they worked through vexing theoretical and practical issues concerning

Dewey's emerging work on the relationships between democracy and education. He was fond of saying that Young was the person who best knew how to implement democratic education in schools. Their collaboration was rich, mutual, and ongoing until Dewey moved to Columbia University in New York. Young's dissertation, *Isolation in the Schools*, which was published by the University of Chicago Press in 1900, is an important intellectual accomplishment that has broad implications for contemporary schooling.[5]

The premise of *Isolation in the Schools* is that schools have become highly differentiated institutions where individuals are dehumanized and separated from their intelligence. Differentiation occurs across a number of parameters such as grade-level divisions and hierarchical strata. For example, in describing the division of schools into kindergartens, elementary and secondary schools, colleges, and universities, she explained that: "The parts have been brought together mechanically, thus making the accepted conception of this great social institution that of an aggregation of independent units, rather than that of an organization whose successful operation depends upon a clearly recognized interrelation, as well as distinction, between its various members and their particular duties."[6] Thus division in what is otherwise a whole and holistic institution creates a degree of isolation in purpose that shows up particularly when children move from one school to the next and face discontinuities in the purpose, structure, and content of schooling.

Young also described the process by which teachers were isolated from their reasoning and decision-making faculties by a class of administrative personnel determined to make all significant educational decisions for them. She was deeply concerned that teachers might be reduced to mere "operatives" subjected to a prescribed course of instruction that "is mapped out in minute details, and the time to be devoted to each part, the order in which the steps are to be taken, and even the methods of teaching, are definitely and authoritatively prescribed. As a result the teacher is not free to teach according to his 'conscience and power,' but his high office is degraded to the grinding of prescribed grists, in prescribed quantities, and with prescribed fineness—to the turning of the crank of a revolving mechanism."[7] She noted the simultaneous evolution of "an extensive 'business of supervision,' because of the effort to have uniformity in teachers and methods; . . . because of the desire of the strong administrative character to guide others rather than to be in the treadmill."[8] Superintendents typically hired a thick layer of administrative assistants, assistant superintendents, and supervisors, who further insulated superintendents from the business of the schools so that when problems inevitably cropped up, they were usually among the last to realize it. Such isolation reduced the effectiveness and humanity of schools, she argued.[9]

Young also carried a lucid vision of how things needed to change, not a simplistic vision, to be sure, but one that hinted at an ongoing process and required the negotiation and reconfiguration of power among persons working in schools. She explained that first, teachers needed to see their situations more clearly. They also needed the power to have their own ideas and to carry them out, that teachers must be entrusted with the freedom and responsibility to implement their duties using their own judgment.

> In cities where the teaching corps has become aroused to the evils ensuing from a differentiation that means isolation, there are greater possibilities of a healthful readjustment in the organization than in those where the tension is not definitely recognized, for the members are reaching that point of view from which they see that it is not liberty in carrying out, it is freedom and responsibility in origination also, that will make the whole corps a force, a power in itself. To predicate freedom for teachers in the superintendent's position, or for teachers in the principal's or the supervisor's position, is not sufficient to establish freedom as an essential; it must be predicated for all teachers. To prove that some cannot teach unless they possess freedom is not enough; it must be predicated that freedom belongs to that form of activity which characterizes the teacher. The schools will be purged of the uncultured, nonprogressive element, the fetters that bind the thoughtful and progressive will be stricken off, when the work is based on an intelligent understanding of the truth that freedom is an essential of that form of activity known as the teacher.[10]

She argued that the responsibilities of teaching so configured could not help but attract truly capable persons while discouraging those disposed toward the mechanical and superficial. And, she maintained, it would not be enough for administrators to give teachers power; teachers needed their own power from the start. For Young, this configuration of power was contingent upon democratic process, actively involving teachers in the intellectual and legislative functions of schools. This process was to be more than merely "giving input" or "having a voice," which are little more than symbolic gestures, but rather involved having real power. This was to be part of a holistic social system with students and other members of the school community also engaged in meaningful democratic process. Otherwise, she warned that schools risked preparing students for predetermined slots in society, squashing individuals' capacity for responsible and free thought, and causing students and teachers to "lose their souls."

Young's vision, however, was not widely shared by other administrators of her time because it demanded that its adherents undertake the difficult and sometimes messy work of sustained intellectual deliberation. It also required administrators to relinquish some of their control, certainly not to allow power to inhere in the position of teacher. Most administrators were far more concerned with enhancing the prestige of their own work, especially as they came under public attack, or were not fully respected by members of the business and professional communities because of their association with women's work.

In the end, Ella Flagg Young held a vision not only of women being "destined to rule the schools of every city," but she also saw the necessity of a process and configuration of power that might fully make a gender shift possible. It was not enough that women simply fill superintendencies or administrative positions; it was also essential that the relationships in schooling change and that the purpose of schooling be reevaluated. After all, she had not lost her vision of the kinds of persons who should work in and emerge from the Chicago schools. She would not separate the process of schooling from the lessons that students and teachers learned in classrooms and took away into their lives.

And so we must be mindful of how schools are structured. Students observe who has power in schools, who makes the rules, who enforces rules, and how those with less power must respond. They understand that administrators are usually men and teachers women; thus they absorb profound lessons about the roles men and women are expected to fill in our larger society. If we continue to support schools that systematically distribute power unequally by sex and gender, we send a forceful message to students about women's worth, their potential, and their place in society. Gross inequities in one part of the educational system will inevitably be perpetuated in others. A truly fair system for female and male students will not exist until we question the deeply rooted tradition of denying women power in public schooling.

And then we must change it.

Appendix: Historical Data on Women's Representation in the School Superintendency

Few women currently serve as American school superintendents, an odd phenomenon since education and teaching have long been known as "women's work." While this simple assertion echoes through discussions, forums, journals, and reports, seldom is substantiation offered beyond anecdotal evidence or data based on statistical studies of sampled superintendent populations that in some cases do not accurately depict the number of women. Few studies of entire superintendent populations have been conducted and of these, none has been undertaken in a systematic, ongoing fashion over the course of the century. As a result, accurate historical data describing the number of women superintendents has been noticeably missing in discussions about superintendent employment trends. This omission seems particularly ironic because, as Tyack and Hansot have observed, school administrators and researchers have collected prodigious amounts of other detailed statistical information throughout the twentieth century.[1]

As a means of addressing this statistical void, I have undertaken a systematic numerical study of the superintendency in the twentieth century. The first step in this project involved locating a comprehensive reference containing information about every school superintendent. Second, I compiled a computer database of the listed superintendents for the years 1910, 1930, 1950, 1970 and 1990. Through analysis of the resulting records for 51,661 persons, trends in superintendent employment by sex have emerged. This appendix describes this study in some detail. First, it includes a brief outline of the history of published studies of the superintendency by sex. Then it reports the methods and results of the study.

Review of Existing Superintendent Data by Sex

Statistical reports describing superintendents by sex have been published only sporadically over the last 150 years. From the mid-1800s through the peak of the suffrage movement, education proponents compiled massive collections of general information about schools that often included data broken down by sex for students and nearly every type of school employee. Federal government reports even occasionally included articles detailing women's progress in school leadership positions. However, as the suffrage movement gained strength, data describing educational administrators by sex virtually disappeared from print. This practice of excluding statistical reports on women in educational leadership positions largely persisted until the early 1970s when the modern women's movement inspired public discussion about women's traditional roles in society. At this time a number of women's advocacy groups, researchers, and some newly created government agencies produced reports designed to fill gaps in the data by sex. Many of these reports conflicted with each other as researchers labored to recreate a past for which only scattered documentation existed.

Early Reports

From the years following the Civil War to the early 1900s, the annually published *Report of the Commissioner of Education* provided a great deal of information about students and school employees by sex, occasionally even including articles describing women's record of attaining superintendencies. The 1873 report, for example, observed that the practice in western states of electing women county superintendents represented a novel experiment that should be watched closely. Accompanying the text was detailed information describing the few women who had won these positions.[2] Otherwise little information on women superintendents was gathered in an ongoing fashion, leading the editor of the 1900–1901 volume to explain that "the number of women serving as district school officers appears to be comparatively large, but there are no complete statistics on this point."[3] Perhaps to remedy this shortcoming, a few subsequent volumes provided data on the sex of persons holding the indistinct position title "supervisory personnel." This data is difficult to interpret, however, since at the time the terms "supervisor" and "superintendent" often were used interchangeably and also may have included assistant superintendents and other administrators. When Philander Claxton assumed the responsibilities of commissioner of education in 1911, however, the annual reports stopped including any information depicting women's representation in the superintendency or other administrative positions. Ironically, this same year the *Report* listed the sex of every reindeer in each Alaskan district since the Bureau of Education bore responsibility for the Alaska Reindeer Service at the time. Where the bureau could compile detailed data on exactly 33,629 reindeer, the sex of some 6,000 superintendents remained undocumented.[4]

Women's rights advocates complained about this lack of officially documented information. Writing in 1919 for the suffragist magazine *The Woman Citizen*, Louise Connolly observed: "You may search the educational literature of the past two decades for this tendency [of superintendents keeping women out of their ranks] and you will search in vain! The journals which they edit, the conventions which they run, and associations which they form, say nothing about it."[5]

Occasionally, isolated writers or representatives of organized women's groups laboriously compiled data on women superintendents themselves. Edith Lathrop, writing for the then newly organized National Council of Administrative Women in Education, in 1922 published her own such informally collected information. Her monograph, *Teaching as a Vocation for College Women*, urged college-educated women to pursue teaching and school leadership because county superintendencies, especially those in the West, offered women opportunities. She reported that 276 women held county superintendencies in 1900, a number that by her count had grown impressively to 857 by 1922. While her data was not comprehensive because it omitted female city, district, and township superintendents, her report offers a rare instance of published suffrage-era data enumerating women superintendents.[6]

A few years after Lathrop's report appeared, an unidentified women's group pressured the Research Division of the NEA to tabulate the number of women superintendents serving across the country. In response, *The School Review* in 1928 printed a brief, two-paragraph article that included tables accurately documenting the number of women county superintendents.[7] Again, however, counts were omitted that might have depicted the comparatively paltry representation of women among local superintendents. Since the NEA did not continue to collect even this limited data, pressure from the unidentified group of women may have provided the main impetus for compiling these statistics. The NEA leadership of the time undoubtedly found other research endeavors to be more worthy of attention.[8]

Women's groups were not the only ones lobbying for information about school administrators. In the face of increasing public malignment, members of the NEA Department of Superintendence sought to "elevate the profession" of school administrators by collecting and publishing statistical information that would bolster their status. The department conducted a series of major surveys that queried thousands of selected superintendents around the country about their personal and professional characteristics as well as their job experiences. The results of the first four such surveys were exhaustively reported in the 1923, 1933, 1952, and 1960 yearbooks of the department. David Tyack analyzed these reports and found that in 1923 and 1933, the report editors did not include sex among survey data relevant for publication. The 1952 survey, however, listed 99.4 percent of superintendents as male. The 1960 study included only men, which overlooked several hundred women county and local superintendents.[9] Clearly, the image that the department sought to portray was not one that included women.

Contemporary Reports

Few other published reports besides those of the Department of Superintendence documented the existence of women superintendents from the 1920s through the 1960s. The 1960s, however, witnessed the emergence of the modern women's movement. President Kennedy's Commission on the Status of Women produced both a tightly organized network of women interested in promoting women's social advancement and a governmental mechanism for collecting data on women's conditions in society; it therefore served as an effective catalyst for future women's advocacy. Two years after the commission published its widely discussed 1963 report, the National Council of Administrative Women in Education released its own study documenting the rapid Cold War–era decline of women elementary school principals.[10] In this atmosphere of heightened awareness of women's recent administrative losses, the Department of Elementary School Principals of the NEA published *The Elementary School Principalship in 1968*, a study that offered historical data broken down by sex describing the number of elementary school principals. Like the NCAWE study, the Department of Elementary School Principals report indicated that the percentage of female elementary school principals had declined rapidly after World War II. Where in 1928 women had accounted for 55 percent of elementary school principals, they held only 41 percent in 1948, 38 percent in 1958, and finally only 22.4 percent in 1968.[11] Hungry for proof of women's declining presence in school leadership, women's advocates eagerly cited these two studies in numerous articles that appeared over the next decade.

Women's movement pressure soon mounted for more exhaustive and ongoing accounting of women's participation not only in the principalship, but also in other educational leadership positions. In 1971, the NEA published a report documenting women's presence in a variety of education positions. This study was based on surveys of school employees and included sex as a category of analysis. Out of 14,379 superintendents in 1970–71, the authors of the study estimated that only ninety, or .6 percent were women.[12] Since the NEA researchers surveyed only a selected subset of the population of superintendents, it missed several hundred women county superintendents.[13] The sampling method was not documented in the report.

In the same year as the NEA study, the AASA released its fifth detailed study of the superintendency. This report continued in the tradition of the earlier Department of Superintendence reports by documenting the personal, demographic, and professional characteristics of the nation's superintendents. Although the 1952 and 1963 Department of Superintendence reports made limited, if any mention of the sex of superintendents, the 1971 AASA report included sex as a category of analysis. The results revealed that women accounted only for around 1.3 percent of all superintendents; however, like the NEA report, this survey missed many of the women who served as county superintendents.[14]

In 1972, the Council of Chief State School Officers weighed in with its own study of school superintendents with data broken down by sex. Unlike the NEA and AASA reports, this study purported to have surveyed all 16,653 school districts in the country. The results indicated that women superintended only 86 local operating districts and 131 intermediate districts.[15] Though the council claimed to have compiled comprehensive statistics, it significantly underrepresented the number of women superintendents, especially those holding county-level positions.[16] Interestingly, the council gathered this information even though Andrew Fishel and Janice Pottker contended in the late 1970s that "the Council of Chief State School Officers . . . has made a persistent effort to get Congress and the executive branch to restrict and limit the collection of data relating to civil rights enforcement."[17] If Fishel and Pottker's assertion is correct, then the council's study arguably might have been intended to reduce the pressure on the federal government to undertake systematic studies of school administrators by sex.

Women's rights activists expressed frustration with these statistical studies, complaining that the data was not complete or detailed enough to be useful in pursuing sex equity policies through the ranks of all school personnel. In an article published in 1971 in the *American School Board Journal*, Betty Friedan and Anne West demanded "the publication of annual reports showing the number of men and the number of women holding school-related jobs at each level of rank and salary."[18] Finding this data difficult to procure from organizations resistant to women's advancement in education, independent researchers Catherine Lyon and Terry Saario attempted to compile the data themselves at the national level. In a 1973 *Phi Delta Kappan* article they detailed the difficulty they faced in this project since many state agencies kept erratic and incomplete data on school administrators by sex.[19] Similarly, Jacqueline Parker Clement attempted to compile this data for her 1975 report, *Sex Bias in School Leadership*, in which she cited the frustration of consulting widely dispersed resources, phoning state officials, and otherwise piecing together what she considered inconclusive statistics.[20] Clearly for such research to have yielded data stringent enough for policy-making and enforcement purposes, significant funding and a bureaucratic mechanism for its management would have been required. The federal government had such a mechanism but routinely used it for other purposes. The former commissioner of education and chair of the federal Task Force on the Impact of Office of Education Programs on Women in 1972 offered this assessment of the situation: "With respect to collecting information on women, OE [the Office of Education] has not fulfilled its oldest mandate. Despite growing concern about sex discrimination, information comparing the status of men and women in education is still limited. Few national statistics have been collected to supplement piecemeal information on sex discrimination has come to light in recent years."[21]

Women's activists then pushed harder for the federal government to keep track of statistics on the sex of school administrators. In response, the commissioner approved a task force plan calling for the agency to "collect more data broken down by sex both on its programs and on the educational system generally," and to "publish an annual summary of data available on women in education." This data, however, was never collected and many parts of the task force plan were simply forgotten.[22]

In 1976, the Department of Health, Education, and Welfare prepared a report that estimated the distribution of full-time public school superintendents and assistants combined as 94.6 percent male and 5.4 percent female.[23] By grouping school superintendents together with assistant superintendents, the report obscured the tendency for women to be hired as assistant superintendents much more frequently than as superintendents; thus it failed to offer information that might challenge the "glass ceiling" between these positions.

Eventually, however, the AASA took seriously the need for accurate data on women superintendents. A 1981 AASA report revealed that women held 9 percent of superintendencies in 1950, 1 percent in 1972 and an estimated .5 percent in 1980.[24] In a more significant effort also sponsored by the AASA, Effie Jones and Xenia Montenegro began collecting data in the late 1970s to determine the representation of persons of color and women in school administration. Their ongoing efforts since then have been published in 1983, 1985, 1988, 1990, and 1993, and perhaps represent the only organizational commitment to this endeavor. Their data, which now extends over a generation, has begun to illuminate recent trends in administrator demographics. For example, while their data reveals that 1 percent of superintendents in 1980 were women, over 7 percent were by 1993 in what appears to have been a steady rise. Interestingly, the period of this increase occured during the years in which Jones and Montenegro compiled these important reports.[25]

Apart from these contemporary AASA projects, little other data has been collected on the numbers of women in school administration, particularly the superintendency. The data that does exist varies widely because each study employed different research and sampling techniques, and occurred at erratic intervals. As a result, it is difficult to interpret at face value even though perhaps it can reveal a great deal about the politics of statistical reportage.

While the AASA is compiling current data, historical information is still needed to create a clearer picture of how educational employment became so highly sex-stratified. For this reason, I undertook a study of my own to determine women's access to the superintendency over the course of the twentieth century. I wanted to know how many, when, and where women served in this school administration position. Then I could explore the particular historical contexts of their work. This statistical study, then, provides the groundwork on which the historical account in this volume is based.

Method

It is likely that there have been few statistical studies describing women school superintendents because persons or institutions with the resources to undertake the work largely have been uninterested, or worse, they have believed that producing the data would invite critique of a relatively closed promotional system. However, part of the reason, too, involves the fact that such data collection requires time, funding, personnel, and significant cooperation from numerous agencies. Until recently, women's advocates have had few of these resources at their disposal. The advent of the personal computer, though, has rendered such a project feasible for motivated researchers.[26] With my computer, database software, a bit of programming, and a consistent reference listing all school superintendents for the century, I have been able to undertake this project that only a few years ago would have proved prohibitively expensive for all but the wealthiest organizations. The following section details how I utilized these resources to produce a comprehensive statistical study of the superintendency with sex as a category of analysis.

Database

The only known source of data on the school superintendency that has been collected systematically and in a consistent manner throughout the twentieth century is *Patterson's American Education*, an annual volume dating from 1904. The editor of one of the first volumes explained that "the aim of this work is to give a complete index to the educational system of the United States and Canada. . . . A complete list of the schools . . . is given, together with information as to the kind of school, class of students admitted. . . . The Public School system is fully covered by complete lists of the State Educational Officials and county superintendents of schools."[27] Among other data, each volume of *Patterson's* lists the names of every school superintendent in the country along with the name of his or her school district. Most volumes also include either district population or enrollment figures. Data in *Patterson's* has been gathered with the consistent help of "school officials, state and national bodies, association members and the many individuals who have answered . . . annual questionnaires, or who have otherwise supplied information."[28]

Over the twentieth century *Patterson's* directories have been used for public reference, as an important source of addresses for targeted mailings from school-related merchandisers, and for research. The influence of *Patterson's* is evident in its participation in the cooperative venture, the Educational Research Service (ERS), an alliance consisting of such important education data collecting organizations as the NEA, AASA, and the U.S. Bureau of the Census.[29] Currently, librarians around the country recognize *Patterson's* as the standard reference for detailed information on school leadership personnel for all districts in the United States. Clearly *Patterson's* directories have established a degree of credibility through the years.

While *Patterson's* has provided consistent data on the names of all school superintendents, their school systems, states, and district population/enrollment, it has not noted the sex of listed superintendents. On its face this presents a serious challenge for a study devoted to tabulating the sex of superintendents through the century. I resolved this problem, however, by determining the sex of each superintendent based on his or her name and any other sex-specific identifying information.

In 1910, this was a straightforward task because nearly every female superintendent's name was preceded either by "Mrs." or "Miss."

First names were also sex-distinct during this year; there was little, if any, overlap between possible male and female names. Finally, males in 1910 were almost invariably listed with their first and middle initials. Because females were not traditionally known by their initials during this time, I assume that none of the superintendents listed by their initials were women.[30]

Name data for 1930 and 1950 were not difficult to differentiate either, because *Patterson's* continued the practice of preceding most women's names with either "Mrs." or "Miss." Rather than using initials during these decades, the editors of *Patterson's* listed most males and females with their first and/or middle names. This convention made sex determination easy because during these years men's and women's names continued to be quite distinct, such as the feminine name "Catherine" or masculine name "Peter." In some cases, I confirmed the traditional gender assignment for obscure names by consulting the *Complete Dictionary of English and Hebrew First Names.*[31] For the few remaining names about which I was still uncertain either because they could have represented either men or women, or because I could not ascertain the sex of persons with highly obscure names, I marked superintendent records as "uncertain" for sex categorization.

The data for 1970 and 1990 were somewhat more difficult to interpret because *Patterson's* included "Miss" or "Mrs." in front of women's names much less frequently than earlier in the century; a larger, uncertain percentage of women are listed with their initials; and greater numbers of persons had androgynous names such as "Jackie," "Pat," or "Terry." Again, I marked records with sex ambiguous or little known names as "uncertain" for sex assignment. Mainly because of women's increased use of initials, the 1970 and 1990 data are less reliable than for 1910, 1930, or 1950.

Using the information in *Patterson's*, I constructed the database with records for every superintendent serving in the years 1910, 1930, 1950, 1970, and 1990. The following information was entered for each superintendent record: complete name, title, sex, year of service, state, district name, type of district, and either district population (given in the 1930, 1950 and 1970 volumes) or pupil enrollment (given in the 1990 volume). Data for a total of 51,661 superintendents was entered into the database. Then several data checks were conducted to assure the accuracy of each record and field. Finally, I queried the database to determine the number and percentage of women superintendents:(*a*) for each of the years of the study, (*b*) by type of district (state, intermediate, or local), (*c*) by state and region, and (*d*) by district population/enrollment.

District Classification

Over the past century numerous types of school districts have existed. To simplify the range of district types for analysis, I employed the following classification scheme:

- *State:* agency designated for supervision of public schools for an entire state or territory
- *Intermediate:* administrative organization between the state education agency and local school district; districts where chief administrators do not directly supervise schools (such as county, intermediate district, parish, district, and division)
- *Local:* administrative unit where the chief administrator provides direct supervision of schools

It is important to note that over the course of this century not every school district has employed a person designated as a superintendent, supervisor, commissioner, or other equivalent title. As a result, the number of superintendents tabulated for each year of this study is smaller than the total number of school districts.

Findings

Table A.1 offers a general summary of my analysis of the superintendent database. With local, intermediate, and state superintendencies combined, women held between 9 and 11 percent of all superintendencies from 1910 to 1950. Then from 1950 to 1970, women's representation in the superintendency declined dramatically to a scant 3 percent. From 1970 to 1990, women made modest progress in attaining superintendencies, increasing their representation from 3 to 5 percent overall (also see figure I.1).

Data by District Type

Intermediate Districts: Women's record of attaining superintendencies has varied significantly by school district type. Throughout the century, women have been relatively successful in becoming intermediate district superintendents, especially county superintendents. Data in table A.1 shows that women have held anywhere from 14.12 percent to just over 27 percent of all intermediate superintendencies during any given year of the study. It is important to note, however, that with school

TABLE A.1

Women Superintendents by District Type, 1910–1990

	1910			1930			1950			1970			1990		
	Wom.	?*	Tot. n	Wom.	?*	Tot. n	Wom.	?*	Tot. n	Wom.	?*	Tot. n	Wom.	?*	Tot. n
State	2	0	46	4	0	48	5	2	48	1	0	50	6	1	51
	4%	0%		8%	0%		10%	4%		2%	0%		12%	2%	
Intermediate	403	20	2854	862	36	3146	718	41	3091	366	20	2554	150	10	651
	14.12%	.70%		27.40%	1.14%		23.23%	1.33%		14.33%	.78%		23.04%	1.54%	
Local	327	21	5284	93	26	5539	85	37	5769	73	92	10,431	477	160	12,099
	6.19%	.40%		1.68%	.47%		1.47%	.64%		.70%	.88%		3.94%	1.32%	
All District Types Combined	732	41	8184	959	62	8733	808	80	8908	440	112	13,035	633	171	12,801
	8.94%	.50%		10.98%	.71%		9.07%	.90%		3.38%	.86%		4.94%	1.34%	

Note: This data describes the number of superintendents rather than the total number of school districts. Many school districts did not employ a person designated by the title "superintendent" (or a similar title such as "commissioner").

*Number of superintendents for whom sex determination cannot be made with certainty.

Appendix

FIGURE A.1

Women Superintendents by District Type, 1910–1990

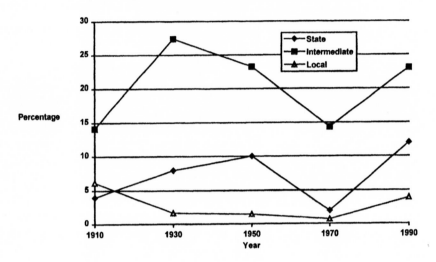

FIGURE A.2

Numbers of Local and Intermediate Districts and
Women Superintendents, 1910–1990

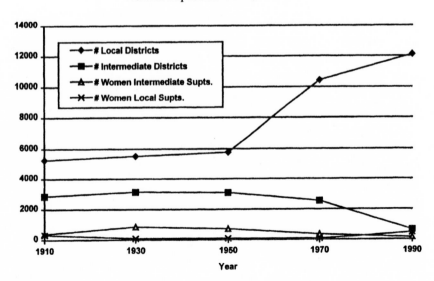

district consolidation, the number of intermediate districts declined significantly from 3,146 in 1930 to 651 in 1990 (see figure A.2). Since women held a greater proportion of these positions than local superintendencies, consolidation affected them to a greater extent than men.

Local Districts: Women have not enjoyed easy access to the local district superintendency during any time in this century. As is demonstrated in table A.1, women have never held more than 6.19 percent of these positions—a level achieved in 1910 and not matched since. In 1910, women served in 327 of 5,284 local school districts. By 1970, women superintended only 73 out of 10,431 local districts, producing a steady decline in representation from 6.19 percent to only .70 percent. Interestingly, however, from 1950 through 1970 the number of local districts more than doubled—and since this position traditionally has been held by men even more than either intermediate or state superintendencies, this increase appears also to have contributed to women's decline in representation. In an apparent reversal of this trend, women started assuming a greater number and percentage of local district superintendencies after 1970. From the years 1970 to 1990, the number of female local district superintendents jumped from 73 out of 10,431 (.70 percent) to 477 out of 12,099 (3.94 percent), representing nearly a sixfold increase. This increase occurred even as the number of local district superintendencies continued to rise.

States: Data describing women in state superintendencies offers less conclusive information than it does for either intermediate or local district positions because there are relatively few state superintendents and small changes in women's numbers from year to year produce great variation in the percentages. With this caveat in mind, the trends in the female state superintendency generally resemble those for the intermediate and local district positions: moderate representation in 1910 (4 percent), higher representation in mid-century (8 percent in 1930 and 10 percent in 1950), sharply lower representation in 1970 (2 percent), and an increase (to 12 percent) by 1990.

Data by Region

Strong regional patterns in the employment of women superintendents have existed throughout the century. Generally, western states have employed more female school leaders than those in any other part of the country. Tables A.2 through A.5 summarize the numbers of women superintendents for each region sorted by state for the years of the study. These tables also indicate for each region and state the total number of superintendents of each district type as well as the number of superintendents for whom sex determination could not be made reliably. Figure A.3 provides a graphical, comparative summary of this data.

Each of the four regions displays a similar overall pattern from 1910 to 1970: moderately high levels in 1910, peak levels in 1930, slightly lower levels by 1950, and very low levels in 1970. In each of these years, the order of the regions is the same: western states with the highest percentage of women superintendents followed by the midwestern states, southern states, and finally the northern states. By 1990, however, the order shifts with the Midwest having the smallest percentage of women superintendents, followed in order by the South, the North, and the West once again with the highest percentage.

Differences by District Population or Enrollment

Among local district superintendents with immediate jurisdiction over schools, patterns in the employment of women are evident when analyzed by district population or enrollment. Table A.6 breaks down by district population the number and percentage of women who held local district superintendencies in 1930, 1950 and 1970. First, in each of these years women's chances of superintending a local district generally decreased as district population increased. In 1930, for example, women held 3.76 percent of superintendencies for small districts with between one and 1,000 residents. However, women held only .44 percent of superintendencies for much larger districts with 25,001 to 100,000 persons. Second, in these decades the pattern of women's declining representation in the superintendency with increasing district population is broken for the very largest districts. The chances of women superintending the largest districts (100,000+ residents) were consistently greater than for medium-large districts (25,001–100,000 residents). Finally, the number of women in each local district population category generally declined through these decades as the overall number of women local district superintendents decreased.

District size data in the 1990 volume of *Patterson's* lists school district enrollment rather than population. Table A.7 details the number and percentage of women superintendents by district enrollment. A trend clearly evident is that the percentage of women superintendents increased with local school district enrollment (also see figure A.5). This represents a different pattern from earlier decades where greater percentages of women served in small districts. In 1990, women held around 3 percent of superintendencies for districts with enrollments under 1,000 students, yet the percentage doubled for districts with enrollments between 25,001 and 100,000 students.

TABLE A.2

Women Superintendents in Northern States, 1910–1990

State	1910 Wom.	1910 ?*	1910 Tot. n	1930 Wom.	1930 ?*	1930 Tot. n	1950 Wom.	1950 ?*	1950 Tot. n	1970 Wom.	1970 ?*	1970 Tot. n	1990 Wom.	1990 ?*	1990 Tot. n
Connecticut															
• Local	0	0	26	2	0	68	2	0	99	0	1	121	10	0	127
• Intermediate	na	na	na	na	na	na	na	na	na	0	0	10	na	na	na
• State	na	na	na	0	0	1	0	0	1	0	0	1	0	0	1
Delaware															
• Local	0	0	2	0	0	11	0	0	12	0	0	16	0	0	19
• Intermediate	0	0	3	na	na	na	na	na	na	0	0	15	na	na	na
• State	na	na	na	0	0	1	0	0	1	0	0	1	0	0	1
District of Columbia															
• Local	0	0	1	0	0	1	0	0	1	0	0	1	2	0	5
• Intermediate	na	na	na	na	na	na	na	na	na	na	na	na	na	na	na
• State	na	na	na	na	na	na	0	0	1	0	0	1	0	0	1
Maine															
• Local	3	0	34	9	0	186	3	0	170	1	0	118	0	0	128
• Intermediate	na	na	na	na	na	na	na	na	na	na	na	na	na	na	na
• State	0	0	1	0	0	1	0	0	1	0	0	1	1	0	1
Maryland															
• Local	na	na	na	0	0	12	0	0	12	0	0	1	1	1	24
• Intermediate	0	0	24	1	0	23	1	0	23	0	0	23	na	na	na
• State	0	0	1	0	0	1	0	0	1	0	0	1	0	0	1

* Number of persons for whom sex determination cannot be made with certainty.

TABLE A.2—*Continued*

State	1910			1930			1950			1970			1990		
	Wom.	?*	Tot. n	Wom.	?*	Tot. n	Wom.	?*	Tot. n	Wom.	?*	Tot. n	Wom.	?*	Tot. n
Massachusetts															
• Local	3	0	185	2	0	242	4	5	232	3	2	227	21	1	271
• Intermediate	na	na	na	na	na	na	na	na	na	na	na	na	na	na	na
• State	0	0	1	0	0	1	0	0	1	0	0	1	0	0	1
New Hampshire															
• Local	0	0	36	0	1	70	0	2	76	0	0	41	2	0	60
• Intermediate	0	0	25	na	na	na	na	na	na	na	na	na	na	na	na
• State	0	0	1	0	0	1	0	0	1	0	0	1	0	0	1
New Jersey															
• Local	0	1	50	1	0	78	0	0	71	1	0	251	16	5	376
• Intermediate	0	0	21	0	0	21	0	0	21	0	0	20	5	0	21
• State	0	0	1	0	0	1	0	0	1	0	0	1	0	0	1
New York															
• Local	1	1	89	9	3	175	7	2	214	1	0	226	33	5	699
• Intermediate	9	3	112	48	0	209	23	0	162	5	0	71	na	na	na
• State	0	0	1	0	0	1	0	0	1	0	0	1	0	0	1
Pennsylvania															
• Local	1	0	101	1	1	264	0	0	221	2	3	274	32	4	497
• Intermediate	1	0	66	0	0	66	0	0	66	1	0	66	3	0	29
• State	0	0	1	0	0	1	0	0	1	0	0	1	0	0	1

* Number of persons for whom sex determination cannot be made with certainty.

TABLE A.2—*Continued*

State	1910			1930			1950			1970			1990		
	Wom.	?*	Tot. n	Wom.	?*	Tot. n	Wom.	?*	Tot. n	Wom.	?*	Tot. n	Wom.	?*	Tot. n
Rhode Island															
• Local	1	na	39	0	0	34	2	0	32	0	0	32	2	0	33
• Intermediate	na	na	na	na	na	na	na	na	na	na	na	na	na	na	na
• State	0	0	1	0	0	1	0	0	1	0	0	1	0	0	1
Vermont															
• Local	2	2	41	6	2	51	2	0	69	4	0	47	2	0	54
• Intermediate	2	2	21	na	na	na	na	na	na	na	na	na	na	na	na
• State	0	0	1	0	0	1	na	na	na	0	0	1	0	0	1
Regional Totals															
• Local	11	5	604	30	7	1192	20	9	1227	12	6	1355	121	16	2293
• Intermediate	12	5	272	49	0	319	24	0	272	6	0	205	8	0	50
• State	0	0	9	0	0	11	0	0	11	0	0	12	1	0	12
• Total	23	10	885	79	7	1522	44	9	1510	18	6	1572	130	16	2355
Total Percentages															
• Local Supts.	1.82%	.83%		2.52%	.59%		1.63%	.73%		.89%	.44%		5.28%	.70%	
• Intermediate Supts.	4.41%	1.84%		15.36%	0%		8.82%	0%		2.93%	0%		16.00%	0%	
• State Supts.	0%	0%		0%	0%		0%	0%		0%	0%		8.33%	0%	
• Overall Supts.	2.60%	1.13%		5.20%	.46%		2.91%	.60%		1.15%	.38%		5.52%	.68%	

* Number of persons for whom sex determination cannot be made with certainty.

TABLE A.3

Women Superintendents in Southern States, 1910–1990

State	1910			1930			1950			1970			1990		
	Wom.	?*	Tot. n	Wom.	?*	Tot. n	Wom.	?*	Tot. n	Wom.	?*	Tot. n	Wom.	?*	Tot. n
Alabama															
• Local	34	0	239	7	0	99	2	0	74	0	3	53	9	1	124
• Intermediate	0	0	67	0	0	66	1	2	67	1	2	67	na	na	na
• State	0	0	1	0	0	1	0	0	1	0	0	1	0	0	1
Arkansas															
• Local	2	1	169	3	0	93	2	1	97	2	7	353	8	6	328
• Intermediate	1	1	79	5	0	74	8	1	75	26	0	70	na	na	na
• State	0	0	1	0	0	1	0	0	1	0	0	1	1	0	1
Florida															
• Local	0	0	11	1	0	20	1	0	24	0	0	2	6	1	67
• Intermediate	0	0	46	3	0	67	2	0	67	0	0	67	na	na	na
• State	0	0	1	0	0	1	0	0	1	0	0	1	1	0	1
Georgia															
• Local	2	0	79	2	0	175	5	1	161	0	1	17	11	4	174
• Intermediate	1	0	146	17	1	161	13	2	159	4	2	158	na	na	na
• State	0	0	1	0	0	1	0	0	1	0	0	1	0	0	1
Kentucky															
• Local	0	0	27	2	1	102	7	1	114	7	0	192	5	1	171
• Intermediate	21	0	119	19	3	120	16	0	119	5	0	120	na	na	na
• State	0	0	1	0	0	1	0	0	1	0	0	1	0	0	1

* Number of persons for whom sex determination cannot be made with certainty.

TABLE A.3–Continued

State	1910			1930			1950			1970			1990		
	Wom.	?*	Tot. n	Wom.	?*	Tot. n	Wom.	?*	Tot. n	Wom.	?*	Tot. n	Wom.	?*	Tot. n
Louisiana															
• Local	na	na	na	0	0	16	0	1	41	0	0	3	3	2	64
• Intermediate	0	0	58	0	1	62	0	1	64	0	0	65	na	na	na
• State	0	0	1	0	0	1	0	1	1	0	0	1	0	0	1
Mississippi															
• Local	3	0	48	0	0	66	3	0	84	1	1	70	4	2	154
• Intermediate	0	1	78	10	1	82	13	2	82	3	2	81	na	na	na
• State	0	0	1	0	0	1	0	0	1	0	0	1	0	0	1
North Carolina															
• Local	1	0	83	0	0	102	1	0	111	0	0	93	6	2	141
• Intermediate	0	0	98	2	0	100	2	0	100	0	1	100	na	na	na
• State	0	0	1	0	0	1	0	0	1	0	0	1	0	0	1
South Carolina															
• Local	1	0	118	0	1	81	2	0	106	0	0	121	9	2	96
• Intermediate	0	0	42	7	0	46	3	0	46	5	0	46	na	na	na
• State	0	0	1	0	0	1	0	0	1	0	0	1	0	0	1
Tennessee															
• Local	0	1	46	2	0	71	2	0	79	1	1	43	8	3	127
• Intermediate	4	1	96	11	2	94	4	0	95	3	2	95	na	na	na
• State	0	0	1	0	0	1	0	0	1	0	0	1	0	0	1

* Number of persons for whom sex determination cannot be made with certainty.

TABLE A.3–*Continued*

State	1910 Wom.	?*	Tot. n	1930 Wom.	?*	Tot. n	1950 Wom.	?*	Tot. n	1970 Wom.	?*	Tot. n	1990 Wom.	?*	Tot. n
Virginia															
• Local	1	0	21	0	0	39	1	0	56	1	0	34	3	2	132
• Intermediate	0	0	117	0	0	119	0	2	108	0	0	96	na	na	na
• State	0	0	1	0	0	1	0	0	1	0	0	1	0	0	1
West Virginia															
• Local	3	0	58	2	1	64	0	0	4	na	na	na	4	1	52
• Intermediate	0	0	55	6	2	55	0	1	55	1	2	55	na	na	na
• State	0	0	1	0	0	1	0	0	1	0	0	1	0	0	1
Regional Totals															
• Local	47	2	899	19	3	928	26	4	951	12	13	981	76	27	1630
• Intermediate	27	3	1001	80	10	1046	62	11	1037	48	11	1020	na	na	na
• State	0	0	12	0	0	12	0	1	12	0	0	12	2	0	12
• Total	74	5	1912	99	13	1986	88	16	2000	60	24	2013	78	27	1642
Total Percentages															
• Local Supts.	5.23%	.22%		2.05%	.32%		2.73%	.40%		1.22%	1.33%		4.66%	1.66%	
• Intermediate Supts.	2.70%	.30%		7.65%	.96%		5.98%	1.06%		4.71%	1.08%		na	na	
• State Supts.	0%	0%		0%	0%		0%	8.33%		0%	0%		16.67%	0%	
• Overall Supts.	3.87%	.26%		4.98%	.65%		4.40%	.80%		2.98%	1.19%		4.75%	1.64%	

* Number of persons for whom sex determination cannot be made with certainty.

Table A.4

Women Superintendents in Midwestern States, 1910–1990

State	1910 Wom.	1910 ?*	1910 Tot. n	1930 Wom.	1930 ?*	1930 Tot. n	1950 Wom.	1950 ?*	1950 Tot. n	1970 Wom.	1970 ?*	1970 Tot. n	1990 Wom.	1990 ?*	1990 Tot. n
Illinois															
• Local	5	0	224	11	3	285	2	4	298	4	6	702	16	13	756
• Intermediate	10	0	102	17	0	102	7	2	102	2	0	102	3	1	57
• State	0	0	1	0	0	1	0	0	1	0	0	1	0	0	1
Indiana															
• Local	9	0	384	1	0	166	1	1	160	0	4	268	6	4	288
• Intermediate	0	1	92	2	2	92	0	2	92	0	0	15	na	na	na
• State	0	0	1	0	0	1	0	0	1	0	0	1	0	0	1
Iowa															
• Local	0	2	178	4	0	249	3	0	280	5	3	455	14	4	419
• Intermediate	27	1	99	60	1	99	26	1	99	4	0	99	0	0	15
• State	0	0	1	1	0	1	0	1	1	0	0	1	0	0	1
Kansas															
• Local	2	0	82	3	0	156	4	1	146	2	6	318	5	7	303
• Intermediate	42	0	105	65	3	104	73	0	104	na	na	na	na	na	na
• State	0	0	1	0	0	1	0	0	1	0	0	1	0	0	1
Michigan															
• Local	0	1	61	2	2	217	3	1	226	1	4	525	9	3	518
• Intermediate	10	0	83	28	1	83	21	2	82	5	1	81	0	0	57
• State	0	0	1	0	0	1	0	0	1	0	0	1	0	0	1

* Number of persons for whom sex determination cannot be made with certainty.

TABLE A.4–Continued

State	1910 Wom.	1910 ?*	1910 Tot. n	1930 Wom.	1930 ?*	1930 Tot. n	1950 Wom.	1950 ?*	1950 Tot. n	1970 Wom.	1970 ?*	1970 Tot. n	1990 Wom.	1990 ?*	1990 Tot. n
Minnesota															
• Local	3	0	196	0	1	228	0	2	228	1	4	448	13	6	401
• Intermediate	24	1	85	46	2	85	42	0	86	19	0	71	na	na	na
• State	0	0	1	0	0	1	0	0	1	0	0	1	1	0	1
Missouri															
• Local	3	0	146	2	1	201	0	0	204	0	5	466	10	7	450
• Intermediate	11	1	114	30	2	114	27	1	114	7	1	34	na	na	na
• State	0	0	1	0	0	1	0	0	1	0	0	1	0	0	1
Nebraska															
• Local	92	5	494	4	0	166	2	1	163	7	2	337	6	1	303
• Intermediate	37	2	90	56	4	93	59	2	93	49	0	90	33	2	92
• State	0	0	1	0	0	1	0	0	1	0	0	1	0	0	1
North Dakota															
• Local	0	0	48	0	0	57	0	0	58	4	1	266	2	3	218
• Intermediate	14	1	46	29	0	53	39	3	53	40	2	53	33	2	50
• State	0	0	1	1	0	1	0	0	1	0	0	1	0	0	1
Ohio															
• Local	1	0	308	2	0	333	3	1	348	2	3	627	34	11	657
• Intermediate	na	na	na	0	0	88	1	0	88	0	0	88	2	0	87
• State	0	0	1	0	0	1	0	0	1	0	0	1	0	0	1

* Number of persons for whom sex determination cannot be made with certainty.

TABLE A.4—Continued

State	1910			1930			1950			1970			1990		
	Wom.	?*	Tot. *n*	Wom.	?*	Tot. *n*	Wom.	?*	Tot. *n*	Wom.	?*	Tot. *n*	Wom.	?*	Tot. *n*
South Dakota															
• Local	0	0	37	2	0	120	0	0	119	2	0	205	0	1	173
• Intermediate	20	1	53	48	0	68	51	0	67	50	0	64	na	na	na
• State	0	0	1	0	0	1	0	0	1	0	0	1	0	0	1
Wisconsin															
• Local	1	0	67	2	0	94	1	1	139	4	1	386	11	3	383
• Intermediate	12	2	73	26	1	71	21	1	72	0	0	19	na	na	na
• State	0	0	1	0	0	1	0	0	1	0	0	1	0	0	1
Regional Totals															
• Local	116	8	2225	33	7	2272	19	12	2369	32	39	5003	126	63	4869
• Intermediate	207	10	942	407	18	1052	367	14	1052	176	4	716	71	5	358
• State	0	0	12	2	0	12	0	1	12	0	0	12	1	0	12
• Total	323	18	3179	442	25	3336	386	27	3433	208	43	5731	198	68	5239
Total Percentages															
• Local Supts.	5.21%	.36%		1.45%	.31%		.80%	.51%		.64%	.78%		2.59%	1.29%	
• Intermediate Supts.	21.97%	1.06%		38.69%	1.71%		34.89%	1.33%		24.58%	.56%		19.83%	1.40%	
• State Supts.	0%	0%		16.67%	0%		0%	8.33%		0%	0%		8.33%	0%	
• Overall Supts.	10.16%	.57%		13.25%	.75%		11.24%	.79%		3.63%	.75%		3.78%	1.30%	

* Number of persons for whom sex determination cannot be made with certainty.

TABLE A.5

Women Superintendents in Western States, 1910–1990

State	1910			1930			1950			1970			1990		
	Wom.	?*	Tot. *n*	Wom.	?*	Tot. *n*	Wom.	?*	Tot. *n*	Wom.	?*	Tot. *n*	Wom.	?*	Tot. *n*
Alaska															
• Local	na	na	na	na	na	na	na	na	na	0	0	32	6	0	52
• Intermediate	na	na	na	na	na	na	na	na	na	na	na	na	na	na	na
• State	na	na	na	na	na	na	na	na	na	0	0	1	0	0	1
Arizona															
• Local	12	1	45	0	0	21	0	2	32	0	1	80	12	1	130
• Intermediate	0	0	13	13	1	14	6	1	14	6	0	14	6	0	15
• State	0	0	1	0	0	1	0	0	1	na	na	na	1	0	1
California															
• Local	0	0	33	3	0	95	4	0	130	3	4	497	53	5	605
• Intermediate	23	0	58	28	1	58	21	1	58	1	0	58	5	0	58
• State	0	0	1	0	0	1	0	0	1	0	0	1	0	0	1
Colorado															
• Local	4	0	86	1	0	68	2	2	67	3	0	174	4	4	174
• Intermediate	34	0	60	55	1	63	52	0	63	24	0	28	na	na	na
• State	1	0	1	1	0	1	1	0	1	0	0	1	0	0	1
Hawaii															
• Local	na	na	na	na	na	na	na	na	na	0	0	10	2	0	7
• Intermediate	na	na	na	na	na	na	na	na	na	0	0	4	na	na	na
• State	na	na	na	na	na	na	na	na	na	0	0	1	0	0	1

* Number of persons for whom sex determination cannot be made with certainty.

TABLE A.5—Continued

State	1910			1930			1950			1970			1990		
	Wom.	?	Tot. n	Wom.	?	Tot. n	Wom.	?	Tot. n	Wom.	?	Tot. n	Wom.	?	Tot. n
Idaho															
• Local	0	0	17	0	0	50	2	0	59	1	2	100	2	0	105
• Intermediate	17	0	23	35	0	44	32	0	44	na	na	na	na	na	na
• State	1	0	1	0	0	1	0	0	1	0	0	1	0	0	1
Montana															
• Local	2	0	57	0	1	64	2	0	67	0	2	165	10	1	170
• Intermediate	25	1	27	52	1	56	48	2	56	49	0	55	39	1	56
• State	0	0	1	1	0	1	1	0	1	1	0	1	1	0	1
Nevada															
• Local	8	0	28	1	0	12	0	0	10	na	na	na	0	0	16
• Intermediate	0	0	5	na	na	na	na	na	na	0	0	17	na	na	na
• State	0	0	1	0	0	1	1	0	1	0	0	1	0	0	1
New Mexico															
• Local	0	0	7	0	0	46	2	0	47	0	0	91	7	1	88
• Intermediate	3	0	26	20	1	31	15	1	31	0	0	3	na	na	na
• State	0	0	1	0	0	1	0	0	1	0	0	1	0	0	1
Oklahoma															
• Local	1	0	72	2	2	222	2	1	216	5	12	425	9	14	451
• Intermediate	19	0	76	28	0	76	17	2	77	11	2	77	20	2	76
• State	0	0	1	0	0	1	0	0	1	0	0	1	0	0	1

* Number of persons for whom sex determination cannot be made with certainty.

Table A.5—*Continued*

State	1910 Wom.	1910 ?	1910 Tot. n	1930 Wom.	1930 ?	1930 Tot. n	1950 Wom.	1950 ?	1950 Tot. n	1970 Wom.	1970 ?	1970 Tot. n	1990 Wom.	1990 ?	1990 Tot. n
Oregon															
• Local	58	2	259	0	1	51	1	2	63	0	0	174	9	1	194
• Intermediate	1	0	34	15	0	36	14	2	36	1	1	35	1	1	29
• State	0	0	1	0	0	1	0	0	1	0	0	1	0	0	1
Texas															
• Local	31	1	610	2	1	299	2	1	299	5	11	1013	26	16	975
• Intermediate	3	0	237	40	3	254	20	4	254	19	2	239	na	na	na
• State	0	0	1	0	0	1	0	0	1	0	0	1	0	0	1
Utah															
• Local	0	0	6	0	0	20	2	1	37	0	1	7	0	3	40
• Intermediate	3	0	29	1	0	35	2	0	35	0	0	35	na	na	na
• State	0	0	1	0	0	1	0	0	1	0	0	1	0	0	1
Washington															
• Local	30	2	297	1	3	157	0	2	151	0	0	249	12	7	253
• Intermediate	18	0	38	20	0	39	20	0	39	7	0	28	0	0	9
• State	0	0	1	0	0	1	1	0	1	0	0	1	0	0	1
Wyoming															
• Local	7	0	39	1	1	42	1	1	44	0	1	75	2	1	47
• Intermediate	11	1	13	19	0	23	18	3	23	18	0	20	na	na	na
• State	0	0	1	0	0	1	1	0	1	0	0	1	0	0	1
Regional Totals															
• Local	153	6	1556	11	9	1147	20	12	1222	17	34	3092	154	54	3307
• Intermediate	157	2	639	326	8	729	265	16	730	136	5	613	71	5	243
• State	2	0	13	2	0	13	5	0	13	1	0	14	2	1	15
• Total	312	8	2208	339	17	1889	290	28	1965	154	39	3719	227	60	3565
Total Percentages															
• Local Supts.	9.83%	.39%		.96%	.78%		1.64%	.90%		.55%	1.10%		4.66%	1.63%	
• Intermediate Supts.	24.57%	.31%		44.72%	1.10%		36.30%	2.19%		22.19%	.82%		29.22%	2.06%	
• State Supts.	15.38%	0%		15.38%	0%		38.46%	0%		7.14%	0%		13.33%	6.67%	
• **Overall Supts**	14.13%	.36%		17.95%	.90%		14.76%	1.42%		4.14%	1.05%		6.37%	1.68%	

FIGURE A.3

Women Superintendents of all District Types Combined by Region, 1910–1990

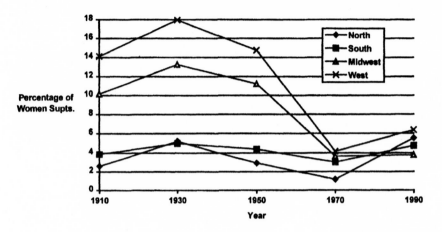

Summary

Generally, women served as superintendents in far greater numbers earlier in this century than at present. The overall percentage of women superintendents remained roughly constant through the suffrage movement and two world wars. In the wake of World War II, however, the number of women superintendents quickly declined to the lowest level of the century by 1970. The years from 1970 to 1990 brought modest improvement in women's representation in the superintendency while falling far short of early century levels.

Women have enjoyed the greatest success in attaining intermediate rather than local district or state superintendencies. From 1910 to 1950, hundreds of women served in these positions. In the 1970s and 1980s, however, large numbers of these districts were dissolved. Meanwhile, women achieved only modest gains in local school district superintendencies.

Women have been more likely to attain superintendencies in the western states than in any other region of the country. Until recently midwestern states have offered relatively good opportunities for women as well. Historically, women have enjoyed the weakest opportunities for superintendencies in northern and southern states, though currently women in the North appear to be making important gains.

TABLE A.6

Women Local District Superintendents by Population, 1930–1970

	District Population					
Year	1-1,000	1,001-2,500	2,501-10,000	10,001-25,000	25,001-100,000	100,000+
1930						
n Local Districts	797	2337	1509	451	225	78
n Women	30	38	15	5	1	1
• Women	3.76%	1.63%	.99%	1.12%	.44%	1.28%
n Uncertain Sex	7	8	7	4	0	2
• Uncertain Sex	.88%	.34%	.46%	.89%	0%	2.56%
1950						
n Local Districts	1025	1901	1854	582	303	91
n Women	22	31	24	7	3	1
• Women	2.15%	1.63%	1.29%	1.20%	.99%	1.10%
n Uncertain Sex	8	15	10	2	1	1
• Uncertain Sex	.78%	.79%	.54%	.34%	.33%	1.10%
1970						
n Local Districts	2968	2083	2144	881	531	136
n Women	26	13	9	6	3	1
• Women	.88%	.62%	.42%	.68%	.56%	.74%
n Uncertain Sex	22	20	18	7	7	2
• Uncertain Sex	.74%	.96%	.84%	.79%	1.32%	1.47%

Even though women have never attained local district superintendencies in high numbers, their chances have been better in smaller districts. In 1990, however, this tendency apparently was reversed as the percentage of women local district superintendents increased with school system enrollment. Though local district population and school district enrollment are not necessarily comparable figures, this change in trend suggests an important area for further study.

Re-evaluation of Common Views

The data presented in this study suggests that common views about women's access to the superintendency need to be reexamined. The notion that women once held many superintendencies but their

FIGURE A.4

Women Local District Superintendents by District Population, 1930–1970

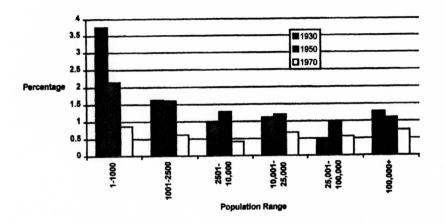

TABLE A.7

Women Local District Superintendents by Enrollment, 1990

	District Enrollment					
Year	1-1,000	1,001-2,500	2,501-10,000	10,001-25,000	25,001-100,000	100,000+
1990						
n Local Districts	5111	3493	2824	488	172	10
n Women	167	137	128	32	12	1
• Women	3.27%	3.92%	4.53%	6.56%	6.98%	10%
n Uncertain Sex	69	55	28	5	3	0
• Uncertain Sex	1.35%	1.57%	.99%	1.02%	1.74%	0%

numbers have since declined steadily is erroneous in that the decline occurred rapidly after World War II.

The notion that women have never held many superintendencies also is disputable since women held around 10 percent of all superintendencies for around half of the twentieth century. While this percentage hardly matches that of women teachers at any point, it is at least significantly higher than the percentage of women superintendents over the past twenty-five years.

FIGURE A.5

Percentage of Women Local District Superintendents by Enrollment, 1990

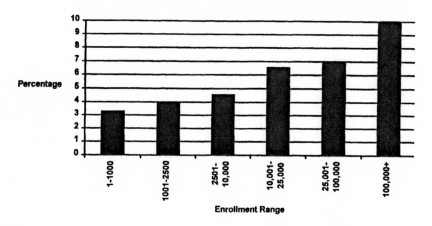

The notion that women are making considerable progress after the modern women's movement is ahistorical and demonstrably false in light of the data in this study. While the percentage of women superintendents has increased since 1970, the increases have been relatively small when compared with data from earlier in the century. Also, the kinds of superintendencies offered to women need to be examined. For example, some of these recent increases have occurred in states like California where school districts have been split into secondary and elementary districts. Women are more likely to lead elementary than secondary districts, which, in effect, creates another gender-stratified administrative category.

Discussion

This statistical study of the public school superintendency addresses gaps left by other reports through the century. Although it attempts to answer some questions about women's access to the superintendency, it also suggests many others such as: What are the patterns of superintendent employment for African American, Native American, Hispanic, and Asian educators? How does the method of selecting a superintendent affect the hiring of racial/ethnic minorities and women? To what extent are superintendent salaries linked with persons of color and women's likelihood of attaining these positions? Have religious or political views influenced superintendent selection?

I believe that numbers ultimately are limited as tools for describing the complexities of lived experience. Numbers fail to express the meanings people attach to their actions, thoughts, and experiences. However, numbers have been deployed as rhetorical weapons in debates about the shape of public education, especially those concerning educational administration, and also as political tools in the campaigns for equitable hiring. Therefore, they must be understood as part of the context and language of the time rather than as ends in themselves. Clearly, to understand women's experiences in seeking superintendencies, arguably positions that have symbolized power in shaping the course of public schooling, a much more intricate and complex exploration beyond the limitations of a statistical report is necessary. This statistical study, however, offers a useful start and has compelled much of the work presented in this volume.

Notes

Introduction

1. "The Highest Salaried Woman in the World," *The Western Journal of Education*, 14 (1909): 515.

2. Patricia A. Schmuck, "Women School Employees in the United States," in *Women Educators: Employees of Schools in Western Countries*, ed. Patricia A. Schmuck (Albany, NY: SUNY Press, 1987), 77.

3. Elisabeth Hansot and David Tyack, *The Dream Deferred: A Golden Age for Women School Administrators*, Policy Paper No. 81-C2 (Palo Alto, CA: Stanford University Institute for Research on Educational Finance and Governance, May 1981).

4. Edith A Lathrop, *Teaching as a Vocation for College Women* (Washington, DC: National Council of Administrative Women in Education Monograph, 1922).

5. Hansot and Tyack, "The Dream Deferred," 13.

1. Their First Great Public Profession

1. Thomas Woody, *A History of Women's Education in the United States*, 2 (New York: The Science Press, 1929), 441.

2. Woody, *History of Women's Education*, 1:129.

3. Willard Waller, *The Sociology of Teaching* (New York: John Wiley and Sons, 1932), 58.

4. Walt Whitman, *Brooklyn Daily Eagle* (Oct. 22, 1845 & Feb. 4, 1847), cited in Geraldine Joncich Clifford, "Man/Woman/Teacher: Gender, Family, and Career in American Educational History," in *American Teachers: Histories of a Profession at Work*, ed. Donald Warren (New York: Macmillan, 1989), 319.

5. Barbara Miller Solomon, *In the Company of Educated Women* (New Haven, CT: Yale University Press, 1985), 2.

6. Abigail Adams to John Adams, in *Adams Family Correspondence*, 2 (Cambridge, MA: Belknap Press, 1963), 94.

7. Cited in Sara M. Evans, *Born for Liberty: A History of Women in America* (New York: Free Press, 1989), 58.

8. Solomon, *Company of Educated Women*, 14–15.

9. Sally Schwager, "Educating Women in American," in *Reconstructing the Academy: Women's Education and Women's Studies*, ed. Elizabeth Minnich, Jean O'Barr, and Rachel Rosenfeld (Chicago: University of Chicago Press, 1988), 157.

10. Solomon, *Company of Educated Women*, 16–17.

11. Ibid., 17–18.

12. Kathryn Kish Sklar, *Catharine Beecher: A Study in American Domesticity* (New York: W. W. Norton, 1973), 59.

13. Anne Firor Scott, "The Ever Widening Circle: The Diffusion of Feminist Values from the Troy Female Seminary, 1822–1872," *History of Education Quarterly* 19 (Spring 1979): 3–6.

14. Susan McIntosh Lloyd, "Mary Lyon," in *Women Educators in the United States, 1820–1993: A Bio-Bibliographical Sourcebook*, ed. Maxine Schwartz Seller (Westport, CT: Greenwood Press, 1994), 294–305.

15. "A Satire on a College for Women in Kentucky," Springfield, Massachusetts *Republican and Journal* (March 14, 1835); excerpted in Sol Cohen, ed., *Education in the United States: A Documentary History*, 3. (New York: Random House, 1974), 1573.

16. Alexis de Tocqueville, *Democracy in America*, 2, sect. 3, chap. 9 (New York: Mentor, 1956).

17. Tocqueville, *Democracy in America*, 2, sect. 3, chap. 10.

18. Schwager, "Educating," 164.

19. Catharine Beecher, *The True Remedy for the Wrongs of Women* (Boston: Phillips, Sampson, 1851), 97–99.

20. Horace Mann, "Report for 1843," *Annual Reports on Education*, 2 (Boston: Horace B. Fuller, 1868), 359.

21. Horace Mann, "Lecture II: Special Preparation a Prerequisite to Teaching," *Lectures and Annual Reports on Education* (Boston: Geo. C. Rand & Avery, 1867), 100.

22. New York Committee, Beecher, and Stowe cited in Woody, *History of Women's Education*, 1:463, 481.

23. Kathryn Kish Sklar, "Catharine Beecher: Transforming the Teaching Profession," in *Women's America: Refocusing the Past*, 3rd ed., ed. Linda K. Kerber and Jane Sherron De Hart, (New York: Oxford University Press, 1991), 173–75.

24. Catharine Beecher, "Petition to Congress," *Godey's Ladies Book* (1853), 176–77.

25. *Pennsylvania School Report* (1865), 121, cited in Ellsbree, *The American Teacher,* 204.

26. *Rhode Island School Report* (1855), 209, cited in Ellsbree, *The American Teacher,* 204.

27. Horace Mann, ed., *Common School Journal* 8 (1846), 117, cited in Ellsbree, *The American Teacher,* 201–2.

28. Richard A. Quantz, "The Complex Visions of Female Teachers and the Failure of Unionization in the 1930s: An Oral History," *History of Education Quarterly* 24 (Winter 1985): 439–58.

29. Spencer J. Maxcy, "The Teacherage in American Rural Education," *The Journal of General Education* (Winter 1979): 271; Marta Danylewycz, Beth Light, and Allison Prentice, "The Evolution of the Sexual Division of Labor in Teaching: Nineteenth Century Ontario and Quebec Case Study," in *Women and Education: A Canadian Perspective,* ed. Jane S. Gaskell and Arlene Tigar McLaren (Calgary, Alberta: Detselig Enterprises, 1987), 51.

30. Mary Hurlbut Cordier, *Schoolwomen of the Prairies and Plains: Personal Narratives from Iowa, Kansas, and Nebraska, 1860s–1920s* (Albuquerque, NM: University of New Mexico Press, 1992), 29–30.

31. Sklar, "Catharine Beecher: Transforming," 173–74.

32. Schwager, "Educating," 169.

33. Stanley K. Schultz, *The Culture Factory: Boston Public Schools, 1789–1860* (New York: Oxford University Press, 1973), 116.

34. Leslie Butler, *The Michigan Schoolmasters' Club: A Story of the First Seven Decades, 1886–1957* (Ann Arbor: University of Michigan, 1958), 14.

35. Willard Waller, *The Sociology of Teaching* (New York: John Wiley and Sons, 1932), 58.

36. David Tyack and Elisabeth Hansot, *Managers of Virtue: Public School Leadership in America, 1820–1980* (New York: Basic Books, 1982), 49; American Institute of Instruction, *Journal of Proceedings 1869,* 7–8; and Paul H. Mattingly, *The Classless Profession: American Schoolmen in the Nineteenth Century* (New York: New York University Press, 1975), 85.

37. Mattingly, *The Classless Profession,* 110–11, 180–81.

38. "Constitution of the NTA," *Proceedings of the National Teachers Association* (1857), 311–12; Ellsbree, *American Teacher,* 254–55.

39. Elizabeth Cady Stanton, Susan B. Anthony, and Matilda Joslyn Gage, eds., *History of Woman Suffrage*, 1 (repr., Salem, NH: Ayer Company, 1985), 513–15.

40. Stanton, Anthony, and Gage, *History of Woman Suffrage*, 515.

41. May Wright Sewall, "Woman's Work in Education," *Proceedings of the National Educational Association 1884* (Boston: J. E. Farwell & Co., 1885), 153.

42. Woody, *History of Women's Education*, 507.

43. Leonard Ayres, "What Educators Think about the Need for Employing Men Teachers in Our Schools," *Journal of Educational Psychology* 2 (January 1911): 91–92.

44. "Are there Too Many Women Teachers?" *Educational Review* 28 (June 1904): 101.

45. Henry Armstrong, "Report," *Reports of the Mosely Educational Commission to the United States* (London: Co-operative Printing Society Limited, 1903; repr. New York: Arno Press & The New York Times, 1969), 13.

46. Myra Strober and David Tyack, "Why Do Women Teach and Men Manage? A Report on Research on Schools," *Signs: Journal of Women in Culture and Society* 5, 3 (1980): 499–500.

47. Schultz, *The Culture Factory*, 107.

48. Ellsbree, *American Teacher*, 200.

49. Bernard and Vinovskis, "The Female School Teacher," 337.

50. Sewall, "Woman's Work in Education," 153–54.

51. David Tyack, *The One Best System: A History of American Urban Education* (Cambridge, MA: Harvard University Press, 1974), 61.

52. Strober and Tyack, "Why Do Women Teach?" 499.

53. Ellsbree, *American Teacher*, 207.

54. Thomas Morain, "The Departure of Males from the Teaching Profession in Nineteenth-Century Iowa," *Civil War History* 26 (June 1980): 165.

55. Wayne Fuller, *Old Country School* (Chicago: University of Chicago Press, 1985), 105.

56. Ellsbree, *American Teacher*, 168–70.

57. Richard M. Bernard and Maris A. Vinovskis, "The Female School Teacher in Ante-Bellum Massachusetts," *Journal of Social History* 10 (1977): 339.

58. Aaron Gove, "Limitations of the Superintendents' Authority and of the Teacher's Independence," *The Journal of Proceedings of the National Education Association 1904* (Winona, MN: National Education Association, 1904), 152–57.

59. Strober and Tyack, "Why Do Women Teach?" 500.

60. Ellsbree, *American Teacher*, 175–76.

61. Margaret K. Nelson, "From the One-Room Schoolhouse to the Graded School: Teaching in Vermont, 1910–1950," *Frontiers* 7, 1 (1983): 14–17.

62. Cordier, *Schoolwomen of the Prairies and Plains*, 17.

63. Thomas Morain, "The Departure of Males," 166.

64. Edward L. Thorndike, *Education: A First Book* (New York: Macmillan, 1912), 156.

65. Tyack, *The One Best System*, 60.

66. C. W. Bardeen, "Why Teaching Repels Men," *Educational Review* 35 (April 1908): 351.

67. John Rury, "Who Became Teachers? The Social Characteristics of Teachers in American History," in *American Teachers: Histories of a Profession at Work*, ed. Donald Warren (New York: Macmillan, 1989), 27.

68. Thomas Morain, "The Departure of Males," 169.

69. Thorndike, *Education*, 156.

70. Waller, *The Sociology of Teaching*, 61.

71. *The Statistical History of the United States from Colonial Times to the Present* (Stamford, CT: Fairfield Publishers, 1965), 208.

72. Bardeen, "Why Teaching Repels Men," 351.

73. Ibid., 352–55.

74. Ella Flagg Young, *Isolation in the Schools* (Chicago: University of Chicago Press, 1900), 20–21.

75. "Are There Too Many Women Teachers?" *Educational Review* 28 (June 1904): 103.

76. *Report of the Commissioner of Education 1891–92*, 2: 668–71, cited in Woody, *History of Women's Education*, 507.

77. Ayres, "What Educators Think ," 92.

78. Ellsbree, *American Teacher*, 206; Mattingly, *The Classless Profession*, 110–11.

79. Mattingly, *The Classless Profession*, 51. Also see Sari Knopp Biklen, *School Work: Gender and the Cultural Construction of Teaching* (New York: Teachers College Press, 1995), 1–6, for a discussion of the tradition among some schoolmasters of idealizing lone martyrs and heroes in education.

80. "Are There Too Many Women Teachers?" 98–99.

81. Ayres, "What Educators Think," 90–91.

82. Courtney Ann Farr and Jeffrey A. Liles, "Male Teachers, Male Roles: The Progressive Era and Education in Oklahoma," *Great Plains Quarterly* 11 (Fall 1991): 234–48.

83. Edwin A. Lee, Committee of Phi Delta Kappa, *Teaching as a Man's Job* (Homewood, IL: Phi Delta Kappa, 1938).

84. Bardeen, "Why Teaching Repels Men," 358.

85. *The Statistical History of the United States*, 208.

86. Danylewycz, Light, and Prentice, "The Evolution of the Sexual Division of Labor," 50–51.

87. Myra H. Strober and Audri Gordon Lanford, "The Feminization of Public School Teaching: Cross-Sectional Analysis, 1850–1880," *Signs: Journal of Women in Culture and Society* 11, 2 (1986): 221.

88. Strober and Tyack, "Why Do Women Teach?" 499.

89. Rury, "Who Became Teachers?" 19.

90. Bureau of the Census, "Teachers," in *Statistics of Women at Work* (Washington, DC: Government Printing Office, 1907), 110–11.

2. A Distinctly Higher Walk

1. David Tyack and Elisabeth Hansot, *Managers of Virtue: Public School Leadership in America, 1820–1980* (New York: Basic Books, 1982), 97; and Paul C. Nagel, "A West that Failed: The Dream of Charles Francis Adams II," *The Western Historical Quarterly* 18 (October 1987): 397–407.

2. Charles Francis Adams, "The Development of the Superintendency," *Addresses and Journal of Proceedings of the NEA 1880* (Salem, OH: Allan K. Tatem, 1880), 65.

3. Ibid., 67.

4. Ibid., 69–71.

5. Fraser's Report, cited in Francis Adams, *The Free School System of the United States* (London: Chapman and Hall, 1875; reprinted New York: Arno Press & The New York Times, 1969), 17.

6. Ellwood P. Cubberley, *Public Education in the United States* (Boston: Houghton Mifflin, 1934), 212–13.

7. AASA, *The American School Superintendency, 30th Yearbook* (Washington, DC: AASA, Dept. of NEA, 1952), 40–41.

8. Theodore Lee Reller, "The Historical Development of School Administration in the United States," in *Educational Progress and School Administration*, ed. Clyde Milton Hill (New Haven, CT: Yale University Press, 1936), 11.

9. Thomas H. Benton, *Annual Report of the Superintendent of Public Instruction of the State of Iowa* (Iowa City: Palmer & Paul, 1848), 3.

10. Francis Adams, *The Free School System*, 43.

11. Cubberley, *Public Education*, 214.

12. Willard Ellsbree, *The American Teacher: Evolution of a Profession in a Democracy* (New York: American Book Company, 1939), 166; and Francis Adams, *The Free School System*, 43–44.

13. Cubberley, *Public Education*, 218; Francis Adams, *The Free School System*, 43.

14. "Institutes and County Superintendency," *Report of the Superintendent of Public Instruction of Iowa* (Des Moines: G. W. Edwards, 1872), 54. Also see Arthur E. Lee, "The Decline of Radicalism and Its Effect on Public Education in Missouri," *Missouri Historical Review* 74 (October 1979): 11–12, for a discussion of the importance of county superintendents' work with Teachers' Institutes.

15. Wayne Fuller, *Old Country School* (Chicago: University of Chicago Press, 1985), 133–34; Cubberley, *Public Education*, 218; Ellsbree, *American Teacher*, 167–68; E. B. McElroy, "County Superintendents—Their Relations and Duties to Teachers," *Journal of Proceedings and Addresses of the NEA*, 1886 (Salem: NEA, 1887), 337–45; and Clarence Ray Aurner, *History of Education in Iowa*, 2 (Iowa City: State Historical Society of Iowa, 1914), 64–66.

16. Ellwood P. Cubberley, *Public School Administration* (Boston: Houghton Mifflin, 1916), 38–39.

17. Cubberley, *Public Education*, 218.

18. "Institutes and County Superintendency," 55.

19. Ellsbree, *American Teacher*, 168; and Lee, "The Decline of Radicalism," 9–10.

20. Aurner, *History of Education in Iowa*, 79.

21. Cited in Fuller, *Old Country School*, 135–36; also see 153.

22. Cubberley, *Public School Administration*, 52–55; and Ellwood Cubberley, "Politics and the Country-School Problem," *Educational Review* 47 (January 17, 1914), 10–13.

23. Ellsbree, *American Teacher*, 170–71; and Lotus D. Coffman, "The American School Superintendent," *Educational Administration and Supervision* 1 (1915): 15.

24. Ellsbree, *American Teacher*, 173–74; and Reller, "Historical Development of School Administration," 19–23.

25. David Tyack, *The One Best System: A History of American Urban Education* (Cambridge, MA: Harvard University Press, 1974), 37–38; and R. W. Stevenson, "City and Town Supervision of Schools," *Addresses and Proceedings of the NEA, 1887* (Salem, MA: NEA, 1887), 283–92.

26. W. H. Maxwell, "City School Systems," *Journal of Proceedings and Addresses, 1890* (Topeka: NEA, 1890), 447–60; and Reller, " Historical Development of School Administration," 24–26.

27. "Teachers," *Biennial Report of the Superintendent of Public Instruction of Iowa* (Des Moines: R. P. Clarkson, 1876), 44–45.

28. Geraldine Joncich Clifford, "Man/Woman/Teacher: Gender, Family, and Career in American Educational History," in *American Teachers: Histories of a Profession at Work*, ed. Donald Warren (New York: Macmillan, 1989), 326–27.

29. Tyack and Hansot, *Managers of Virtue*, 34–39.

30. Stanley K. Schultz, The *Culture Factory: Boston Public Schools, 1789–1860* (New York: Oxford University Press, 1973), 127, 146–47.

31. Schultz, *The Culture Factory*, 146–47.

32. Cited in David Tyack, *Turning Points in American Educational History* (Waltham, MA: Blaisdell Publishing, 1967), 322.

33. J. L. Pickard, *School Supervision* (New York: Appleton, 1890), 1–2; quoted in H. Warren Button and Eugene Provenzo, *History of Education & Culture in America*, 2nd ed. (Englewood Cliffs, NJ: Prentice Hall, 1989), 136.

34. William H. Payne, *Chapters on School Supervision: A Practical Treatise on Superintendence: Grading; Arranging Courses of Study; the Preparation and Use of Blanks, Records, and Reports; Examinations for Promotion, Etc.* (Cincinnati: Van Antwerp, Bragg & Co., 1875), 13–18.

35. Tyack, *The One Best System*, 24.

36. Gail Hamilton, *Our Common School System* (Boston: Estes and Lauriat, 1880), 91.

37. "Weak Places in Our School System," *Addresses and Journal of Proceedings of the NEA, 1881* (Salem, OH: Allan K. Tatem, 1881), 73.

38. Hamilton, *Common School System*, 91.

39. Joan Burstyn, "Catharine Beecher and the Education of American Women," *New England Quarterly* 47 (1974): 398.

40. Cited in ibid., 398.

41. Comment on the structure of school administration cited in Michael Katz, "The New Departure in Quincy, 1873–81: The Nature of 19th Century Educational Reform," in *Education in American History*, ed. Michael Katz (New York: Prague, 1973), 73.

42. Elisabeth Hansot and David Tyack, *The Dream Deferred: A Golden Age for Women School Administrators*, Policy Paper No. 81-C2 (Palo Alto, CA: Stanford University Institute for Research on Educational Finance and Governance, May 1981), 8.

43. *Report of the Commissioner of Education* (Washington, DC: Government Printing Office, 1874), 124.

44. William E. Chancellor, "The Selection of County Superintendents," *N.E.A. Bulletin* 3, 6 (May 1915): 175–79.

45. May Wright Sewall, "Woman's Work in Education," *Proceedings of the National Educational Association*, 1884 (Boston: J. E. Farwell & Co., 1885), 155.

46. Mrs. George Bass, "Mrs. Young and the Chicago Schools," *School and Society* 2 (October 23, 1915): 605–6.

47. Fuller, *Old Country School*, 140.

48. Emerson White, "Department of Superintendence of the National Educational Association: Brief Sketch of Its Early History," *Journal of Proceedings and Addresses*, 1901 (Washington, DC: NEA, 1901), 233–36.

49. "Why Superintendents Lose Their Jobs," *American School Board Journal* (May 1916): 18–19; and Merrill E. Gates, "Popular Criticisms and Their Proper Influence upon School Superintendence," *Journal of Proceedings and Addresses*, 1890 (Topeka: NEA, 1890), 468–79.

50. Tyack and Hansot, *Managers of Virtue*, 129–67.

51. Harry Kursh, *The United States Office of Education: A Century of Service* (Philadelphia: Chilton Books, 1965), 7, 10.

52. Cited in Kursh, *The United States Office of Education*, 11.

53. Kursh, *The United States Office of Education*, 12–16.

54. Donald R. Warren, *To Enforce Education: A History of the Founding Years of the United States Office of Education* (Detroit: Wayne State University Press, 1974), 165.

55. AASA, "The Centennial Story," 88.

56. From hearings on S. 291 and H.R. 5000, pp. 380–89. 69th Congress, 1st Session. February, 1926; cited in Julia E. Johnsen, *Federal Department of Education* (New York: H. W. Wilson, 1926), 112–13.

57. Payne, *Chapters on School Supervision*, 13–18.

58. Ibid., 75.

59. Tyack, *The One Best System*, 135–36.

60. Ella Flagg Young quoted in *Educational Review* 46 (1913): 540.

61. Robert H. Morrison, "Qualities Leading to Appointment as School Supervisors and Administrators," *Educational Administration and Supervision Including Teacher Training* 12, 8 (November 1926): 510.

62. Joan Wallach Scott, *Gender and the Politics of History* (New York: Columbia University Press, 1988), 113–15.

63. American Association of School Administrators, *The American School Superintendency: Thirtieth Yearbook of the American Association of School Administrators* (Washington, DC: AASA, 1952); and for an analysis of these early reports on the superintendency, see David Tyack, "Pilgrim's Progress: Toward a Social History of the School Superintendency, 1860–1960," *History of Education Quarterly* 16 (Fall 1976): 257–300.

3. Out of Politics

1. Mary Wollstonecraft, *A Vindication of the Rights of Woman* (1792; repr. New York: W. W. Norton, 1988), 21.

2. Margaret Fuller, *Woman in the Nineteenth Century* (1845; repr. New York: W. W. Norton, 1971).

3. Thomas Woody, *A History of Women's Education in the United States*, 2 (New York: Science Press, 1929), 415.

4. Marie Mitchell Olesen Urbanski, *Margaret Fuller's Woman in the Nineteenth Century: A Literary Study of Form and Content, of Sources and Influence* (Westport, CT: Greenwood Press, 1980), 146.

5. "Declaration of Sentiments, "*History of Woman Suffrage*, ed. Elizabeth Cady Stanton, Susan B. Anthony, and Matilda Joslyn Gage, 1 (New York: Fowler & Wells, 1881; repr. Salem, NH: Ayer, 1985), 70–71.

6. Kathleen Barry, *Susan B. Anthony: A Biography of a Singular Feminist* (New York: Ballantine, 1988), 39–45.

7. Louise Rosenfield Noun, "Carrie Lane Chapman Catt and her Mason City Experience," *Palimpsest* 74 (Fall 1993): 130–44.

8. "Betsey Mix Cowles," *Notable American Women*, ed. Barbara Sicherman, Carol Hurd Green, Ilene Kantrov, and Harriette Walker (Cambridge, MA: Belknap Press, 1980), 393–94.

9. T. A. Larson, "Wyoming's Contribution to the Regional and National Women's Rights Movement," *Annals of Wyoming* 52, 1 (Spring 1980): 9.

10. Susan B. Anthony and Ida Harper, eds., *History of Woman Suffrage*, 4 (1900; repr. Salem, NH: Ayer, 1985), 37.

11. Patricia Smith Butcher, "Education for Equality: Women's Rights Periodicals and Women's Higher Education, 1849–1920," *History of Higher Education Annual* 6 (1986): 63–74.

12. Ibid., 64–67.

13. Anne Firor Scott, " The Ever Widening Circle: The Diffusion of Feminist Values from the Troy Female Seminary, 1822–1872," *History of Education Quarterly* 19 (Spring 1979): 8.

14. Ibid., 20.

15. Joan Burstyn, "Catharine Beecher and the Education of American Women," *New England Quarterly* 47 (1974): 386.

16. Mary Beth Norton, "The Paradox of 'Women's Sphere'," in *Women of America: A History*, ed. Carol Ruth Berkin and Mary Beth Norton (Boston: Houghton Mifflin, 1979), 145.

17. Burstyn, "Catharine Beecher," 387.

18. Norton, "The Paradox of 'Women's Sphere'," 145.

19. May Wright Sewall, "Woman's Work in Education," *Proceedings of the National Educational Association*, 1884 (Boston: J. E. Farwell & Co., 1885), 155.

20. May Wright Sewall, *Debate on Woman Suffrage in the Senate of the United States, 2d Session, 49th Congress, January 25, 1887.* Also see Edith M. Phelps, ed., *Selected Articles on Woman Suffrage*, second and revised edition (Minneapolis: H. W. Wilson, 1912), 77–78.

21. Alice S. Blackwell, "Do Teachers Need the Ballot?" in *Selected Articles on Woman Suffrage*, second and revised edition, ed. Edith M. Phelps (Minneapolis: H. W. Wilson, 1912), 74–82; Mary Sumner Boyd, "The Woman Educator and the Vote," in *The Woman Suffrage Yearbook*, 1917 (New York: National Woman Suffrage Publishing Company, 1917), 165–67; Helen L. Grenfell, "The Ballot and the Schools," *Political Equality* leaflets (Warren, OH: National American Woman Suffrage Association, 1904); Alice S. Blackwell, "Progress of Equal Suffrage," *Political Equality* leaflets (Warren, OH: National American Woman Suffrage Association, 1904); Ellen H. E. Price, "School Suffrage and Other Limited Suffragists in the United States," Hearing on House Joint Resolution 68,

House Judiciary Committee (February 15, 1898), 3–5; and Woody, *History of Women's Education*, 2:441–44.

22. "Woman Suffrage in School Affairs," *Annual Report of the Secretary of the Interior*, 1894 (Washington, DC: Government Printing Office, 1896), 1416.

23. Frances M. Bjrkman and Annie G. Porritt, eds., *The Blue Book: Woman Suffrage History, Arguments, and Results* (New York: National Woman Suffrage Publishing Co., 1917). For information on states granting women full suffrage, see "Woman Suffrage a Success," *The Woman Voter* 6, 11 (1914): 14–16.

24. John Eaton, "Women as School Officers," *Report of the Commissioner of Education 1873* (Washington, DC: Government Printing Office, 1874), CXXXIII.

25. "School Legislation in the United States," Report of the Commissioner of Education, 1894–95 (Washington, DC: Government Printing Office, 1896), 960; Woody, *History of Women's Education*, 1:516.

26. Anthony and Harper, *History of Woman Suffrage*, 4:627–28; and "Woman Suffrage in School Affairs," 1417.

27. Woody, *History of Women's Education*, 2:443.

28. Anthony and Harper, *History of Woman Suffrage*, 4:375.

29. Jean Christie, "Sarah Christie Stevens: Schoolwoman," *Minnesota History* 48 (Summer 1983): 250. Also see Kathleen C. Berkeley, "'The Ladies Want to Bring About Reform in the Public Schools': Public Education and Women's Rights in the Post–Civil War South," *History of Education Quarterly* 24 (Spring 1984): 45–58, for a discussion of how organized women in Memphis in 1872–73 rallied to support the election of a highly qualified woman candidate for superintendent. Though this effort failed, Berkeley describes how it served as an awakening among the women to their need for suffrage.

30. Christie, "Sarah Christie Stevens," 252.

31. Carrie Chapman Catt, "The Cave Man Complex vs. Woman Suffrage," *The Woman Citizen* 8 (April 5, 1924): 16.

32. Rev. John Todd, *Woman's Rights* (Boston: Lee and Shepard, 1887).

33. For a description of Strachan's efforts on behalf of the Interborough Association of Women Teachers, see David Tyack and Elisabeth Hansot, *Managers of Virtue: Public School Leadership in America, 1820–1980* (New York: Basic Books, 1982), 185. Strachan's detailed arguments and strategies to win some measure of sex equity in school employment are recounted in her work, *Equal Pay for Equal Work* (New York: B. F. Buck & Co., 1910).

34. Anthony and Harper, *History of Woman Suffrage*, 4:575–78.

35. Helen Laura Sumner Woodbury, *Equal Suffrage* (New York: Collegiate Equal Suffrage League, 1909), 128–44.

36. Kathleen Underwood, "Schoolmarms on the Upper Missouri," *Great Plains Quarterly* (Fall 1991): 225–33, especially 227.

37. "Women as Voters and School Officers," *Report of the Commissioner of Education 1880* (Syracuse, NY: C. W. Bardeen, 1901), 26.

38. Frances M. Bjrkman and Annie G. Porritt, eds., "The Blue Book," *Woman Suffrage History, Arguments, and Results* (New York: National Woman Suffrage Publishing, 1917), 30–40.

39. *The Woman Suffrage Yearbook, 1917* (New York: National Woman Suffrage Publishing, 1917), 166.

40. Winnifred Harper Cooley, *The New Womanhood* (New York: Broadway Publishing, 1904), 129–30. Also, a scarcely noted woman state school superintendent was Emma J. McVicker of Utah, who completed the term of a state superintendent who died in office in 1900. McVicker filed a report that year detailing such problems as misappropriated teacher salary money, pervasive business mentality among school board members at the expense of sound educational considerations, incompetence of male teachers, and a series of other problems. Carol Ann Lubomudrov describes McVicker's brief term in "A Woman State School Superintendent: Whatever Happened to Mrs. McVicker?" *Utah Historical Quarterly* 49, 3 (1981): 254–61.

41. Woody, *History of Women's Education*, 1:517.

42. *Report of the Commissioner of Education 1900–1901*, 2 (Washington, DC: Government Printing Office, 1902), 1228–229.

43. "Women in Our Public Schools," *American Educational Review* 34 (March 1913): 289–90, and *Woman Suffrage Yearbook*, 1917, 165–67.

44. Ida Husted Harper, ed., *History of Woman Suffrage*, 5 (1920; repr. Salem, NH: Ayer, 1985), 103–5.

45. Anthony and Harper, *The History of Woman Suffrage*, 4:1042–44.

46. Ibid.,4:1045.

47. Ibid., 4:1043–44. For census data, see Bureau of the Census, 1900.

48. Anthony and Harper, *The History of Woman Suffrage*, 4:1042–43.

49. Joan N. Burstyn, "Historical Perspectives on Women in Educational Leadership," in *Women and Educational Leadership*, ed. Sari Biklen and Marilyn Brannigan (Lexington, MA: Lexington Books, 1980), 71.

50. Anthony and Harper, *The History of Woman Suffrage*, 4:1071–72.

51. Ibid., 4:1050, 1052, 1071.

52. Nancy Cott, *The Grounding of Modern Feminism* (New Haven, CT: Yale University Press, 1987), 87.

53. Mrs. O. Shepard Barnum, "The Past, Present, and Future of the Patrons' Department," *Proceedings of the NEA 1917* (Washington, DC: NEA, 1917), 639–45; Marjorie Murphy, *Blackboard Unions* (Ithaca, NY: Cornell University Press, 1990), 59.

54. Mrs. Barnum, "The Past, Present, and Future," 639–45; and Burstyn, "Historical Perspectives," 70–72.

55. Anthony and Harper, *The History of Woman Suffrage*, 4:1071.

56. "Arthur Capper," *The Woman Citizen* (September 8, 1923): 29.

57. *The Woman Voter* 5, 1 (1914): 26.

58. U.S. Office of Education, *Biennial Survey of Education 1916–1918* (Washington, DC: Office of Education, 1921), 10.

59. "Women Teachers' Clubs," *Journal of Education* 37, 14 (April 6, 1893): 216.

60. "Celestia Susannah Parrish," *Notable American Women*, ed. Sicherman, Green, Kantrov, and Walker, 18–20; Marcia G. Synnott, "Celestia Susannah Parish," *Women Educators in the United States, 1820–1993: A Bio-Bibliographical Sourcebook*, ed. Maxine Schwartz Seller (Westport, CT: Greenwood Press, 1994), 359–67.

61. Barbara Sicherman, Carol Hurd Green, Ilene Kantrov, and Harriette Walker, eds., *Notable American Women: 1607–1950* (Cambridge, MA: Belknap Press, 1980).

62. Joan Smith, *Ella Flagg Young: Portrait of a Leader* (Ames, Iowa: Educational Studies Press and the Iowa State University Research Foundation, 1979), 164–173. When she died a few years later, the annual NEA proceedings made little mention of her passing or of her monumental contributions to the association. See "Resolutions," *Addresses and Proceedings of the NEA 1919* (Washington, DC: NEA, 1919).

63. Mrs. George Bass, "Mrs. Young and the Chicago Schools," *School and Society* 2 (October 23, 1915): 605–6.

64. Ibid.

65. B. V. Hubbard, *Socialism, Feminism, and Suffragism, the Terrible Triplets Connected by the Same Umbilical Cord and Fed from the Same Nursing Bottle* (Chicago: American Publishing, 1915), 282–84.

66. For a discussion of Young's difficulties with the Chicago school board, see George Herbert Mead, "A Heckling School Board and an Educational Stateswoman," *Survey* 31 (1914): 443–44. Helen Christine Bennett described Young's tenure in the Chicago superintendency in *American Women in Civic Work* (New York: Dodd, Mead and Co., 1915), 255–77.

67. Susan M. Dorsey, "Relations of the Superintendent of Schools to the Teaching Corps," *Addresses and Proceedings of the National Education Association*, 1924 (Washington, DC: National Education Association, 1924), 869–75, especially 871.

68. Bennett, *American Women*, 261–77; Smith, *Ella Flagg Young*, 122–27.

69. Mrs. W. S. Griswold, "The Rural School's Friend," *The Woman Citizen* 8 (June 16, 1923): 10.

70. Griswold, "The Rural School's Friend," 10. See Spencer J. Maxcy, "The Teacherage in American Rural Education," *The Jorunal of General Education* 30, 4 (Winter 1979): 267–74, for a discussion of the origin of teacherages and their parallels to parsonages. Preston served as the president of the NEA in 1920.

71. "Report of the National Council of Administrative Women in Education," *Proceedings of the NEA 1933* (Washington, DC: NEA, 1933), 270.

72. "The Work of a Local Branch," *Proceedings of the NEA 1934* (Washington, DC: NEA, 1934), 268.

73. George S. Counts, *The Social Composition of Boards of Education: A Study in the Social Control of Public Education* (Chicago: University of Chicago Press, 1927), 43.

74. Counts, *The Social Composition*, 42–45.

75. Helen L. Grenfell, "The Constitution of the Ideal School Board," *American School Board Journal* 38 (1909): 26.

76. "It's 'No Accident' That Men Outnumber Women on School Boards Nine to One," *American School Board Journal* 161 (May 1974): 53. For more recent data, see "Leadership," *American School Board Journal* 177 (December 1990): A12–13.

77. Margaret Gribskov, "Feminism and the Woman School Administrator," in *Women and Educational Leadership*, ed. Sari Knopp Biklen and Marilyn Brannigan (Lexington, MA: Lexington Books, 1980), 77.

78. Sara M. Evans, *Born for Liberty: A History of Women in America* (New York: Free Press, 1989), 187.

79. Eleanor Flexner, *Century of Struggle: The Woman's Rights Movement in the United States*, revised edition (Cambridge, MA: Belknap Press, 1975), 340.

80. Raymond Callahan, *Education and the Cult of Efficiency* (Chicago: University of Chicago Press, 1962).

81. Callahan, *Education and the Cult of Efficiency*, 150.

82. Emphasis added. "Iowa Teachers," *Journal of Education* 39 (January 18, 1894): 44.

83. Underwood, "Schoolmarms," 227.

84. "Colorado," *Journal of Education* 39 (May 31, 1894): 348.

85. Emphasis added. "Colorado Teachers," *Journal of Education* 39 (January 11, 1894): 28.

86. Emphasis added. "Colorado," *Journal of Education* 39 (March 8, 1894): 156.

87. "Colorado," *Journal of Education* 39 (May 3, 1894): 284.

88. "Colorado School Election," *Journal of Education* 39 (May 17, 1894): 312.

89. *The Woman Suffrage Yearbook,* 1917, 165. Also see Sumner Woodbury, *Equal Suffrage,* 122–46; and Joseph G. Brown, *The History of Equal Suffrage in Colorado, 1868–1898* (Denver: News Job Printing, 1898), 16–52.

90. David Snedden, "Elective vs. Appointive Educational Officials," *Educational Administration & Supervision* 1, 1 (1915): 65–66.

91. "Out of Politics," *American School Board Journal* 38 (March 1909): 6.

92. Emphasis added. "Hiring a Superintendent," *American School Board Journal* 37 (August 1908): 8.

93. Lee L. Driver, "Report of the Committee on the County Superintendents' Problems," *Addresses and Proceedings of the National Education Association, 1922* (Washington, DC: National Education Association, 1922), 293–303, especially 303.

94. Ellwood P. Cubberley, *Public School Administration* (Boston: Houghton Mifflin, 1916), 38–39.

95. "Legal Status of the School Superintendent," *National Education Association Research Bulletin* 29 (October 1951): 128.

96. Murphy, *Blackboard Unions,* 57–58.

97. Margaret A. Haley, president of the National Federation of Teachers, Chicago, "Why Teachers Should Organize," in *Journal of Proceedings and Addresses of the National Educational Association 1904* (Winona, MN: National Educational Association, 1904), 145–52.

98. Aaron Gove, Superintendent of Denver Schools, "Limitations of the Superintendents' Authority and of the Teacher's Independence," in *Journal of Proceedings and Addresses of the National Educational Association 1904* (Winona, MN: National Educational Association, 1904), 152–57.

99. "Notes and News," *Educational Review* 28 (June 1904): 107.

4. A Change in Fashion

1. Louis I. Dublin, "The Higher Education of Women and Race Betterment, " in *Eugenics in Race and State*, 2 (Baltimore, MD: Williams & Wilkins, 1921), 384–85.

2. Joe L. Dubbert, "Progressivism and the Masculinity Crisis," *Psychoanalytic Review* 61 (1974): 443–55.

3. John K. Folger and Charles B. Nam, *Education of the American Population: A 1960 Census Monograph*, (Washington, DC: U.S. Bureau of the Census, 1967), 81.

4. Folger and Nam, *Education of the American Population*, 81.

5. Kathryn Kish Sklar, "Catharine Beecher: Transforming the Teaching Profession," in *Women's America: Refocusing the Past*, 3rd ed., ed. Linda K. Kerber and Jane Sherron DeHart (New York: Oxford University Press, 1991), 177.

6. Catharine E. Beecher, *The True Remedy for the Wrongs of Women* (Boston: Phillips, Sampson, 1851), 52–60, quoted in David Tyack and Elisabeth Hansot, *Learning Together: A History of Coeducation in American Public Schools* (New York: Russell Sage Foundation, 1992), 41.

7. Geraldine Joncich Clifford, "Daughters into Teachers: Education and Demographic Influences on the Transformation into 'Women's Work' in America," *History of Education Review* 12 (Spring 1983): 15–28; Richard M. Bernard and Maris A. Vinovskis, "The Female School Teacher in Antebellum Massachusetts," *Journal of Social History* 10 (1977): 336–37.

8. David Tyack and Myra Strober, "Jobs and Gender," in *Educational Policy and Management: Sex Differentials*, ed. Patricia A. Schmuck, W. W. Charters Jr., and Richard O. Carlson (New York: Academic Press, 1981), 131–52.

9. The term "spinster" originated in Europe, where unmarried women commonly employed their time literally by spinning thread. In general parlance, "spinster" eventually came to mean a single woman. From 1850 to around 1950 in this country, so many school teachers were single women that the terms "spinster" and "teacher" became popularly linked. See Judy Grahn, *Another Mother Tongue* (Boston: Beacon Press, 1984), 111–13.

10. Catherine Goggin, "Early Days," quoted in Marjorie Murphy, *Blackboard Unions: The AFT and the NEA, 1900–1980* (Ithaca, NY: Cornell University Press, 1990), 73.

11. Richard A. Quantz, "The Complex Visions of Female Teachers and the Failure of Unionization in the 1930s: An Oral History," *History of Education Quarterly* 25 (Winter 1985): 446.

12. Grace Strachan, "Two Masters Cannot be Served," *The Woman Voter* 5, 12 (1914): 12.

13. "Employment of Married Women as Teachers," *Research Bulletin of the NEA* 10 (1932): 17.

14. For data on the marital status of women teachers, see Folger and Nam, *Education of the American Population*, 81.

15. Howard K. Beale, *Are American Teachers Free?* (New York: Charles Scribner's, 1936), 384–85.

16. Thomas Woody, *A History of Women's Education in the United States*, 1. (New York: Science Press, 1929), 509.

17. Elisabeth Hansot and David Tyack first described the tendency among some urban women superintendents to serve while single, divorced, or widowed in *Managers of Virtue: Public School Leadership in America, 1820–1980* (New York: Basic Books, 1982), 196. See Kellie Wilkinson McGarrh, "Hangin' in Tough: The Life of Superintendent Mildred E. Doyle, 1904–1989," (Ph.D. diss., University of Tennessee, Knoxville, 1995), for a rich biographical portrait of Knoxville's Mildred Doyle. Brief biographical sketches of the remaining listed superintendents can be found in Barbara Sicherman, Carol Hurd Green, Ilene Kantrov, and Harriette Walker, eds., *Notable American Women* (Cambridge, MA: Belknap Press of Harvard University Press, 1980).

18. David Tyack, "Pilgrim's Progress: Toward a Social History of the School Superintendency, 1860–1960," in *History of Education Quarterly* 16 (Fall 1976): 257–300.

19. William H. Payne's *Chapters on School Supervision: A Practical Treatise on Superintendence; Grading; Arranging Courses of Study; the Preparation and Use of Blanks, Records, and Reports; Examinations for Promotion, Etc.* (Cincinnati: Van Antwerp, Bragg & Co., 1875), 47–53.

20. NEA Department of Superintendence/AASA surveys were published in 1923, 1933, 1952, 1960, and 1971. For an excellent descriptive summary of the first four of these surveys, see David Tyack, "Pilgrim's Progress," 257–300. For discussion on the dual marriage standards for school administrators, see Hansot and Tyack, "The Dream Deferred," 22–23.

21. Daniel H. Mundt, "How We Selected a Superintendent," *American School Board Journal* 146 (April 1963): 13.

22. For an extensive treatment of the connections between masculinity and the U.S. economy, see Julie A. Matthaei, *An Economic History of Women in America: Women's Work, the Sexual Division of Labor, and the Development of Capitalism* (New York: Schocken Books, 1982), especially 105–6.

23. For a discussion of the masculinity crisis, see Dubbert, "Progressivism and the Masculinity Crisis," 443–55.

24. Joe L. Dubbert, *A Man's Place: Masculinity in Transition* (Englewood Cliffs, NJ: Prentice Hall, 1979); George Chauncey, "From Sexual Inversion to Homosexuality: Medicine and the Changing Conception of Female Deviance," *Salmagundi* 58–59 (1983): 114–46.

25. Herbert Branston Gray, "Report," *Reports of the Mosely Educational Commission to the United States* (London: Co-operative Printing Society, 1904; repr. New York: Arno Press and the New York Times, 1969), 166.

26. Horace Coon, *Coquetry for Men* (New York: Amour Press, 1932), 110–11, quoted in Christina Simmons, "Companionate Marriage and the Lesbian Threat," *Frontiers* 4 (Fall 1979): 55.

27. G. Stanley Hall, *Adolescence*, 2 (New York: D. Appleton and Company, 1931), 623.

28. Tyack and Hansot, *Learning Together*, 165–200.

29. "Male Teachers Needed," *American School Board Journal* 37 (December 1908): 8.

30. Edward L. Thorndike, *Education: A First Book* (New York: Macmillan, 1912), 155.

31. Dublin, "The Higher Education," 384–85.

32. Ibid., 381–82.

33. Walter M. Gallichan, *The Great Unmarried* (London: T. Werner Laurie, 1916), 72–73.

34. "Notes and Notices," *Eugenics Review* 11 (April 1919): 47.

35. Nathan G. Hale, *The Rise and Crisis of Psychoanalysis in the United States: Freud and the Americans, 1917–1985* (New York: Oxford University Press, 1995), 3–9.

36. Chauncey, "From Sexual Inversion to Homosexuality," 114–46; Lillian Faderman, "The Morbidification of Love between Woman by 19th-Century Sexologists," *Journal of Homosexuality* 4 (Fall 1978): 73–90.

37. Faderman, "The Morbidification of Love between Women," 73–90.

38. Vern L. Bullough, "Katharine Bement Davis, Sex Research, and the Rockefeller Foundation," *Bulletin of the History of Medicine* 62 (Spring 1988): 78–79.

39. Katharine Bement Davis, *Factors in the Sex Life of Twenty-Two Hundred Women* (1929; repr., New York: Arno Press and New York Times, 1972), 247, 263.

40. Willard Waller, *The Sociology of Teaching* (New York: John Wiley and Sons, 1932), 143.

41. Margaret Korzitzer, *The Modern Woman and Herself* (London: Jonathan Cape, 1932), 247–49.

42. Andrea Weiss, *Vampires & Violets: Lesbians in Film* (New York: Penguin Books, 1992), 8–11.

43. Waller, *The Sociology of Teaching*, 147–49.

44. Lillian Faderman, "Nineteenth-Century Boston Marriage as a Possible Lesson for Today," in *Boston Marriages: Romantic but Asexual Relationships among Contemporary Lesbians*, ed. Esther D. Rothblum and Kathleen A. Brehony (Amherst, MA: University of Massachusetts Press, 1993), 29–42.

45. Blanche Wiesen Cook, "Female Support Networks and Political Activism: Lillian Wald, Crystal Eastman, Emma Goldman," *Chrysalis* 3 (1977): 43–61.

46. See Alison Oram's excellent article, "'Embittered, Sexless or Homosexual': Attacks on Spinster Teachers 1918–39," in *Not a Passing Phase: Reclaiming Lesbians in History 1840–1985* (London: The Women's Press, 1989), 99–118, for a discussion of how the image of the spinster schoolteacher was conflated with that of the "embittered" lesbian. For a description of Young's relationship with Brayton, see Joan Smith, *Ella Flagg Young: Portrait of a Leader* (Ames, Iowa: The Educational Studies Press, 1979), 186–96.

47. "Marriage as Related to Eligibility," *NEA Research Bulletin* 20 (March 1942): 61.

48. Leo M. Chamberlain and Leonard E. Meece, "Women and Men in the Teaching Profession," *Bulletin of the Bureau of School Service* (University of Kentucky) 9 (March 1937): 57.

49. "Marriage as a Basis for Termination of Service," *NEA Research Bulletin* 20 (May 1942): 108

50. Ibid., 107–8.

51. "Marriage as Related to Eligibility," 60.

52. Ibid.

53. Ferdinand Lundberg and Marynia Farnham, *Modern Woman: The Lost Sex* (New York: Harper & Brothers, 1947), 364–65.

54. Statistics from the 1943 and 1962 volumes of *Patterson's American Education Directory* (Mt. Prospect, IL: Education Directories Inc.). Kansas was cho-

sen because it is one of the only states that consistently listed women superintendents with titles (Mrs., Dr.) over the years in question. Other states often
omitted titles or included them erratically.

55. Regina Markell Morantz, "The Scientist as Sex Crusader: Alfred C.
Kinsey and American Culture," *American Quarterly* 29 (1977): 563–89.

56. Alfred Kinsey, Wardell B. Pomeroy, and Clyde E. Martin, *Sexual Behavior in the Human Male* (Philadephia: W. B. Saunders, 1948), 5.

57. Kinsey, Pomeroy, and Martin, *Sexual Behavior,* 625. Kinsey employed a
taxonomic approach in selecting his study participants, rather than random
sampling.

58. John D'Emilio, *Sexual Politics, Sexual Communities, 1940–1970: The Making of a Sexual Minority* (Chicago: University of Chicago Press, 1983), 32–37.

59. Ibid., 33–37.

60. Allan Berube and Jóhn D'Emilio, "The Military and Lesbians during
the McCarthy Years," *Signs: Journal of Women and Culture in Society* 9 (Summer
1984): 759–75; see also Allan Berube, *Coming Out under Fire: The History of Gay
Men and Women in World War Two* (New York: Penguin, 1990).

61. 81st Congress, 2nd Session, comments by Robert F. Rich (Representa-
tive from Pennsylvania), "Perverts in Federal Agencies Called Peril to United
States Security," *Congressional Record* (Washington, DC: Government Printing
Office, 1950), Appendix 7755.

62. Ibid.

63. "Mail Snooping, *"The New Republic* (August 21, 1965): 6–7.

64. D'Emilio, *Sexual Politics,* 40–49.

65. Ibid., 44.

66. Florida Legislative Investigation Committee, *Homosexuality and Citizenship in Florida: A Report* (Tallahassee, FL: Author, 1964).

67. Jonathan Katz, *Gay American History,* revised ed. (New York: Meridian,
1992), 125.

68. Karen Harbeck, "Gay and Lesbian Educators: Past History/Future
Prospects," in *Coming Out of the Classroom Closet: Gay and Lesbian Students, Teachers and Curricula,* ed. Karen Harbeck (New York: Harrington Park Press, 1992),
125–26. Also, for an outstanding history of the social and legal concerns of gay
and lesbian teachers, see Karen Harbeck's doctoral dissertation, "Personal Free-
doms/Public Constraints: An Analysis of the Controversy over the Employment of Homosexuals as School Teachers," 2 vols. (Ph.D. diss., Stanford
University, 1987).

69. Harbeck, "Gay and Lesbian Educators," 125–26.

70. Harbeck, "Personal Freedoms," 153.

71. Eugene E. Levitt and Albert D. Klassen, "Public Attitudes toward Homosexuality: Part of the 1970 National Survey by the Institute for Sex Research," *Journal of Homosexuality* 1 (1974): 33.

72. Lillian Faderman, *Odd Girls and Twilight Lovers: A History of Lesbian Life in Twentieth-Century America* (New York: Penguin, 1991), 156.

73. See Madiha Didi Khyatt, *Lesbian Teachers: An Invisible Presence* (Albany, NY: SUNY Press, 1992), for an exhaustive accounting of the experiences of nineteen lesbian teachers and how they balanced their hidden identities with their public images in schools.

74. Charol Shakeshaft, *Women in Educational Administration*, updated edition (Newbury Park, CA: Sage, 1989), 48.

75. Clare Broadhead, James E. Heald, Stanley E. Hecker, Donald J. Leu, and Herbert C. Rudman, "The Woman Principal—Going the Way of the Buffalo?" *The National Elementary Principal* 45 (April 1966): 6.

76. Shakeshaft, *Women*, 48.

77. Sakre Kennington Edson, *Pushing the Limits: The Female Administrative Aspirant* (Albany, NY: SUNY Press, 1988), 109.

78. The comparison between marriage rates of the general population and of male superintendents is elaborated in C. Emily Feistritzer, *Profile of School Administrators in the United States* (Washington, DC: National Center for Education Information, 1988), 17.

79. W. W. Carpenter, *The Administrator's Wife* (Boston: Christopher Publishing House, 1941), cited in David Tyack and Elisabeth Hansot, *Managers of Virtue*, 191. Also see "What is the Role of the School Administrator's Wife?" *Official Report of the American Association of School Administrators 1960* (Washington, DC: American Association of School Administrators, 1960), 221–39.

80. Janne and Clyde E. Blocker, "The School Executive's Wife," *American School Board Journal* 146 (May 1963): 12.

81. McGarrh, *Hangin' in Tough*, 115–24.

82. Arlie Hochschild, *The Second Shift* (New York: Avon Books, 1989).

83. Alice S. Barter, "The Status of Women in School Administration," *Educational Digest* 25 (October 1959): 40–41; Harris A. Taylor, "Women in Administration," *American School and University* 38 (December 1963): 21–23; and Claire Broadhead, James E. Heald, Stanley E. Hecker, Donald J. Leu, and Herbert Rudman, "The Woman Principal: Gone the Way of the Buffalo?" *The National Elementary Principal* 45 (April 1966): 6–11.

84. Jean Stockard, "Sex Inequalities and the Experiences of Students," in *Sex Equity in Education*, ed. Jean Stockard, Patricia Schmuck, Ken Kempner, Peg Williams, Sakre Edson, and Mary Ann Smith, (New York: Academic Press, 1980), 29–30.

85. For an excellent discussion of the connections between homophobia and sex discrimination, see Suzanne Pharr, *Homophobia: A Weapon of Sexism* (Inverness, CA: Chardon Press, 1988).

5. The Way of the Buffalo

1. National Council of Administrative Women in Education, "Needed: More Women in School Administration," *Senior Scholastic Teachers' Edition* 86 (April 8, 1965): 1.

2. Clare Broadhead, James E. Heald, Stanley E. Hecker, Donald J. Leu, and Herbert C. Rudman, "The Woman Principal—Going the Way of the Buffalo?" *The National Elementary Principal* 45, 5 (April 1966): 6–11.

3. Ibid., 6.

4. Norma Q. Hare, "The Vanishing Woman Principal," *The National Elementary Principal* 45, 5 (April 1966): 12–13.

5. Broadhead, Heald, Hecker, Leu, and Rudman, "The Woman Principal," 8.

6. Willard Waller offers a lengthy discussion of the problems of returning war veterans in *The Veteran Comes Back* (New York: Dryden Press, 1944), 92–191.

7. For a discussion of the political forces that shaped the G.I. Bill, see J. M. Stephen Peeps, "A B.A. for the G.I. . . . Why?" *History of Education Quarterly* 24 (Winter 1984): 513–525.

8. Keith W. Olson, *The G.I. Bill, the Veterans, and the Colleges* (Lexington, KY: University Press of Kentucky, 1974), 43–56.

9. Barbara Miller Solomon, *In the Company of Educated Women* (New Haven, CT: Yale University Press, 1985), 188–97.

10. Roald F. Campbell, Thomas Fleming, L. Jackson Newell, and John W. Bennion, *A History of Thought and Practice in Educational Administration* (New York: Teachers College Press, 1987), 54.

11. Victor Leonard, "No Man's Land," *American School Board Journal* 113 (September 1946): 21–22.

12. Raymond E. Callahan, *Education and the Cult of Efficiency: A Study of the Social Forces That Have Shaped the Administration of the Public Schools* (Chicago: University of Chicago Press, 1962), 262.

13. Alice S. Barter, "The Status of Women in School Administration," *Education Digest* 25 (October 1959): 40.

14. "The Organized Teaching Profession," in *Education in the States: Nationwide Development since 1900*, ed. Edgar Fuller and Jim Pearson (Washington, DC: NEA, 1969), 667.

15. Joan Kalvelage, "The Decline in Female Elementary Principals since 1928: Riddles and Clues" (Eugene, OR: Sex Equity in Educational Leadership Project, 1978), 1; Suzanne S. Taylor, "Educational Leadership: A Male Domain?" *Phi Delta Kappan* 55 (October 1973): 124.

16. Robert I. Wessel, "Athletics and Their Effects on Female Teachers in Public Schools in Iowa," *Iowa State Journal of Research* 55, 3 (1981): 245–252.

17. Betty Friedan and Anne Grant West, "Sex Bias: The Built-In Mentality that Maims the Public Schools," *The American School Board Journal* 159 (October 1971): 16–20.

18. Vynce A. Hines and Hulda Grobman, "The Weaker Sex is Losing Out," *American School Board Journal* 132 (March 1956):100.

19. AASA Commission on the Preparation of Professional School Administrators, *The American School Superintendent: An AASA Research Study*, ed. Stephen J. Knezevich (Washington, DC: American Association of School Administrators, 1971), 25–27, 48.

20. Carol Poll, "It's a Good Job for a Woman (and a Man): Why Males and Females Choose to be Elementary School Teachers," paper presented at the annual meeting of the American Sociological Association (1979), cited by Charol Shakeshaft, *Women in Educational Administration* (Newbury Park, CA: Sage, 1989), 50.

21. Roald F. Campbell, "The Superintendent—His Role and Professional Status," in *An Introduction to School Administration: Selected Readings*, ed. M. Chester Nolte (New York: Macmillan, 1966), 316–17.

22. Hazel Davis and Agnes Samuelson, "Women in Education," *The Journal of Social Issues* 6, 3 (1950): 32–34; Marguerite Wykoff Zapoleon, "Women in the Professions," *The Journal of Social Issues* 6, 3 (1950): 20; J. W. Campbell, "Women Drop Back In: Educational Innovation in the Sixties," in *Academic Women on the Move*, ed. A. S. Rossi and A. Calderwood (New York: Russell Sage Foundation, 1973), 93–124, cited in Jean Stockard, "Sex Inequities in the Experiences of Students," in *Sex Equity in Education*, ed. Jean Stockard, Patricia A. Schmuck, Ken Kempner, Peg Williams, Sakre K. Edson, and Mary Ann Smith (New York: Academic Press, 1980), 29–30.

23. AASA, *The American School Superintendent*, 25–27, 48.

24. Myra Strober, "Toward a General Theory of Occupational Sex Segregation: The Case of Public School Teaching," in *Sex Segregation in the Workplace:*

Trends, Explanations, Remedies, ed. Barbara F. Reskin (Washington, DC: National Academy Press, 1984), 149–50.

25. Council of State Governments, *The Forty-Eight State School Systems* (Chicago: Council of State Governments, 1949), 165.

26. David Tyack and Elisabeth Hansot, *Managers of Virtue: Public School Leadership in America, 1820–1980* (New York: Basic Books, 1982), 220.

27. AASA, *The American School Superintendency 30th Yearbook* (Washington, DC: AASA, Department of the NEA, 1952), 62.

28. Arthur D. Morse, "Who's Trying to Ruin Our Schools?" *McCall's* 78 (September 1951): 26–27, 94, 102, 108–9.

29. AASA, "The Centennial Story," in *An Introduction to School Administration: Selected Readings,* ed. M. Chester Nolte (New York: Macmillan, 1966), 96.

30. Jack A. Culbertson, "A Century's Quest for a Knowledge Base," in *Handbook of Research on Educational Administration,* ed. Norman J. Boyan (New York: Longman, 1988), 15.

31. AASA, "Research in Administrative Theory," in *An Introduction to School Administration: Selected Readings,* ed. M. Chester Nolte (New York: Macmillan, 1966), 334–45.

32. Culbertson, "A Century's Quest," 15; AASA, "Research in Administrative Theory," 334–45.

33. AASA, "The Centennial Story," 99–100.

34. M. Chester Nolte, *Introduction to School Administration: Selected Readings* (New York: Macmillan, 1966), 333.

35. Jack Culbertson, *Building Bridges: UCEA's First Two Decades* (University Park, PA: University Council for Education Administration, 1995), 96–102.

36. James W. Garrison, David J. Parks, and Mary Jane Connelly, *Defining the "Philosophical and Cultural Values" Performance Domain,* Report for the National Commission for the Principalship (1991), 84–85. Also see Spencer Maxcy, *Educational Leadership: A Critical Pragmatic Perspective* (New York: Bergin & Garvey, 1991), 14.

37. Evelyn Fox Keller, *Reflections on Gender and Science* (New Haven, CT: Yale University Press, 1985), 3–4; Garrison, Parks, and Connelly, *Defining the "Philosophical and Cultural Values,"* 84–85; Maxcy, *Educational Leadership,* 14. Also for an analysis of the exclusion of women authors in the UCEA's featured journal, see Charol Shakeshaft and Marjorie Hanson, "Androcentric Bias in the *Educational Administration Quarterly,*" *Educational Administration Quarterly* 22, 1 (Winter 1986): 68–92.

38. The National Council of Administrative Women in Education released a report, *Administrative Opportunities for Women in School Systems* (June 1951), which indicated that in cities with policies favoring the promotion of teachers to administrative positions, there were proportionately more women in administration. Conversely, women fared less well in systems that favored outsiders, or that demonstrated no promotional preference (pp. 11–12). A 1932 study of Ohio school administrators also indicated that women tended to be promoted from within the system. See Earl W. Anderson, "The Woman School Executive," *The School Executive* 57 (March 1938), 332.

39. *Digest of Education Statistics,* 1975 and 1980, cited in Flora Ida Ortiz and Catherine Marshall, "Women in Educational Administration," in *Handbook of Research on Educational Administration,* ed. Norman J. Boyan (New York: Longman, 1988), 129.

40. Catherine Dillon Lyon and Terry N. Saario, "Women in Public Education: Sexual Discrimination in Promotions," *Phi Delta Kappan* 55 (October 1973): 121.

41. Culbertson, *Building Bridges,* 160–68.

42. Campbell, "The Superintendent," 315–16.

43. AASA, *The American School Superintendent,* 15–16, 21–22.

44. Broadhead, Heald, Hecker, Leu, and Rudman, "The Woman Principal," 8.

45. AASA, *The American School Superintendency,* 231.

46. Willard S. Ellsbree, *The American Teacher* (New York: American Book Co., 1939), 517.

47. William Spalding, "Teachers' Organizations are Poor Stuff," *The Nation's Schools* 37 (March 1946): 41.

48. AASA, *The American School Superintendency,* 11–12.

49. Marjorie Murphy, *Blackboard Unions: The AFT & the NEA, 1900–1980* (Ithaca, NY: Cornell University Press, 1990), 209–31.

50. Tyack and Hansot, *Managers of Virtue,* 240–41.

51. Allan M. West, *The National Education Association: The Power Base for Education* (New York: Free Press, 1980), 83–84.

52. Ruth Milkman, "Gender at Work: The Sexual Division of Labor during World War II," in *Women's America: Refocusing the Past,* 3rd ed., ed. Linda K. Kerber and Jane Sherron De Hart (New York: Oxford University Press, 1991), 438–49.

53. Bureau of the Census, *Historical Statistics of the United States,* pt. 1 (Washington, DC: U.S. Government Printing Office, 1975).

54. Eva Moskowitz, "'It's Good to Blow Your Top': Women's Magazines and a Discourse of Discontent, 1945–1965," *Journal of Women's History* 8, 3 (Fall 1996): 66–98.

55. Marynia Farnham and Ferdinand Lundberg, *The Modern Woman: The Lost Sex* (New York: Harper & Brothers, 1947), 355–77.

56. Harris A. Taylor, "Women in Administration," in *An Introduction to School Administration: Selected Readings*, ed. M. Chester Nolte (New York: Macmillan, 1966), 404.

57. Ibid.

58. Ibid.

59. S. Taylor, "Educational Leadership," 124.

60. H. Taylor, "Women in Administration," 404.

61. Broadhead, Heald, Hecker, Leu, and Rudman, "The Woman Principal," 8.

62. Barter, "The Status of Women," 40–41.

63. Broadhead, Heald, Hecker, Leu, and Rudman, "The Woman Principal," 10.

64. Ibid., 11.

65. S. Taylor, "Educational Leadership," 124–28.

66. Suzanne S. Taylor, "The Attitudes of Superintendents and Board of Education Members in Connecticut toward the Employment and Effectiveness of Women as Public School Administrators" (Doctoral dissertation, University of Connecticut, 1971), cited in Taylor, "Educational Leadership," 124–28.

67. *Report of the New York State Commission on the Quality, Cost, and Financing of Elementary and Secondary Education*, 3 (1972), 13–100, cited in Lyon and Saario, "Women in Public Education," 120–23. Also see Hare, "The Vanishing Woman Principal," 13; and Wiles, Kimball, and Brogman, Hulda Gross, "Principals as Leaders," *Nation's Schools* 56 (October 1955): 75.

68. H. Taylor, "Women in Administration," 404.

6. Is This All?

1. Betty Friedan, *The Feminine Mystique* (Dell, 1963), 11.

2. Linda K. Kerber and Jane Sherron De Hart, eds., *Women's America: Refocusing the Past*, 3rd ed. (New York: Oxford University Press, 1991), 479–80.

3. Patricia Schmuck, "Context of Change: The Women's Movement as a Political Process," in *Sex Equity in Education,* ed. Jean Stockard, Patricia Schmuck, Ken Kempner, Peg Williams, Sakre Edson, and Mary Ann Smith, (New York: Academic Press, 1980), 172–75; Andrew Fishel and Janice Pottker, *National Politics and Sex Discrimination in Education* (Lexington, MA: Lexington Books, 1977), 2; and Sara M. Evans, *Born for Liberty: A History of Women in America* (New York: Free Press, 1989), 274–75.

4. Evans, *Born for Liberty,* 274–77.

5. Ibid., 278.

6. Cited in ibid., 287.

7. "*Ms.*: 20 Years of the U.S. Women's Movement," *Ms.* 3, 1 (July-August 1992).

8. Betty Friedan and Anne Grant West, "Sex Bias: The Built-in Mentality that Maims the Public Schools," *American School Board Journal* 158 (October 1971): 16.

9. Joan Hoff, *Law, Gender, and Injustice: A Legal History of U.S. Women* (New York: New York University Press, 1991), 21–48.

10. Wendy W. Williams, "The Equality Crisis: Some Reflections on Culture, Courts, and Feminism [1982]," in *Feminist Legal Theory: Readings in Law and Gender,* ed. Katharine T. Bartlett and Rosanne Kennedy (Boulder, CO: Westview Press, 1991), 16–17.

11. Ibid., 16–17.

12. Hoff, *Law, Gender, and Injustice,* 83, 87–90.

13. Williams, "The Equality Crisis," 16–17.

14. Leslie Friedman Goldstein, *The Constitutional Rights of Women: Cases in Law and Social Change,* new edition (Madison, WI: University of Wisconsin Press, 1988), 66–67.

15. The opinion of the court delivered by Justice Miller, *Myra Bradwell v. State of Illinois,* 83 U.S. (16 Wall.) 130 (1873).

16. Comments of Justice Bradley, *Myra Bradwell v. State of Illinois,* 83 U.S. (16 Wall.) 130 (1873).

17. Ibid.

18. Claire Sherman Thomas, *Sex Discrimination,* 2nd ed. (St. Paul, MN: West Publishing, 1991), 74–75.

19. *Sail'er Inn, Inc. v. Kirby,* P.2d 329 (1971).

20. Ibid.

21. Cynthia Stoddard and Antoinette Little, *Sex Discrimination in Educational Employment: Legal Strategies and Alternatives* (Holmes Beach, FL: Learning Publications, 1981), 7.

22. Mary Moran, " Up against the Glass Ceiling: Sex Discrimination Can Cost Your Board Big Money in Court, and That's Just the Beginning," in *American School Board Journal* 179 (February 1992): 39.

23. Moran, " Up Against the Glass Ceiling," 38.

24. Flora Ida Ortiz and Catherine Marshall, "Women in Educational Administration," in *The Handbook of Educational Administration,* ed. Norman J. Boyan (New York: Longman, 1988), 128–29.

25. Roald F. Campbell, Thomas Fleming, L. Jackson Newell, and John W. Bennion, *A History of Thought and Practice in Educational Administration* (New York: Teachers College Press, 1987), 187.

26. Karen Diegmueller, "Sidelined: More Girls are Playing Sports, but Fewer Women are Coaching Them," *Teacher Magazine* (October 1992): 12.

27. Ibid., 12.

28. Charlotte Shapiro, "We'll Sue Your School Board to Win Equity for Women Administrators," *American School Board Journal* 171 (May 1984): 43–47.

29. Marilee C. Rist, "Response: Progress Takes Time," *American School Board Journal* 171, 5 (May 1984): 45.

30. Robert K. Robinson, Billie M. Allen, Geralyn McClure Franklin, and David L. Duhon, "Sexual Harassment in the Workplace," *Public Personnel Management* 2 (April 1993): 123; Equal Employment Opportunity Commission, "Policy Guidance on Current Issues of Sexual Harassment" (N-915035, October 25, 1988).

31. Moran, "Up against the Glass Ceiling," 39.

32. Goldstein, *The Constitutional Rights of Women,* 455–56.

33. Dissenting opinion of Justice Rehnquist, *Cleveland Board of Education v. LaFleur,* 414 U.S. 632 (1974).

34. Charol Shakeshaft, *Women in Educational Administration,* updated ed. (Newbury Park, CA: Sage, 1989), 43.

35. Goldstein, *The Constitutional Rights of Women,* 540–41.

36. Dissenting opinion of Justice Marshall, *Personnel Administrator v. Feeney,* 442 U.S. 256 (1979).

37. Fishel and Pottker, *National Politics and Sex Discrimination*, 84.

38. Rist, "Response: Progress Takes Time," 45.

39. D. Timpano, "How to Tell if You're Discriminating Against Would-Be Women Administrators and What to Do about It if You Are," *American School Board Journal* 163 (June 1976): 19.

40. Sakre Kennington Edson, *Pushing the Limits: The Female Administrative Aspirant* (Albany, NY: SUNY Press, 1988), 205.

41. Ibid.

42. Fishel and Pottker, *National Politics*, 15, citing Education Commission of the States, *State Education Priorities: A Poll of State-Level Education Policymakers* (Denver: ECS, 1974), 3.

43. Women's Educational Equity Act Program, U.S. Education Department, *Survey: Attitudes toward Women as School District Administrators Summary of Responses to a Survey of a Random Sample of Superintendents and School Board Presidents*, Prepared for AASA by ERS, Inc. (Newton, MA: WEEA Publishing Center, 1981), 44.

44. Julie Underwood, "End Sexual Harassment of Employees, or Your Board Could Be Held Liable," *American School Board Journal* 174 (April 1987): 43.

45. Fishel and Pottker, *National Politics*, 12.

46. Women's Educational Equity Act Program, *Survey: Attitudes toward Women*, 9–10, 23–24.

47. Betty Friedan, *The Second Stage* (New York: Summit Books, 1981).

48. Patricia A. Schmuck, "Advocacy Organizations for Women School Administrators, 1977–1993," in *Women Leading in Education*, ed. Diane M. Dunlap and Patricia A. Schmuck (Albany, NY: SUNY Press, 1995), 199–224.

49. Amie Revere, "A Description of Black Female School Superintendents," a paper presented at the Annual Meeting of the American Educational Research Association, San Francisco, CA, 1986, 1–6.

50. Nancy Arnez, "Selected Black Female Superintendents of Public School Systems," *Journal of Negro Education* 51, 3 (1982): 309–17.

51. Kofi Lomotey, Kim Allen, Dianne Mark, and Shariba Rivers, "Research on African American Educational Leaders: The State of the Art," a paper presented at the American Educational Research Association, New York, 1996.

52. Xenia Montenegro, "Women and Racial Minority Representation in School Administration" (Arlington, VA: AASA, 1993), 2.

53. Charles Moody, "On Becoming a Superintendent: Contest or Sponsored Mobility?" *Journal of Negro Education* 52, 4 (1983): 383–97.

54. Catherine Marshall, *The Assistant Principal: Leadership Choices and Challenges* (Newbury Park, CA: Corwin Press, 1992), 66–71.

55. "Leadership," *American School Board Journal* 177 (December 1990): A 12–13.

56. Lorraine Collins, "About Those Few Females Who Scale the Heights of School Management," *American School Board Journal* 163 (June 1976): 26; Charlotte Shapiro, "We'll Sue Your School Board," 43–47.

57. Charlotte Shapiro, "We'll Sue Your School Board," 43–47.

58. Marilyn Tallerico and Joan N. Burstyn, "Retaining Women in the Superintendency: The Location Matters," *Educational Administration Quarterly* 33 (February 1997).

7. Conclusion

1. Linda K. Kerber, "Separate Spheres, Female Worlds, Woman's Place: The Rhetoric of Women's History," *The Journal of American History* 75 (1988): 30–37.

2. Estelle Freedman, "Separatism as Strategy: Female Institution Building and American Feminism, 1870–1930," *Feminist Studies* 5 (Fall 1979): 512–29.

3. My thinking about the connections between caring and the structure of school administration is heavily influenced by Nel Noddings's theoretical work on the nature of caring, although she certainly deserves no blame for my interpretations! Particularly important are *Caring: A Feminine Approach to Ethics & Moral Education* (Berkeley, CA: University of California Press, 1984) and *Women and Evil* (Berkeley, CA: University of California Press, 1989). I have discussed some of these connections in "Caring and the Open Moment in Educational Leadership: An Historical Perspective," *Caring in an Unjust World*, ed. Deborah Eaker-Rich and Jane Van Galen (Albany, NY: SUNY Press, 1996), 13–29.

4. Arlie Hochschild, *The Second Shift* (New York: Avon Books, 1989).

5. Ella Flagg Young, *Isolation in the Schools* (Chicago: University of Chicago Press, 1900).

6. Ibid., 7.

7. Ibid., 12–13.

8. Ibid., 13.

9. Ibid., 13–14.

10. Ibid., 16–17.

Appendix

1. David Tyack and Elisabeth Hansot, *Managers of Virtue* (New York: Basic Books, 1982), 187; Charol Shakeshaft, *Women in Educational Administration* (Newbury Park, CA: Sage, 1987), 19–23; Jacqueline Parker Clement, *Sex Bias in School Leadership* (Evanston, IL: Integrated Education Associates, 1975), 3–8. Since the early 1980s, the AASA has undertaken the task of compiling statistics on the representation of women and persons of color in school administrative positions. The 1993 report, compiled by Xenia Montenegro, indicates that this is the only known such systematic, ongoing reporting effort. See Xenia Montenegro, *Women and Racial Minority Representation in School Administration* (Washington, DC: AASA, 1993), 6.

2. *Report of the Commissioner of Education* (Washington, DC: Government Printing Office, 1873).

3. "Status of Women with Respect to the Direction of Public Education in States and Territories," *Report of the Commissioner of Education 1901*, 2 (Washington, DC: Government Printing Office, 1901), 1228–30.

4. "The Alaska Reindeer Service," *Report of the Commissioner of Education 1911* (Washington, DC: Government Printing Office, 1911), 1395–97.

5. Louise Connolly, "Is There Room at the Top? For Women Educators?" *The Woman Citizen* (March 8, 1919): 840–43.

6. Edith Lathrop, *Teaching as a Vocation for College Women* (Washington, DC: National Council of Administrative Women in Education, 1922), 3–4.

7. I say that these figures are accurate because they agree well with my data for 1930. See table A.1.

8. "Women in Educational Administration," *The School Review* 36 (May 1928): 326–27.

9. David Tyack, "Pilgrim's Progress: Toward a Social History of the School Superintendency, 1860–1960," *History of Education Quarterly* 16 (Fall 1976): 257–300. Also, see table A.1.

10. *President's Commission on the Status of Women* (Washington, DC: Government Printing Office, 1963). For discussion of the NCAWE report on the elementary school principalship, see chapter 5 above.

11. NEA Department of Elementary School Principals, *The Elementary School Principalship in 1968* (Washington, DC: National Education Association, 1968), 11.

12. "Professional Women in Public Schools, 1970–71," *NEA Research Bulletin* 49, 3 (October 1971): 67–68.

13. See table A.1 for comparison data from the present study.

14. Stephen J. Knezevich, ed., *The American School Superintendent: An AASA Research Study* (Washington, DC: American Association of School Administrators, 1971), 20. Also, see table A.1 for comparative data.

15. Catherine Dillon Lyon and Terry N. Saario, "Women in Public Education: Sexual Discrimination in Promotions," *Phi Delta Kappan* (October 1973): 120–23.

16. See table A.1 for comparative data.

17. Andrew Fishel and Janice Pottker, *National Politics and Sex Discrimination in Education* (Lexington, MA: Lexington Books, 1977), 149.

18. Betty Friedan and Anne Grant West, "Sex Bias: The Built-in Mentality That Maims the Public Schools," *American School Board Journal* 158 (October 1971): 16–20. Also see Paul Tractenberg, ed., *Selection of Teachers and Supervisors in Urban School Systems* (New York: Agathon Publication Services, 1972), 482–83.

19. Lyon and Saario, "Women in Public Education," 120–23.

20. Clement, *Sex Bias*, 5–6.

21. Report of the Commissioner's Task Force on the Impact of Office of Education Programs on Women, "A Look at Women in Education: Issues and Answers for HEW," (U.S. Department of H.E.W., 1972), 58, cited in Clement, *Sex Bias*, 3.

22. Fishel and Pottker, *National Politics*, 58.

23. B. Foster and J. Carpenter, *Statistics of Public Elementary and Secondary Day Schools*, cited in Jean Stockard, Patricia A. Schmuck, Ken Kempner, Peg Williams, Sakre K. Edson, and Mary Ann Smith, *Sex Equity in Education* (New York: Academic Press, 1980).

24. Cited in Flora Ida Ortiz and Catherine Marshall, "Women in Educational Administration," in *Handbook of Research on Educational Administration*, ed. Norman J. Boyan (New York: Longman, 1988), 127. The data for 1950 agrees closely with the data I collected for the same year. See table A.1. However, the more recent data conflicts with my findings.

25. E. H. Jones and X. P. Montenegro, *Perspectives on Racial Minority and Women School Administrators* (1983), *Women and Racial Minorities in School Administration* (1985), and *Women and Minorities in School Administration* (1988, 1990) (Arlington, VA: AASA); and Xenia Montenegro, *Women and Minority Representation in School Administration* (Arlington, VA: AASA, 1993).

26. I thank Ann Highsmith Fleming for her kind, careful, and meticulous help in completing the superintendent database for this project. I also am grateful to the Spender Foundation for its generous support of my doctoral work with a Dissertation Year Fellowship. This funding allowed me to purchase the equipment and supplies for this work.

27. *Patterson's American Education* (Chicago: American Educational Company, 1910), 3.

28. *Patterson's* (1970).

29. Clement, *Sex Bias*, 4. The ERS explains in its current promotional literature that it is an "independent, nonprofit research foundation providing objective, reliable, up-to-date research and information for school instructional, operational, and policy decisions. School districts enrolling half of the nation's public school pupils currently maintain annual orders for ERS services." ERS is sponsored by the American Association of School Administrators, American Association of School Personnel Administrators, Association of School Business Officials, Council of Chief State School Officers, National Association of Elementary School Principals, National Association of Secondary School Principals, and National School Public Relations Association.

30. During the early decades of the twentieth century, some women writers and other career women chose to be known only by their initials and last name as a way of minimizing sex discrimination in their professional lives. However, public officials like school superintendents were well known in their communities and could not so readily disguise their sex through use of initials.

31. *Complete Dictionary of English and Hebrew First Names* (Middle Village, NY: Jonathan David Publishers, 1984).

INDEX